MISSION VETS

by
ARTHUR L. DORMINY

Front cover picture-Sculpture **Mission Vet** by John Gilliam who resides in Lenore, Idaho.

MISSION VETS

by
ARTHUR L. DORMINY

Christian Veterinary Mission
19303 Fremont Avenue North
Seattle, WA 98133 USA
Current Book Information at:
www.cvmusa.org
PHONE: (206) 546-7569 FAX: (206) 546-7458

Raising Healthy Animals Series

Every year, thousands of people around the world struggle to survive because they don't have the right knowledge, skills and resources to care for their animals. Christian Veterinary Mission (CVM) sends veterinary professionals to live and work alongside many of these people to encourage them and provide them with not only much needed veterinary expertise, but also the hope that is only found in Christ. CVM veterinarians build lasting relationships with individuals and communities, helping them be transformed through Christ's love.

CVM, in its effort to be meaningfully involved in work in the developing world, quickly found there was little appropriate educational material available. CVM set about developing basic resource materials in animal husbandry for farmers and agricultural workers. Apparently, they met a real need, as these books have been accepted throughout the developing nations of the world.

The series of books published by Christian Veterinary Mission includes the following in order of publication:

Raising Healthy Pigs *	Drugs and Their Usage
Raising Healthy Rabbits *	Where There Is No Animal Doctor
Raising Healthy Fish	Raising Healthy Horses
Raising Healthy Cattle	Zoonoses: Animal Diseases That Affect Humans
Raising Healthy Poultry *+	Raising Healthy Honey Bees
Raising Healthy Goats *	Slaughter and Preservation of Meat
Raising Healthy Sheep	Disease and Parasite Prevention in Farm Animals

[Also available in: * Spanish   + French].

CVM fieldworkers have also developed specific training materials for the countries in which they work.

All of these books have been put together by Christian men and women; in a labor of love and service, for people in need throughout the world. It demonstrates dedication to their profession, service to humanity and a witness to their faith. We hope that they are a help to you in developing an appropriate livestock program to meet your needs. We pray God's blessing on their use.

Leroy Dorminy
CVM Founder

Dedication

This book is dedicated to my wife, Tina; to our sons, Bruce and Blair; our daughter-in-law Betsy; and our grandson, Sterling.

It is also dedicated to those committed and faithful servants of the Lord who work under difficult and sometimes dangerous conditions, ministering to the needy of the world through the profession of veterinary medicine.

And to that wonderful corps of volunteers: faithful men and women who have served on short term shuttles; people serving as region, state, and school representatives; partners who have faithfully supported CVM's ministry so generously through the years; volunteers who work in the central office and throughout the country; contributors in the production of educational material; and to all who serve the Lord, living out their lives in service to Him.

To God be the Glory!

Additional Dedication

In memory of my grandfather, W. I. Patrick, a church planting Baptist missionary in South Georgia, following the Civil War. To the memory of my mother, Fannie Lois Patrick Dorminy, who was a missionary in her own right in the community where she lived and to my father, Emory Sphere Dorminy, who was a successful and prudent farmer. Together they raised three daughters, Susie, Vivian and Jo; five sons Albert, Luther, Herman, Drew and Arthur. All the sons served in the navy, in the active theater of war in the Pacific, during WWII.

Table of Contents

Acknowledgements ix

Chapter 1—The Vision 1

Chapter 2—The Call 10

Chapter 3—The Challenge 18

Chapter 4—The Merger 28

Chapter 5—Early Years 34

Chapter 6—Reaching out 43

Chapter 7—Long Term Service 51

Chapter 8—More Assignments 65

Chapter 9—Worldscope 75

Chapter 10—The Cost of Mission Service 86

Chapter 11—Millionaires 98

Chapter 12—Sharing Skills 118

Chapter 13—Defining Relationships 129

Chapter 14—On The Road Again 136

Chapter 15—Asia Discovered 146

Chapter 16—Well Done 155

Chapter 17—Facilitating Others 164

Chapter 18—Christmas 172

Chapter 19—Shifting Gears 176

Chapter 20—Gourmet Ministry 190

Chapter 21—A Time to Weep and A Time to Laugh 203

Chapter 22—Milestones and Miracles 217

Chapter 23—Comings and Goings 232

Chapter 24—Encouragement Post-Communism 246

Chapter 25—Twenty-Five Years 259

Acknowledgements

A special 'thank you' to my wife Tina, who did the initial editing and proofing of the book. Many of the rough spots were identified and cleared out or rewritten. She did the early grammatical and punctuation proofing at the same time.

Tammy Dodd offered general advice on the contents, since she had an intimate working knowledge of CVM and its players. This helped to give me some guidance in the project. I had to make a decision on what I should and could include, since I could not possibly cover all the material.

Dr. Diane Marshall did extensive editing and proofing of the entire document once, and parts of it the second time. I did not always take her advice on some of the material edited, so if you see some things included that shouldn't be, you can credit that to my account.

Drs. Keith Flanagan and Ivan Barineau reviewed some of the Haiti material. Some of the early events were before their time. I had to wing it there, using some of the documents that were still available.

Dr. Todd Cooney did the cartoon. Dr. Kelly Ward did an evaluation review before the final printing of the book.

When I talk about the field workers I am sure they wonder why in the world I chose that particular material for inclusion in the book. Most of it was used because it emphasizes a point or gives the reader the 'feel' of conditions on the field.

The cutoff date for all the material is June 30, 1999. I hope those who have gone on the field on shuttles and long term assignments since that time do not feel slighted. They will make the next twenty-five years issue.

I wish I could have used a photograph of each and every long-term field worker and shuttle, but space did not permit that. My apologies to those of you, who were not included.

Christian Veterinary Mission (Publisher of this book)

Our vision is to see

Christ's love expressed through veterinary medicine.

Our mission is to

challenge, empower and facilitate veterinarians to serve through their profession, living out their Christian faith.

CVM also provides education and encouragement for those who desire to minister through service, prayer, relationship building, and modeling Christ's love.

About CVM

Christian Veterinary Mission (CVM) is a ministry of CRISTA Ministries, a registered non-profit Christian Service Organization 501(c)(3) based in Seattle, Washington, U.S.A.

CVM was founded in 1976 by Dr. Leroy Dorminy who came to realize the impact that veterinarians could have by integrating their faith with their practice, both locally and around the world. In 2008, CVM had nearly 30 veterinary professionals serving full-time internationally and over 200 veterinary professionals and student volunteers serve on short-term cross-cultural mission trips annually. CVM sponsors fellowship & prayer breakfasts at over 20 U.S. veterinary meetings each year and reaches out to veterinary students through Christian Veterinary Fellowship (CVF) groups in every veterinary school in the U.S. by encouraging them in spiritual growth and professional development.

There are over 3,500 veterinarians affiliated with CVM in the U.S. CVM also partners with organizations and networks in other countries that are focused on empowering Christian veterinarians. CVM has a volunteer advisory board of veterinarians who guide its vision, mission, and programming.

CVM books and the free International Animal Health Newsletter were written with small farmers, veterinarians, and agricultural development workers in mind. Our desire is that they would help individuals and groups develop an appropriate livestock program to meet community needs. CVM's Endowment Fund was started in the early years of the organization's life. The fund provides for meaningful programs that could not be funded by the regular budgeting process.

CHAPTER 1

The Vision

A brochure came in the mail, saying that the 1975 Baptist World Alliance (BWA) was meeting in Stockholm, Sweden. Something about the notice intrigued me. Now, I get flyers every day with fantastic offers to visit here and there, to do this and that; but for some reason I didn't throw this one away. Stockholm is a beautiful city; I knew this from visiting before. I had never attended the BWA, so there was no strong attraction there. But something in my heart stirred, and counseled me not to throw it away. I kept it.

It is often difficult for us to discern the Spirit of the Lord at work in our lives. But it is there, nevertheless. We can count on that. In retrospect, God had a plan. He began to unveil it slowly, gradually, even though I was unaware of exactly what it was at the time.

I showed the brochure to my wife, Tina. I asked her if she was interested in going to the Baptist World Alliance in Stockholm, and taking our sons. My family is interested in world travel, so the idea immediately hit a hot button. Together, we began to explore the options, and to formulate a plan to make it happen. As is sometimes the case, small fish grow large fast. Before I knew it, the trip had expanded. After attending the convention, we would drive down through Europe to return from Paris.

Once I had verbally committed, there was no turning back. Things just seemed to escalate. We pursued our passports together. At this point, about all I had to do was hold on. Tina began making travel arrangements—plane, car, hotel. Nightly, we held a family tribal council to get updates on what needed to be done next.

Finally, everything was arranged. We would fly to New York, and from there to Stockholm. We had hotel reservations for Stockholm (a good idea when arriving from a long and tiring trip) and we reserved a car for the drive down through Sweden, Denmark, Germany, (including East and West) and France. It was going to be a fun family trip.

Since graduating from the University of Georgia School of Veterinary Medicine in 1950, I had been doing a mixed practice in Ocilla, Georgia. It was a rural practice with most of the work involving food animals, some horses, and a few pets. In later years the focus shifted more toward companion animal practice. I enjoyed my work but after 25 years I was beginning to ask myself if the Lord was calling me to something else. Maybe I was searching and this was an opportunity to extend that search.

We drove to Atlanta, parked the car, and flew to New York. Murphy's law began to take effect almost immediately! We were scheduled to leave New York at 6:30 in the evening. When that time arrived, nothing happened. Unspecified delays can drag on into forever, it seems. We finally left at 3:30 A.M. and arrived in Stockholm the next evening.

When we landed, jet lag was taking its toll on the family. Luckily, we had those hotel reservations. We were not able to function very well, acting more like zombies than living human beings. Anyone who has traveled overseas recognizes this feeling. After a night's rest and some nourishment, we began to emerge from our state of suspended animation.

Stockholm is an exciting city with many beautiful buildings and bridges. During July and August, natives leave the city in droves, for summer vacations. The tourists probably outnumber the residents during that time. At least Stockholm is considerate enough to leave a few hosts in the city to give directions.

The Baptist World Alliance Convention was a huge affair. More than 10,000 delegates attended, from 84 different countries. Luckily for us, the official language was English, although there were speakerphones available for other languages. It was a great time of fellowship for believers. The love of Christ crosses all barriers. As we prayed and sang, each in our own languages, we could feel the warmth and camaraderie. A banner across the front proclaimed reconciliation in Jesus Christ. It was exciting and heady stuff.

Though the larger group was awesome and thrilling, a more effective way of communicating and growing spiritually was through small group Bible studies. They helped to break the large crowd into more personal, appropriate, and effective groups. There was meaningful dialogue this way. It happened to me in an unforgettable way.

There were about fifteen or twenty of us participating in one small group. We were discussing a particular point in scripture. In the group was a woman from one of the emerging nations of Africa.

Our discussion leader turned to her and asked, "How can we, Christians of the developed world, help you, in the developing countries?"

Quick as a flash came her reply, *"Come and teach us your skills, that we may do things for ourselves."*

What a practical and common sense answer! How profound in its simplicity. That question got larger and larger in my mind, as I pondered her response. More importantly for me, it became specific—what can I, as a veterinarian, do to help?

From that moment on, the general convention became less important than concentrating on my personal relationship and responsibility as God's agent for change. Oh, I immensely enjoyed the rest of the sessions, but it was the beginning of an odyssey.

"And what does the Lord require of you? To act justly, love mercy and to walk humbly with Your God." Micah 6:8.

After the convention ended, we picked up our car and began the trek down through Sweden. It was delightful at that time of the year. We felt free to explore, with no agenda. We only had one deadline—our departure from Paris two weeks later. We developed a rotating system of assigned tasks for the trip. One person drove, one navigated, one read from Fodor's travel guide about places to stay, eat, and see. That left one person free to criticize the other three!

There was something about our car, we were to discover many times over, that piqued the interest of many Europeans. Something about it was funny to them. Maybe it was that we reminded them of the Beverly Hillbillies! Another peculiar car kept appearing wherever we went. It was a car with a pair of horns mounted on it. We began to refer to it as "Old Antlers".

3

. . . In the back of my mind, scrambling to be heard, were the woman's words: "Come teach us your skills that we may do things for ourselves."

"But what does that mean for me? Lord, are you speaking to me? How do you expect me to respond? Why don't you lay out the blueprint for my life, so I can quit wondering and worrying about this?" . . .

From Sweden we traveled to Copenhagen, entering through the Harbor of the Mermaid. It was an interesting city, with its beautiful and exciting Tivoli Gardens. They present an unusually pretty night-time picture. The different colored and gaily lighted lanterns hung throughout the gardens. Families were enjoying their outings. There was something for everyone.

Working our way south from Copenhagen, we drove along the beaches for a while. It was difficult for me to understand how people could be swimming when I was not warm with a coat on even though it was the middle of July! I suppose some people take advantage of a fine and pleasant misery whenever the opportunity presents itself.

We had an enjoyable side trip to the Island of Aero. We took the ferry over from Svenberg and drove around, exploring the small farms and villages. Picking one out of the many windmills we saw, we headed up the narrow road and through a field, to explore close up. We stopped, went inside and visited with a somewhat startled Danish farmer. He was unable to speak English nor we Danish, but he finally understood our desire to observe him grinding grain with the windmill. He was friendly and obliging.

Suddenly, we realized that the last ferry was soon to leave the island. Saying a quick farewell, off we went. Unfortunately, we got out of the hard-packed ruts into the soft dirt, and we were stuck! We hurried back to the farmer's house to borrow a shovel. It took many animated demonstrations for him to realize our problem. Finally, we were successful in getting out. We thanked him in a hurry, and scampered off for the ferry landing. We made the last ferry by one car!

. . . Still, many questions filled my thoughts. If the need were overseas, how would I participate? I had a very rural, mixed solo practice in a small town in South Georgia. Little did I know how well this had prepared me for work in the Third World. . . .

Entering the border between Denmark and Germany, I was reminded of the events of World War II when Hitler's hordes so ruthlessly swarmed into this small defenseless country. Many Danes who lived there during the war were involved in efforts to thwart the Nazi war machine. Voices from the past seemed to speak of intrigue, betrayal, and courage. Of people living out their lives in times of great uncertainty and danger.

Hamburg was the first large city we saw after leaving Denmark. It was impressive because of its bustling economy, busy people, and new landscape—built after World War II. It was simply amazing the way the city had recovered from the devastation 19 years earlier. We found it a bit daunting trying to navigate its immense size, but local citizens came to our rescue. They were quite helpful when they saw us wandering around with our map in our hands.

Driving through Hamburg on the way to the border, we were stopped by police. My oldest son, Blair, was driving.

"Give me your driver's license!" The officer said harshly." You were driving too fast!"

Blair, thinking he was being cooperative, said, "O.K."

"It's not O.K.!" the angry officer shouted.

This American family, non-chalantly vacationing and not showing the proper respect, was more than his system could take. Especially with an old gray-head, sitting in the back seat, chewing gum. The officer was obviously on overload.

> . . . *My thoughts kept drifting back. How do I volunteer my services and to whom? Like many others in the South, I belonged to the Baptist Church. So would I look in this direction?. . .*

Driving from Hamburg to Berlin, we had to go through the communist-held portion surrounding the city. It was chilling to see the effects that system had on the people and their outlook. To go through intense scrutiny at the checkpoint was intimidating but revealing. Border guards used rifles, mirrors, and dogs. Entering the East zone, the custom officials were hostile and intimidating. They made it as difficult as possible to get through the system. It was not designed to help, but to interfere.

5

Once inside East Germany, we drove along the road to Berlin. The buildings and the people reflected the system most graphically. There was no joy, no enthusiasm evident. There was only stark, gray reality! It was not living, but only existing. No wonder those walls had to be built to keep the people in! There was no way anyone would stay voluntarily.

West Berlin itself was an oasis of freedom in the desert of tyranny! It was simply amazing, how the city had rebuilt under the combined authority of the U.S., U.S.S.R., France, and the U.K., even though there were tension and threats.

Going through "Checkpoint Charlie" into East Berlin required the same restrictions as getting into the country. Mirrors were pushed under the tour bus to detect anyone who might be underneath. People used every possible way to escape. This kept the communists constantly devising more and stricter methods to detect and deal with defectors.

Getting back to West Berlin, we gave thanks for the freedom that was so evident there. It was an ever-present testimony to the people who made it so! God grant that there will always be people who hold liberty dear enough to champion its cause. This whole episode of the west vs. east; communism vs. capitalism; freedom vs. oppression made an impact on us all.

> . . . *Should I contact the foreign mission board to see if I could volunteer my time as a veterinarian overseas? And could I do this and retain a practice? Should I consider long time service or should I go for a short period only? What about my family, would they buy into such a venture?*. . .

We drove down to Nuremberg. It was the scene of the infamous war crimes trial following World War II, where many of Hitler's henchmen received more consideration than they ever gave. It was a vivid reminder of the terrible crimes against humanity that people can commit when God is left out, and we are left to our own prejudices, excesses, and lust for power. Our track record seems to say that we never learn.

Munich was our next stop. To my age group, this place is a reminder of Britian's Neville Chamberlain capitulating to the Nazis and Fascist powers under the guise of permanent peace. In fact, when Englishmen were ridiculing Rudolph Hess for parachuting into England, in a rather dumb and naïve effort to secure a cease fire in 1941, Germans responded by taking an umbrella and jumping off a chair, yelling "Chamberlain".

We found the time to enjoy the very fine Pintatoeke Museum. From there, we headed west toward Stuttgart, but not before stopping at the former prison and gas chamber at Dachau. It was another vivid reminder of the indescribably horrible detention and extermination centers for the Jews.

One barracks was left standing as visible evidence of the conditions inside. It represented one of many identified by the concrete slabs remaining. Most repulsive was the crematorium that housed the gas chambers. When in operation, they were insidiously disguised as the showers. The stench remained, whether in my mind or for real. It was sickening. It left me saddened and depressed. God surely must have been ashamed of his creation at that point in time.

On the way out of Dachau, we walked through a series of buildings that had many pictures along the walls, depicting conditions in the camp. I was contemplating the scenes as I moved along. Suddenly, someone with a harsh voice broke the silence. I looked around to see a German guard in his hat and uniform, not unlike what they wore back then. He was only being helpful to me by offering to answer my questions. I realized how frightened the inmates must have been of their guards. What terrible experiences they suffered at the hands of those guards.

> . . . *Now that I had made a decision in my own heart, I needed to follow through. I would answer the call for help from the lady in Africa and others like her. How? I had not worked through the details. I trusted in the Lord to show me the way, His way, in due time. From now on, that was to be my over-riding goal. . . .*

Augsburg had a McDonalds restaurant! American fast foods had arrived in Europe. Now it won't take three hours to eat a meal! However, at this restaurant and at this time, I could not eat. Dachau-the scenes, the smell, the sad recall, was still too much on my mind.

7

We skirted Stuttgart and headed for the region of Alsace Lorraine, the area of much contention in World War I. Dividing the two countries of Germany and France were the Seigfried Military Defense Line on the German side, and the Maginot Military Defense Line on the French side. Both were supposed to be impenetrable. As always, new methods of warfare like "Blitzkrieg" and old methods of warfare like an "end run" made those miles of concrete and pill boxes obsolete and useless. This was another example of the staggering costs to wage war. Huge sums were wasted on man's worst inventions, when they could have done so much for human kind. If only people would learn.

Now it was on to France! We left "Old Antlers" behind and headed for "Gay Paree." Once we were inside the border, we stopped at a small town to eat lunch. None of us spoke French. We ordered the "meal du jour". Not realizing it was a four-course meal, I tried to pay for it after the first course by asking for 'La Addition'.

I thought the waiter was going to have a heart attack for sure, "No! No! Monsieur, Entree! Dessert! Fromage!"

We had a good laugh.

. . . *First, I will write to the Foreign Mission Board and offer my services. That's it, they will know. After all, they have been coordinating missions for a very long time. Haven't I been reading about that in the Christian Index since I was a kid? If they want references I can point to the fact that my grandfather was a church planting home missionary. . . .*

Now, one thing I don't recommend is driving into Paris at night in a rented car (could that have started my heart trouble?). It is an endless game of "chicken" in the turning circle around Place de la Concorde. To cap it off, we had no reservations. We had to try to find a hotel! Everybody pray.

We finally checked in at the Intercontinental. I could see four nights costing me a month's earnings, but I was so exhausted that I would have agreed to anything. It was nice, and further more we met a former Methodist preacher from our hometown in the lobby. Maybe it wouldn't be so expensive after all.

During our stay, I went over to the airline counter to check on our flight home. I heard a familiar drawl engaged in a heated discussion with a French accented airline employee. It was a fellow from Mississippi who had driven in from Italy. Now, after being robbed of all his luggage, he was trying to figure out a way to get home. I joined his side. Since both parties had decided to take no prisoners, we paused from this impossible standoff and retired to another area of the lobby.

In our private discussion, the subject of the American Embassy came up. I related my unsuccessful call to them inquiring about American cemeteries in Paris. This brought the idea up of visiting one just outside the city. We agreed to go together. I would navigate, and he would drive. We looked like something out of a movie, with this van wandering around as an impediment to French traffic (if that's possible). We found the cemetery and, much to our surprise, a Parisian, not an American, was supervising it. He treated us royally.

The best-laid plans can go awry. I took a detailed map of Paris to determine our best route to D'Orly Airport for the next day's departure. The trouble was that it showed nothing concerning one-way streets. The ones I had planned to take were coming in instead of going out. This took extra time as we found our way. We came to Paris in a frenzy and left in one. Dropping off Tina, Bruce, and Blair at the curb, I scurried to return the car. I jumped out of it and sprinted back to the gate, just making it in time. What a trip!

The trip home allowed me time to reflect on the whole experience. Not just the trip, but the BWA, its meaning, and the challenge it presented to me. Deep down, I could sense satisfaction and feel excitement growing as I anticipated my next steps. It was going to mean work, seeking the Lord's will, and at some point stepping out in faith and obedience to His commands. Finally, it was going to mean a rearrangement of my priorities. Daunting as these steps were, I prayed that I would be up to the challenge.

CHAPTER 2

The Call

Bam! A sharp crack, and the glass shattered into a million pieces. Quickly, the driver pulled over to the side of the road. The entire quartz rubble collapsed into our laps. We took sticks, and poked out the remainder of what, minutes before, was the windshield of our jeep. We brushed off the seat and cleared our clothes of shattered glass before continuing.

We were on the way to the Santa Domingo Airport so I could catch a plane back to the United States. I had just spent two of the most exciting weeks of my life, working in the valley around Bonao. It is a beautiful valley, half way between Santa Domingo and Santiago in the Dominican Republic. Much of the area has 1-3 acre subsistence farms. Livestock plays an important part of the day to day living on these small farms.

Earlier that summer, at the state veterinary convention in Jekyll Island, Georgia, I met with Christian veterinarians from around the state. They endorsed the idea of veterinary missions and started a fund to help make that happen. Dr. Felix Smith, of Perry, Georgia, was selected as secretary/treasurer. We collected $335 at this first meeting. This more than financed the medicines I took on my trip to the Dominican Republic. Several members of that original group have continued their support of CVM through the years.

Shortly thereafter, I received the request for a veterinarian in the Dominican Republic. It was an answer to prayer and an opportunity of a lifetime. It allowed me to use my skills as a veterinarian, and to make use of my practice experience.

Charley Purtle was a Baptist missionary from Oklahoma. He had requested help with some of the animal husbandry problems he was encountering. I had volunteered my services to the Baptist Foreign Mission Board for overseas service. It was difficult to place veterinarians who had a desire to serve the Lord through their profession. Providentially, the opportunity arose for me to help Charlie on a short-term basis.

I had no real knowledge of how to proceed, as these were uncharted waters. The only information I had was the type of animals the farmers owned. How would I prepare? Well, I knew they were poor, that was a given. I assumed that they were many years behind the times and were poorly educated, both of which proved to be true. How could I help? What could I do? What should I take? I needed answers for these questions before I could plan effectively.

August 8, 1976.

Dear Charlie,

"I'm very excited and grateful for the opportunity to come and help in the area of veterinary medicine. I look forward to working with you and the Baptist team. Please give me any general information concerning any medicines that might be particularly beneficial in your area."

One advantage for me was that I started my practice many years before, in rural Georgia. The times and conditions that some of my clients faced then were like those of the farmers in the Dominican Republic. This was an assumption I made then that has proven to be true many times since.

One thing we see the world over are great numbers of poor people, inadequately educated, and disenfranchised for many reasons. Some problems are of their own making; many are not. It's hard to escape when you are born into poverty. Many of these people feel hopeless. That is the saddest thing of all, because everyone needs to have hope!

> *. . . Charlie, one reason I am so eager to participate is to find out what role veterinarians can play in mission work and food production in underdeveloped countries. This should give me great insight. There has been much enthusiasm on the part of veterinarians in Georgia and across the United States.*

Now that the "call" was given, how would I go about responding to that call? For starters, I researched the Dominican Republic. I learned as much as I could about the country, its climate, history, and people. Next, I wrote to the missionary, asking for information on the types of animals in the area where he worked. They had most of the animals that I practiced on every day. That was a relief! It gave me a place to start when planning what to take.

I put a practice bag in my surgery. Slowly, I began filling it with things that would have been appropriate in the early days of my practice. I added medicines and supplies that are needed universally— medicines for wounds, and a simple, but complete surgical pack. (It will always be used, if for nothing else but for spaying the local missionary's cat on the table. That happened on the final day for me.) Antibiotics, and, of course, de-worming medicines for all species. Don't leave home without them!

Extreme parasitism and malnutrition are cooperating culprits in every country of the developing world. They were made for each other; or more accurately, they were made because of each other. Reflected in that, is the corresponding state of health in animals and people. They reflect the good or bad conditions of each other!

An unusual thing I included when packing my bag were some rubber balloons. My receptionist, Vivian Martin, who was most helpful, suggested them. I also took some chewing gum and candy. I knew there would be plenty of kids who never had such things, or had even seen them. This was a great hit with the kids and an icebreaker with the people.

The Dominican Republic is a beautiful island with tropical growth and great potential, but it is woefully lacking in efficient technology. It is an undeveloped country. The town of Bonao is typical. It is nestled in a gorgeous valley, modern looking but deceptive. Its water supply is unsafe and the electricity is undependable.

Here lived Charlie Purtle, a missionary sympathetic to the poor small farmer; someone who was interested in their hunger and their pain. It was quite a different attitude from the government whose leader had erected a monument to himself! His enemies were fed to the sharks, while the people suffered because of his mismanagement and cruelty.

As in most developing countries, the literacy rate was very low. This was an impediment to learning. Other common problems are extreme parasitism and malnutrition. These are culprits in every country of the developing world, and reflect the state of health in the animals and the people. Family planning is not practiced because of religious views, poverty, and ignorance.

After I arrived and settled in with the Purtles, we began to make plans for beginning the work. Community leaders were called together and told about the services that would be available for the next few weeks. Since the farms were so small, it was easy to go from one to the next, examining livestock and treating sick animals, vaccinating and de-worming.

One experiment that I started early on, began when I identified a community leader in a strategic location. I convinced him to place four of his pigs in a pen for a de-worming and feeding test. We administered piperazine and substituted an improved ration. We made sure the new feed was already available locally. It took only four or five days for those scrawny pigs to show visible improvement.

This showed me the importance of learning by seeing, of having the community participate in the process. You are familiar with the adage "a picture is worth a thousand words". How much better is a learning experience that is happening to you or to something you own.

After the pig experiment, I held a training session on parasites for the local farm chapter. There were 50 men and one woman. They were very interested in the training, because they could see the results of the de-worming and the improved ration. (The roundworms can be seen in the feces in a few hours after de-worming).

During the following week, I led another session on nutrition. I again used the pigs in the test, to demonstrate how a balanced ration for the pigs makes a difference in their growth and weight gain. I tried to equate the various components of a good ration to things that the farmers could relate to in their own meals.

The pigs also ate leftovers, if there were any. Pigs are scavengers and garbage disposals. I wanted to impress upon the farmers that when a pig roots, he is looking for something that is missing in his diet and not just necessarily having fun. If a few necessary ingredients were provided, the pigs could do fairly well on almost anything else. It was not ideal pig husbandry, but workable.

The farmers' interest level and response was overwhelming! I had more to do than I could accomplish, because I was only one person (now we send shuttle vets in pairs, incidentally that is scriptural). The workload was tremendous.

For various reasons, I could only bring a certain amount of medicine with me. An interesting thing happened when we finally ran out of medicine. We went to Santiago in search of a supply. I found a well-stocked animal health store, which would have been first class anywhere in the United States. The problem was that the farmers did not have the money to buy, or the knowledge to use the products in that store. It was a catch-22. The important question is where do you start to rectify the situation. What do you do first? The answers are as many and varied as the number of people you ask.

I suppose we could expound endlessly on why there is so much need in the world, and so few resources to meet those needs. That is not the issue. The Gospel of Christ teaches us clearly what our response should be, when we see that need. To respond will move us out of our comfort zone. Anyone who has lived or worked in these situations could tell of many moving experiences. There were some especially poignant and heartrending scenes from my perspective.

One day, Charlie had to go into town. I was left to fend for myself. I found a young boy who could speak a little English, and we set out. I began working the small farms, using him as translator. Many children accompanied us. So many, in fact, that I must have looked like the Pied Piper, making my way from one farmer's house to another. It was an exhilarating day, but very wearing. The weather was hot, and the needs were unending.

Late that afternoon, I had exhausted most of my supplies so I made one final stop. The last family was a large one, with children everywhere. Family planning is an omnipresent need in every developing nation of the world. Unfortunately, it is such an emotional issue involving layers of tradition, religious, political, economic and gender overtones that it becomes a most difficult one with which to deal.

I asked the farmer in my very limited Spanish, "How many children do you have?"

"Dies y ocho (18)," he replied.

"Did I misunderstand?" I asked my young translator. "I thought he said eighteen."

"Yes, that's right, he said eighteen."

Can you imagine the stress on their mother during these years? The strain on their meager resources just to provide food and clothing, much less adequate housing, must have been enormous.

I remembered the balloons in my bag, hidden beneath the gauze. I began to give them away. Children crowded around in excitement and anticipation. One of the farmer's little girls wanted one so badly. Her father scolded her sharply for pushing in too close. I will never forget the look on her face. She was agonizing over her options, the threat of her father's wrath and the possibility she might not get a balloon. It was heartrending. I made very sure she received one.

How many times have I recalled that incident, and thanked God for the things I enjoy and take for granted? It was a very humbling experience for me.

John's words came to mind: "We know and to some extent, realize the love of God for us, because Christ expressed it in laying down His life for us. We must in turn express our love by laying down our lives for those who are our brothers". 1 John 3:16

His next sentence puts it into everyday practical terms: "But as far as the well-to-do man who sees his brother in want but shuts his eyes and his heart; how could anyone believe that the love of God lives in him? Let us not love with words or tongue but with deed and truth." 1 John 3-17,18

Do you and I demonstrate the love of God in deed?

One day, a man on a horse came riding down from the hills. He said that he had heard there was a veterinarian who was treating animals for the farmers. He wanted to know if the vet would come to his community and treat their animals. Poverty was even worse in the mountains than down in the valley. Was it because things grew better in the valley? Did the hill people miss training opportunities because of the remoteness of their region?

One young hill farmer had one sow and a litter of pigs. The sow was too thin and too parasitized to give adequate milk for her pigs. They were beginning to dwindle and die. I tried my best to explain the cause of the problem. Again, the condition of their animals are reflected in the people's health. As we approached the house, out came his twins with pale faces and swollen stomachs.

In a moving effort to show his appreciation, the farmer offered to pay me with two eggs. I, of course, declined and showed him instead how to make a nutritious mixture with the eggs and some powdered milk, which he would receive the next day.

I thought of the simple measures that come naturally to trained veterinarians, that could be life saving to so many people. What a wonderful and fulfilling way God had provided for me to share my skills in response to the needs of the poor, the hungry, and the disenfranchised of the world.

I had two weeks of action packed, heart warming, heart breaking, real life experiences. It was a time of extreme exhilaration and a time of sheer exhaustion. It was a time for looking outward and forward, and a time for introspection and examination. Most of all, it was a time to thank God for how He touches our hearts and says, "as you do it to the least of these, you do it unto me". Matthew 25:40

What had I meant to these Dominicans? What did this experience mean for me? One thing was for sure; there was no returning to my former ways. This experience was etched into my memory forever. More importantly, it would change my perspective on service to my brothers and sisters in need. God was calling me to use my talents in service to Him.

As Charlie and I bounced along the rough track to the airport, Charlie said, "Leroy, I guess you know you have made a mess".

"Probably," I answered, "but exactly how?"

"Before you came, I had more than I could do. But now, so much interest has been created, I will never get done!"

It was evident that we had struck a responsive chord with the people. More importantly, God had struck a responsive chord with me.

When we arrived at the Santa Domingo airport, I went through emigration and customs without any problem, even though I was carrying a large box with my microscope inside. As I passed through the gate to board the plane, a security guard stepped in front of me.

While holding his gun across his chest, he pointed to the bag and said, "No. Es Grande."

I responded, "No Es Grande. It's breakable and valuable, I brought it down here, why can't I take it back?"

We stared at each other for a minute, and then he stepped aside and motioned me on.

A huge black cloud was coming from the south, heading for the airport. I hoped we wouldn't have to fly through that. Everyone boarded quickly, and the plane taxied to the southern end of the runway and turned around. The pilot gunned the engines and we were on our way. Once again, I said "thank you" to the Lord for that and for all other times He had looked after me on this trip. God is good and answers prayer. Isn't that reassuring to know?

Arriving in Miami, I suffered culture shock in reverse. In the short time I had been gone, it seemed to me that the cars had grown twice as big. Then the tears came flowing down my cheeks. It was just too much for me at that moment, because of the poverty I had encountered. I knew that God had humbled my heart and that His Spirit was speaking to me. Now it was unmistakably clear; this was His call for my life.

CHAPTER 3

The Challenge

It never entered my mind that we would not get a charter for the organization or that we could not develop a modus operandi to make it happen. The challenge, as I saw it, was to identify veterinarians who had a desire to be involved in veterinary missions. Until now, there was no such organization.

My first thought was to share my experiences with veterinarians that I knew were Christians. I chose Macon, Georgia, because of its central location in the state. Then I called friends from across the state, asking them to meet with me. About a dozen people arrived on Sunday afternoon, October 31, at the Hilton Hotel. I showed slides of the Dominican farmers, and talked about my Dominican Republic experiences. I offered more enthusiasm than answers about veterinarians working overseas. However, a nucleus was formed. Although some may have responded more out of a desire not to puncture the balloon I was flying aloft on, than a desire to get involved.

I shared at that meeting the good news that Christian Veterinary Mission was now chartered. The Secretary of State of Georgia issued the charter on September, 13, 1976. The Judge of the Superior Court of Irwin County, Georgia, recognized CVM'S incorporation on September 21, 1976 and this was legally published in The Ocilla Star, Ocilla, GA, on September 23, 1976. The official process was complete.

We reviewed our financial position and organizational structure. We discussed the organization's needs, and ways to develop a roster of veterinarians who were interested in missions. We also began to identify short-range and long-range objectives. I drove home, amazed at how God had blessed and guided our effort. Without Him, it would never come to be. With Him, it would be successful and grow to fruition.

The life-blood of a non-profit organization is its tax-exempt status. Everyone should enjoy the quest for this special privilege once in his or her life. With the help of my accountant, we worked toward that goal. We reached the finish line sooner than we expected—the first half of 1977. It was another fine and pleasant misery along the way.

We decided that if we were going to dream, we would dream big. Since we were chartered, and up and running, I wrote a letter to about sixty Ministers of Agriculture in developing countries. My senator, Sam Nunn, supplied their addresses. While I was at it, I even challenged the Food and Agriculture Organization of the United Nations to call on us for our services. More interesting postage stamps than substance came with the replies. At least our name was out there!

Another essential ingredient for our organization was a logo. My neighbor and friend, Frank Crouch, had a niece who was an artist. Sandra Irons illustrated the theme I had outlined—the world, a rural farmer, a calf, and a syringe, overlaid with a shadow of the good shepherd (see figure below). I thought it was good. I still think it represents the heart and soul of CVM, though later it was replaced by our present logo, which I love very much.

Old Logo

Requests for help began to trickle in, mostly from South and Central America. We helped fund a goat project in Honduras. We also began to make plans for short-term shuttles. We sent out a newsletter to veterinarians in Georgia, and asked them to join us in our efforts.

A pattern began to emerge for me. I practiced during the day, and at night, I would get on the phone to talk with friends and acquaintances about mission work for veterinarians. Occasionally, I would cold-call strangers—following any lead to identify veterinarians who were interested in missions. I learned that if the person I spoke to had no interest, they usually knew someone who might. Slowly, a network began to emerge—not just in Georgia, but around the country as well.

Around this time, I met Dr. Earle Goodman, from Turbeville, South Carolina. He had been to Bolivia, where he saw the need and the potential for veterinarians to serve others. He had been working through his denomination, but the mission committee failed to catch a vision for veterinary missions. He felt frustrated, but he sent me all of his files and offered his help. Were we dreaming, or were veterinary missions legitimate?

Who were these dreamers, the founding members of CVM? They were products of small town life from the Southeast and the South, and later from the Midwest. They were from towns with names like Shiloh, Turbeville, and Ocilla. Before long, the movement would include the Pacific Northwest, in places like Edmonds and Ballard. These founding members grew up close to the church. They had strong religious convictions, nurtured by generations of faithful parents and grandparents.

They grew up close to the land, following family traditions. They were children who worked alongside their parents, to make a living and a way of life. Most children coming from rural areas, both rich and poor, worked along with their families. They made the farms productive and were influenced tremendously by the work. It nurtured a reverence for family, creation, and the Creator.

At that time, animals were an indispensable part of farm life. They were necessary for producing meat, milk, and eggs. They also provided cash and items for barter, allowing needed purchase of staples. These animals also provided power for operating farm equipment, and served as practical local transportation. Sickness or death of these farm animals often affected the quality of life for a family and their future.

Most farm children of that day developed a great love for animals, and an almost instinctive understanding of their habits and nature. They learned by observing older family members as they cared for and worked with animals. Most children were assigned chores like milking and feeding, where the relationship became even more intimate. It sealed forever within them their love for animals.

It is little wonder that to some, veterinarians were their earliest heroes, next to their dads. The wonderful things that the vet could do for their animals amazed these young kids. While other children dreamed of becoming firefighters or pilots, many farm children dreamed of becoming veterinarians.

Another profound influence in rural areas was the role of religion in family life. Yearly revivals usually took place in the spring or fall. On occasion, the speaker for the week's services was a returning missionary. The missionaries and their families stayed in church members' homes. They came from far-away places like Africa. They told stories of living with the people, suffering hardships, and experiencing great adventures in and through the Lord's work. This sparked an interest in many who heard. Their sharing planted seeds for future harvest.

Little did that generation know that these warm and everyday life experiences during their early years would serve them well in the future. They were prepared to support an organization that would some day play a unique role in addressing the basic needs of people around the world. The war on hunger in undeveloped areas of the world wasn't even on the horizon at that time, much less in the awareness of these dreamers.

CVM had its roots in Georgia, but the implications for service were less provincial. I thought, "If this is a viable option, should we be confining our organizational efforts to Georgia?" Early correspondence documents this.

Many veterinarians, who never had this kind of opportunity, were eager to be involved. As the network of interested individuals began to expand, I became aware of a spiritual stirring within the veterinary profession, manifested in a small group of individuals. It was as if they were coming out of their shells, emerging from a long dormancy. This served as an eye opener to many, to learn of other Christians out there, in their midst! It was encouraging to see people begin to express their beliefs without fear of ridicule.

At that time, the head of Christian Veterinary Fellowship (CVF) was Dr. George Burch, from Indianapolis, Indiana. Dr. Tim Blair, from Knoxville, Tennessee, and his wife Sarah served as editors of the CVF newsletter. This group was organized just a short time before our mission efforts, when 4 or 5 veterinarians got together for prayer and fellowship. They had progressed to a regular functioning group that was able to have a spiritual presence at many veterinary meetings. This group did not have an overseas mission interest at that time. It seems that this was a place reserved for us—it had Christian Veterinary Mission written all over it.

I began to explore a possible relationship between CVM and CVF. We approached each other with an unfamiliar and somewhat wary eye. Were there common or conflicting interests? Dancing around like courting flamingos, we gradually began to learn more about each other. After discovering that there was certainly no competition, we considered ways that CVM and CVF might even compliment each other.

Dr. Tim Blair and Dr. Felix Smith.

In 1976, we shared our story with CVF members in Cincinnati at the American Veterinary Medical Association (AVMA) meeting, at the Auburn University Short Course, the American Animal Hospital Association (AAHA) meeting in Boston, and in the CVF newsletter. We were using all avenues at our disposal to get the message out. What a blessing organized veterinary medicine was as we made plans for CVM.

As the Lord would have it, the AVMA was scheduled to meet in Atlanta in July of 1977. We knew that the Lord had orchestrated this long before we discovered His plan. I organized a mission breakfast to coincide with this event.

Georgia CVF-CVM Breakfast
Monday, July 11, 1977 at 7:00 am
(Don't panic—it's not as long as it looks!)

Breakfast prayer (Doxology)
Devotion—Dr. Raiford Claxton, from Girard, Georgia
Home Missions—Dr. Leroy Penner, from Tsaile, Arizona
Short-term Missions Overseas—Dr. Earl Goodman, from Turbeville, South Carolina
Long-term Missions Overseas—Dr. Gordon Hatcher, from Tegucigalpa, Honduras
Business and Sharing
Financial Report of CVM—Dr. Felix Smith, from Perry, Georgia
Information Sheet Report (volunteers for service)—Dr. Dan Fincher, from Rome, Georgia
Resolutions—Dr. Dave Tyler, from Athens, Georgia
Election of new CVF president elect for Georgia
Installation of incoming president—Dr. W.F. Bozeman, from Adel, Georgia
Closing prayer
       *Doxology
     Praise God from whom all blessings flow
     Praise Him all creatures here below
     Praise Him above ye heavenly host
     Praise Father, Son, And Holy Ghost, Amen.

Seventy-eight people who had an interest in CVM attended this breakfast. Our financial statement revealed a balance of $729.88, after purchasing goats for a Honduran project. I thought this was an auspicious start!

```
MEMO:

TO:    Christian Veterinary Fellowship Advisory Board

FROM: Christian Veterinary Mission

While continuing to enlarge the network of
veterinarians nationwide, we recognize a need to
nurture the relationship between CVF and CVM. We
propose:

(a) That a resolution be formulated and put forth
that would call for the adoption, support, and
promotion of CVM and its goals by CVF.

(b) That CVF would nominate and elect six additional
directors to serve CVF/CVM with the three from
Georgia.
```

The stage was set.

On July 12, 1977, more than 200 veterinarians crowded into and around the room where the CVF breakfast was being held in the Regency Hyatt House in Atlanta. It was the largest Christian meeting of veterinarians I have ever attended. I introduced the resolution and suggested the slate of directors. It passed overwhelmingly. Now we were in business as a national organization.

```
The new slate of directors for CVF/CVM:
Three-year term:
Dr. A.L.Dorminy, of Ocilla, Georgia-Chairman
Dr. W.F. Bozeman, of Adel, Georgia
Dr. Felix Smith, of Perry, Georgia
Two-year term:
Dr. Larry Swango, of Auburn, Alabama
Dr. Earle Goodman, of Turbeville, South Carolina
Dr. Dick Perkins, of Edmonds, Washington
One-year term:
Dr. Clarence Mannasmith, of Morrilton, Arkansas
Dr. Tom Loafman, of St. Louis, Missouri
Dr. Dave Tyler, of Athens, Georgia
```

```
Advisory Committee:
Dr. Mac Barksdale, of Ft. Lauderdale, Florida
Dr. Raiford Claxton, of Claxton, Georgia
Dr. Ed Ames, of Oak Park, Illinois
Dr. C.W. Doney, of Seattle, Washington
Dr. Leroy Penner, of Idaho
Dr. Langdon Davis, of Augusta, Maine
Dr. John Hartsough, of Indiana
Dr. Robert Kirk, of Ithaca, New York
Dr. Larry Edwards, Oklahoma
Dr. Gary McIntosh, of Lewiston, Idaho

Committee Chairs:
Dr. Dick Perkins-Finance
Dr. Larry Swango, Volunteers for Service
Dr. Tom Loafman, Home Missions.
```

The program for the CVF breakfast included:

Christian Veterinary Fellowship

AVMA Breakfast

Opening prayer—Dr. Mel Swenson, Iowa

Welcome—Dr. Bill Bozeman, Georgia

Announcements—Dr. Tim Blair, Tennessee

Speaker I—Dr. Q.L. Darbyshire, Georgia

Music—Kitty Kay,introduced by Dr. Mac Barksdale, Florida

Speaker II—Dr. Ralph Henderson, Alabama

Christian Veterinary Missions—Dr. A.L.Dorminy, Georgia

Prayer—Dr. Ed Richards, Tennessee

Closing prayer—Dr. Clarence Mannasmith, Arkansas

The breakfast was held on my birthday. What a wonderful gift from the Lord! On this day, we established a mission effort in the profession on a national level. God is so good. There was one important detail—we needed to get to work!

On the home front, things were beginning to fall into place. Dr. Tom and Fredda Lois Loafman, from St. Louis, Missouri, initiated a project with Native Americans. They worked with Navajo people for a month in the summer of 1977 and returned in 1978. In the fall of 1977, Susan Price, a veterinary student from Purdue, went as well. From this initial work with the Navajo, we expanded to serve on other reservations. This relationship has continued through the years.

The Ministers of Agriculture in developing countries began responding to my letter, which explained CVM's community rural development involving livestock. Other people were learning about us as well. Some mission groups asked for information, and many expressed interest in pursuing a relationship with CVM. We explored these contacts, and did in depth studies of the needs and the appropriate responses for each community.

In the fall of 1976, Dr. Q. L. Darbyshire, of Moultrie, Georgia began developing relationships with some mission agencies. One of these agencies was Wycliffe, an organization involved in Bible translation for unreached people groups.

I received a letter from John Hostetler, a Wycliffe missionary in the jungles of the Amazon:

Dear Leroy,

Our work involves 10 different tribes. The death rate among their cattle is high. They are plagued with ticks. There is a need for tick fever medicine and sprays. They also have other domesticated animals such as ducks, chickens, and pigs. A visit to our area would be most welcome.

Sincerely, John

This is typical of the needs of the people and their interest in CVM's work. Many contacts with other Wycliffe workers revealed other places of interest as well. It was incredible how opportunities and challenges presented themselves. From these contacts, we began to develop a pool of field openings for veterinarians.

In October of 1977, I attended a meeting of the Southern Veterinary Medical Association in Knoxville, Tennessee. Each new meeting gave me the opportunity to acquaint other veterinarians with the concept of missions. I would encourage them to at least sign up on the CVM mailing list. Even though there was genuine interest, and a hunger to be involved, there was some skepticism as to the integrity of this new organization (which I think is healthy). That's why our organization must always be the embodiment of good stewardship.

Some Christian veterinarians are interested in a fellowship, but do not have a missions focus. One of our tasks was to identify those individuals who would be willing to support missions. They were easily identified, once they learned about CVM. Another challenge was that there was not always a balance between positions and candidates. It's like syrup and biscuits; it never comes out even—you need more of one or the other!

As the year 1977 ended, we had:

- Secured tax-exempt status.
- Become the official mission arm of the CVF.
- Elected a board of directors and officers.
- Adopted an official Statement of Faith.
- Defined our objectives, ministry, membership qualifications for missions, types of ministry, and support.
- Developed a roster of opportunities for service.
- Promoted CVM's ministry to many institutions.
- Added additional resources to CVM.
- Identified CVM representatives in about half of the states.

I wrote to these representatives at that time: "The seed has been planted. Apollos can water, but only God can make the garden grow." And grow it has, as the Lord has blessed it mightily.

CHAPTER 4

The Merger

Now that we had the skeleton of an organization, the next step was to flesh it out. For this animal to live and breathe, it had to grow some vital organs. It needed a heart to pump blood to all the parts. This required connecting arteries and veins to transmit blood. It needed life-sustaining oxygen in a planned and controlled manner. It needed power and direction. We had the framework. We needed now to fill in the details.

Exploring all avenues, we turned to our Christian brothers in medicine. Dr. Don Piermattei, of Fort Collins, Colorado, was active in the Christian Veterinary Fellowship. Don told me about the Christian Medical Society, and their involvement in missions. They were meeting in Wichita, so he and I attended. CMS resembled the United Nations in organization, sitting around the room in desks with placards indicating the area they represented. I was impressed. At that point, they were light years ahead of us—they had salaried employees to manage the organization. One person oversaw the mission program.

We enjoyed the fellowship and the Bible lectures; one was about the gift and high cost of unexpected love. It was a poignant reminder of the tremendous price that was paid for each of us, so that we might enjoy the gift of eternal life through Jesus Christ, our redeemer. We liked CMS's spiritual emphasis. We were not sure that we could or should duplicate their organizational pattern.

After returning home, I sat down to figure out what our needs were and how best to meet those needs. Of course, we had to have veterinarians who were willing to serve as missionaries. That posed no problem in my mind. I was sure veterinarians would be lining up to go. But where? Wherever they are needed? How would they be paid? Would they donate their time and resources?

To answer all those pesky questions, I decided I would make board assignments. That's the solution, board assignments!

I did make board assignments. That was the easy part. Helping board members to function effectively and efficiently was the difficult part. Trying to make all of these things happen after work, by phone, was too much. I was still trying to practice veterinary medicine and run an organization at the same time. Could it be that I was a bit naive?

I was brought up sharply one night. I was talking to the newly appointed finance chairman, Dr. Dick Perkins, of Edmonds, Washington.

After we exchanged a few niceties, he said, "I think this idea of veterinary missions is a neat one. I am most certainly in favor of it, but don't you think we need someone—or an organization—to help us make this work?"

He told me about a relief and development organization in Seattle, called World Concern (WC). This group was already sending personnel and supplies overseas. They had a medical group as a part of their organization. Dick thought that they might be interested in adding a veterinary group, as well.

There was a long silence. I said, "Let me think about it."

It is difficult to have someone tell you something you are not eager to hear, but already suspected. Something you push into the deeper recesses of your mind, hoping it will go away. However, I did not want to lose our momentum. The Lord had brought us a long way in a short period, and I could not see that going to waste.

I talked with other members of the Board. They seemed surprised to learn that I did not have all the answers. They were unusually cautious in their replies. Out of friendship and respect for me, they did not want to hurt my feelings. Most of them just said, "Whatever you think, Leroy, we are with you." It was reassuring, but not very guiding.

I thought it was worth exploring and we might even learn something. Dick set up an appointment with the director of World Concern, Rev. Art Beals. In September of 1977, we sat down with Art and

Crista Administration Bldg.

Mr. Don A. Gilkison, director of management and planning. It seemed that they were only a half step ahead of us; they had organized a few months earlier. They were part of a group of ministries called King's Garden.

Dick and I worked with Art and Don to craft a proposal:

The proposal for the association of Christian Veterinary Missions Foundation, Inc. with World Concern, King's Garden.

With the consummation of this merger proposal, World Concern will begin to implement plans leading to involvement of CVM members in mission (both domestic and foreign). This will include expanding the membership, defining the ministry options, establishing criteria for service in short term assignments, as well as fellowship and financial opportunities at home, and the establishing of a network for communication among members as to professional challenges and Christian service opportunities.

These opportunities might include such things as: speaking on behalf of CVM to local, state and national gatherings; creating an information resource network for guidance in specialized veterinary medicine applications in mission assignments; and establishing and promoting the collection of veterinary sample medicines and surplus supplies for shipment to veterinarians working in mission assignments abroad.

This agreement will be in effect following review and ratification by both the Board of Directors of the CVM Foundation, Inc. and King's Garden inc."

You can see from the wording of the document that we both were tiptoeing through the tulips, not knowing exactly where we were going. It made us rely on the Lord. As it says in, Joshua 3:3: "Keep your eye on the Ark of the Covenant, follow it because you have not been this way before". No truer words had ever been spoken about our pilgrimage in veterinary missions.

In addition to meeting with World Concern, I met with Dr. Dick Perkins, Dr. Bob Otto, and Dr Bud Doney. We spent some time together, going over some of the core beliefs we felt vital to the ministry. It included the vision statement which still remains the same. We developed some general guidelines on how to conduct the ministry that have served us well in the ensuing years.

During the next few months, through numerous phone conversations and mailed communications, we considered many options. These were reviewed by consulting members of the CVM Board. This document does not reflect all the changes, or the fine points that required definition. It does reflect the net result of that process.

For the next four months, I spent time in thought and prayer, trying to decide the proper course. I discussed it with members of the board, considered the implications, and weighed the pros and cons. Should we join forces with WC, or continue alone? It was a big decision!

Finally, I reached a conclusion. Maybe the catalyst was a remark that Dick Perkins made.

He said, *"Leroy, it depends on how big your ego is, as to whether you go with World Concern."*

That did it. I wasn't doing this for an ego trip, but because I believed that the Lord had spoken to me. This was an assignment that He had given me personally—to be involved in Veterinary Missions. I knew what we wanted, but I also recognized that we needed a jump-start to make it happen quickly.

It is interesting, how we go through the agony to make a decision, but when we make it, right or wrong, the tension dissipates and we are at peace. That was the case. In February of 1978, Danny Martin, Director of Medical Ambassadors for WC, flew to Georgia and we consummated the agreement.

There was much more work to be done. First of all we alerted all the veterinarians in the U.S. to the news that there was an organization totally dedicated to facilitating veterinarians in missions. With a check in his hand to finance the first national mailing, Danny headed west to begin preparations.

The AVMA allowed us to buy their mailing list. At that time, it had around 40,000 veterinarians. I wrote a letter, which was sent along with the promise of a small booklet for those who responded. The booklet was John Stott's **Who is My Neighbor**. It emphasized 1 John 3:17,18: "But whoever has the world's goods, and beholds his brother in need and closes his heart against him, how does the love of God abide in him? Little children, let us not love with word or tongue but in deed and truth." It reminded me of the little girl in the Dominican Republic.

We touched a sensitive chord, and the Lord revealed a hunger in the hearts of the recipients. They returned more than 2, 000 responses.

"Unprecedented! Amazing! Unbelievable!" fellow workers in World Concern commented.

The response turned heads. Prior to this, many people believed that there was no place for veterinary missions. Now we had their attention.

We also needed to educate mission organizations about the value of veterinary missions. Like veterinarians in practice, we would teach these "clients" about the skills and expertise of veterinarians, and

explain how they could best use our services. We also needed to educate mission groups overseas, even those doing rural development!
It was unbelievable how unaware many of them were about the
appropriateness of veterinarians for mission work.

I believe veterinarians are uniquely qualified for the task. Think
about the training and experience veterinarians need to be successful in practice. Based on the number of requests we receive now, it
seems that the word is out.

The merger was complete, and we were on our way. We firmly
believed that the Lord was directing our paths.

CHAPTER 5

The Early Years

In a letter to the veterinarians on our mailing list, Dan Martin emphasized the partnership between our organizations.

> *". . . World Concern is not taking over CVM. We both serve the same Master. Christ has given some of us the gift of administration, whereby we offer ourselves in service to those whose gifts lie in the area of veterinary medicine. We trust that by combining our efforts, World Concern and CVM will be enabled to serve our Lord more effectively than either could do individually".*
>
> *Sincerely,*
>
> *Dan Martin*

Linda Pillo was the administrative assistant who helped with general correspondence. Our first objectives were to make veterinarians aware of the opportunities available for mission service, and to facilitate trips as they went. This meant that we had to look at CVM's organizational needs, literature development, and funding. We also had to find prospective candidates for short-term and long-term service. We needed to develop a pattern of doing business that would bring glory to God, and challenge our brothers and sisters in the veterinary profession to be involved in His Kingdom's work.

Prior to the merger, we started a short-term shuttle program in the U.S. We followed the Biblical admonition: Acts 1:8 "You will be

my witness in Jerusalem, and in all Judea, Samaria and to the utter-
most parts of the world." Jerusalem refers to home missions. Unless
we care for our neighbors at home, it is unlikely we will care for our
neighbors when we are overseas.

Shuttles have always been a self-funded venture. They have played
a significant role in the life and work of CVM. For one thing, shuttles
personalize missions like nothing else can. They give a taste of mission work for people who cannot serve long term. Shuttles develop
enthusiasm for the veterinary mission program. They offer a world
perspective and encourage the local focus for missions.

Since my first shuttle experience in the Dominican Republic,
CVM had not ventured out of the country. Rather, we concentrated
on activities at home. With the help of Gordon Hatcher, we arranged
a shuttle to Honduras. Dr E.D.Ver Steeg, of Iowa, went to Catacamas,
Olancho, Honduras to work at the El Sembrador School for Boys.
World Gospel Mission (WGM) operated the school. A dairy and
swine farm was associated with the school. We were elated that one
method of operation was being revealed to us.

Dr. Tom Loafman, Dr Ver Steeg, and their families were the
first of what would become a continuous stream of veterinarians,
students, and technicians to more than 35 countries of the world.
These shuttle participants and long term missionaries have worked
with people in more than 20 language groups. They have helped with
livestock and community development. The focus of their efforts has
been to teach and to train so that others may learn to do things for
themselves.

I have talked to hundreds of veterinarians, students, and technicians after they have returned from a short-term mission. Their
words are often the same, "Leroy, I don't know whether I did them
any good, but it was certainly a blessing to me".

Their joy had been made complete by service in and for the Lord.

We continued to hear from governments, schools, and organizations around the world. They all wanted to know more about CVM's
activities and objectives, and how they could participate with us. We
evaluated each letter, and considered if, and how, CVM could be involved. The number of opportunities began to grow, until the trickle
became a stream.

Haiti was the first country I visited to explore opportunities for service. Haiti was once known as the "Pearl of the Antilles". Not any more. It was a poverty stricken land. I thought the Dominican Republic was bad when I worked there, but it looked very promising in contrast to Haiti. On a later trip, I visited Hospital Albert Schweitzer (HAS). I saw kids exhibiting kwashiorkor, a severe protein deficiency malnutrition, which results in bloated stomachs and reddish hair.

From the original settling of the country by foreigners, to the present, Haiti's leaders have inflicted untold misery upon its people. This includes some leaders from their own people who, when overthrowing foreign tyrannical rule, supplanted it with their own brand, which may be even worse.

Unfortunately, many Haitian people embrace voodoo. This impedes true progress in development and objective thinking.

My contact was Charles Morrow, with Heifer Project International. He helped me contact as many organizations as possible during my short stay. I met with representatives of Rotary International, who were concerned because the animal shipments they financed had a mortality rate greater than 40%. I went to the Department of Agriculture, and learned that only four veterinarians worked in the country of Haiti, and they were almost totally without equipment or medicines. The Methodist, Baptist, and Nazarene missions within the country also received visits from me. Everywhere I went, people needed veterinarians to help with their livestock needs.

At the end of my visit, I was scheduled to fly to the Dominican Republic from Port- au- Prince. Wes Stafford, representing World Concern in Haiti, insisted that I join him for a meal at his favorite restaurant. He assured me that it was o.k. to eat there. I should have suspected something when several chickens came in quite calmly, as if they lived there. Apparently they did. I hurriedly ate and caught the flight to Santa Domingo. The cramps arrived the same time I did. I barely made it through customs before the "Haitian Plague" hit. I spent the entire three days in the bathroom and bed of a missionary friend, Arthur Haylock. It was an unforgettable experience—that I wish was forgettable.

After recovering, I returned to Miami and soon was scheduled to go to Belize. I was still weak; only taking in soup at this point. About

15 minutes out of Miami, the pilot announced over the intercom that a hurricane was predicted to hit Belize the next day. (Due to the short time between my arrival and re-departure, I was unaware of any unusual weather in the area). I looked out the window to the east and sure enough, the storm clouds were rolling in.

We landed at a nearby airport, and I took a taxi into the city—only to learn that the hurricane was going to hit there soon. They were boarding up the hotel. I pulled an old army maneuver, and took the return flight to Miami. I "limped" home to completely recover from the devastating trip to Haiti. I had received my indoctrination under fire, and felt like a seasoned but somewhat weakened veteran.

We began collecting commodities (veterinary instruments, medicines, and supplies), using World Concern's Supply Service warehouse as a collection point. We got some quizzical looks when strange and exotic looking instruments and unusually large 'pills' began arriving at the Supply Service warehouse. They decided it was best to segregate these items from their human collection. As always, the two worlds of veterinary and human medicine have many commonalities, but there are some necessary and obvious differences.

World Concern was most fortunate; the person in charge of the commodities program was Elaine Leslie, a nurse. She was the "Bionic Woman" personified. Elaine had limitless energy, and she could really motivate people. She commanded a corps of volunteers who collected, sorted, boxed, and shipped tons of donated goods.

Elaine's power of persuasion is awesome. At her retirement party (although I doubt she will ever retire), I told the group that some people motivate with love, some with fear. Elaine uses both methods! Her husband, Earl, is a gentle and compassionate man. Earl is retired, but he doesn't realize it because Elaine keeps him so busy—but he loves the work and her. She is a wonderful lady, and I am proud to call her my good friend and "sister" in Christ.

Literature and educational material were very important, if we hoped to motivate people to join us. One of the first things we produced, in order to get the story of CVM out, was a slide-tape presentation called "Bless the Beasts and the Children." It graphically and poignantly contrasted the world of disease, poverty, hunger, and sin with God's desire for our well being; in harmony with Him and His

Creation. Some of the scenes were from India, where we were assisting a veterinarian, Dr. Christopher. Pictures and music can say things words can never convey.

Activity erupted on all fronts. We began organizing intensively at home. One built-in advantage was the infrastructure that existed in the veterinary profession. This allowed us to contact veterinarians throughout the United States, and to attend conventions and meetings, sharing with veterinarians about CVM.

We were invited by Dr. Edward "Bud" Ames, of the AVMA, to participate in the Auto-Tutorial Program. The annual AVMA meeting was in Dallas in July 1978. This was our first opportunity to share with veterinarians from throughout the United States at one event. We are grateful to the AVMA for all of the times that they have given us that opportunity. We are grateful to all the organizations that allow us to participate in their meetings.

It was time to make our literature look more professional. We needed to rework our first brochure. For the second brochure, we featured a rural farmer, a food animal, and one of our expatriate workers. That photo summarized the ministry. It is hard to overstate the importance of animals in the lives of people in developing countries. Animals do not just supply meat, milk, and eggs. The people's total physical needs revolve around their animals. The brochure briefly explained CVM's work and listed the CVM advisory board. It was a start. The brochure has been revised many times since, but has always stuck to our original goal—an accurate reflection of the ministry.

Dan Martin and I went to Dallas armed with our slides-and-tape show, our new brochures, and an unbridled enthusiasm to share our vision with all who would listen. Once there, we participated in the prayer breakfast that Tim and Sarah Blair had organized for CVF. We tried to take advantage of every opportunity and we left the convention with more names and more contacts. We were greatly encouraged by it all.

In addition to the AVMA, we began to contact individuals in state veterinary organizations. We requested opportunities to visit conventions and participate in meetings. I was invited to the South Carolina and North Carolina meetings, and the Florida meeting. Everywhere

I went, I shared the theme "Christ's Love Expressed Through Veterinary Medicine." I never left a meeting without picking up additional names for the mailing list and identifying veterinarians with genuine interest in serving. New names were added to the mailing list daily. At the end of 1977 we were mailing to nearly 300 veterinarians.

I read the book <u>Rich Christians in an Age of Hunger</u> by Ron Sider. It articulated what I had also experienced in my short walk with CVM. The book reinforced in me that the people who had resources, skills, and talents needed to share them with others, especially people in great need.

What was it again that the lady from Africa suggested? "Come share with us your skills, that we may do things for ourselves."

Each milestone brought new challenges as we traveled down the road with faith and perseverance. The tremendous response to the mail-out about CVM left me in a state of euphoria. It revealed an interest in mission work by a profession that had been overlooked by missions.

As we continued networking across the United States, we saw that certain individuals had more than just a passing interest. They could be counted on to take an active role in the organization. A corps of volunteers emerged and began filling leadership roles in areas of the United States.

By the fall of 1978, we had identified openings for veterinarians in Bangladesh, Bolivia, Colombia, Botswana, the Philippines, Mexico, and Zaire. The need was apparent. Now we needed to link the need with the individual whom God had called to meet that need. We were not lacking here, either. We had 80 applicants for service overseas. It reminded me of Matthew 25, which says, in effect, that the Spirit sensitizes us to the needs of others. Apparently, many were sensitized. We need to stay in communion with God's Spirit for direction in our lives. What a joy to see Him working.

As 1978 ended, we thanked the Lord for the tremendous strides CVM had made. It truly was a benchmark year. The Lord had confirmed our step of faith in so many ways; He had done amazing things among us. Our first year's income was $29,000. With confidence in the Lord's direction we even made a start toward establishing a foundation!

Now that the dust had settled from the initial flurry of activity, it was time to hit the road again. This time our destination was Africa. Dan Martin, Director of Medical Missions, Dr. Bob Otto, a practice partner of Dr. Dick Perkins and I headed for Nairobi, Kenya in the spring of 1979. One family we enjoyed visiting very much was that of Dr. Tom and Mrs. Betty Wanous. Tom, Betty, and their five children were from Minnesota. Tom divided his time between Daystar (an organization for developing national leadership), and helping the Turkana people in the northern part of Kenya. Tom was instrumental in helping us establish our work with the Maasai.

Dan and I headed out of Nairobi on a commercial airline to Juba, Sudan. We had assurance from ACROSS, a consortium working there, that if we were unable to get out of the country by a commercial airline they would get us out with their transportation. Juba is on the Nile River which is the lifeblood of the area. It was interesting to see the contrasting green along the winding river, while the rest of the country was a desert brown.

Dr. A. L. Dorminy—Maasai, Kenya.

Our host in Juba went north with Dan, leaving me to enjoy his home while they were gone. Except for one meal that I was invited to the first night after their departure, I fasted for two days. There were no provisions in the house, and no place to purchase any. I was able to identify with the hungry, at least on a short-term basis. The only companions I had were the friendly lizards that infested the house (it was impossible to keep them out). One night as I attempted to turn on a light, I thought the switch was unusually soft and movable. Sure enough, one of my lizard friends was perched there.

The next day, I went to visit the Vaccine and Parasitology Laboratory, financed by the World Bank. The lab was built at the outskirts of Juba. It was a scene straight out of an alien world. A local herdsman, attired in his birthday suit, had taken the ashes from his night camp and had completely smothered himself and his cattle in them, in a heroic effort to keep away the mosquitoes and bugs. His color blended with the gray dawn breaking. His silhouette revealed a tall majestic figure, silently going about his daily chores and tending his animals.

As we walked across the grass surrounding the buildings, a wave preceded us like a Kansas wheat field blowing in the wind, only the air was as calm as the horse latitudes. The "blowing" effect came from lizards and varmints of all descriptions. They were traveling in waves ahead of us. Inside the newly completed buildings were some of the same creatures that infested the house where I was staying. Again, it was impossible to keep them out.

This whole project, I felt, was well intended. Unfortunately, it was never used. We can learn volumes from such failed attempts at development. Progress has to be appropriate, and managed by the people, or it will be a great boondoggle- a waste of time and money.

The group returned to Juba two days later. We immediately left for Nairobi, flying in a small plane with the pilot, Dan, and two nurses. I sat in the navigator's seat. Dan was crammed in the back, and the nurses were in the center of the plane. It was a memorable trip. We taxied down to the end of the runway, only to discover that we couldn't reach the control tower by radio. Honestly, the runway was not that long! It was not a reassuring way to begin.

The pilot was not the greatest confidence builder in the world. He continually voiced his apprehensions:

about being overloaded—"This is more than we are supposed to carry", about the fuel supply—"I'm not sure we have enough to reach Nairobi", and about the weather—"I don't know if we can get over those clouds and we can't go through them".

I took the map and attempted to do some dead reckoning navigation. I pointed to where I thought we were at the time, and he responded by quickly pointing to a rock and stabbing his finger on the map, saying that this is where we are. So much for latitude and longitude and all that good stuff, but what happens when it is cloudy?

We made it back to Nairobi after a four hour unsettling flight. We came to a Methodist guesthouse, where we had just missed lunch. They did serve tea and cookies in the middle of the afternoon. The English influence, you know. It was a gourmet meal for me; I could have eaten anything. Even those lizards were beginning to look promising before we left Juba!

The group split up, each person exploring options for service. Bob Otto went to Malawi, and I went to South Africa and then to Bophuthatswana. The small plane allowed me to view the countryside. We flew to Taung, where I met Dr. Dale Beighle, a Southern Baptist Veterinary Missionary from Kentucky. He was teaching at an agricultural school. I accompanied him on some farm calls

A bull was sick and before we arrived he had already expired. In fact, by the time we got there, the people had skinned and eaten a good bit of him. They were cutting the rest of the bull into small pieces to dry and preserve. They weren't wasting anything. There was not enough of the bull left to make a diagnosis. I have often wondered what killed that bull. It could have been Anthrax or another communicable disease. With scant food and no refrigeration, food options are limited.

Our group met again in Johannesburg, and flew back to the United States. Our introduction to Africa had been a good one. Because of this trip, we identified three long-term positions. Our networking in Africa had begun. It would now be easier to establish and nurture relationships with many of the agencies in Africa. This was important to us, because established agencies have infrastructure in place. This keeps missionaries' costs down, and expedites projects.

CHAPTER 6

Reaching Out

In early September of 1977 while returning to Georgia from Seattle. I stopped in St. Louis to visit with the Loafman family. Tom and Fredda Lois had completed a month in the Navajo reservation. Now they were helping Sue Price, a student from Purdue, prepare for a follow-up trip. This gave us a good opportunity to learn more about doing effective short-term work at home. It was also good training for working overseas. We have had shuttles going to the Navajo Reservation ever since.

Later, we sent shuttles to other Native American tribes, like the Cheyenne, Crow, and Blackfeet. We also had several different shuttle sites within the Navajo Reservation. The Reservation is huge; it covers a large part of both Arizona and New Mexico. There are unlimited opportunities.

Shuttle—now there's a word for you. Gloria Hollefreund coined it. When CVM operated within World Concern, she was in charge of processing candidates. The shuttle program has meant so much to CVM—both to the participants, and to the recipients.

Not everyone is able or suited to do long term mission work. Those who are not should not feel guilty. Shuttles do, however, let a person get a 'feel' for mission work and learn about the challenges involved. It is a rewarding experience for Christians who are trying to live out their faith. It broadens their horizons, and helps develop a balanced perspective for world missions, to which, I think the Bible unquestionably calls us. The focus of the New Testament after the resurrection is definitely on missions.

In the spring of 1979, Dr. George Grimes, of Memphis, Tennessee, went to Costa Rica to work. It was a good shuttle; it helped to identify ways that short-term vets could be involved in teaching. George taught in a 'hands on' manner, through castrations and hernia operations. On a shuttle, each person utilizes his or her own God-given talents. In this case, George's teaching skills and visual aids were valuable.

When he returned, George showed others how they, too, could be involved. 1 Peter 4:10 says, "Each one should use whatever gift he/she has been given to serve others, faithfully administering God's grace in its various forms." Can you believe that God would use us to administer His grace? This is CVM's refrain, using your God given talents in service to Him and His children!

In April, the American Animal Hospital Association (AAHA) meeting was in New Orleans. We secured booth space, and shared it with CVF. The response from the AAHA veterinarians was more reserved. Maybe it was because of their perception that small animal veterinarians would not be able to participate in the work.

I am often asked, "How can a small animal veterinarian participate in veterinary missions?"

My response is, "If you learn to ride a bike, you never completely forget. The same is true with large animal medicine or any other basic skills that we learned during veterinary school."

We do suggest doing some refresher work, if possible. Our policy of sending teams of two people, in this case, a small animal vet with a large animal vet, seems to work nicely. Generally, the work is so basic that most veterinarians feel competent, regardless of their experience since graduation. In more recent days we have begun to work in former communist countries that have a veterinary infrastructure but desire to upgrade their skills. This requires a more sophisticated approach.

Many small animal practitioners have made great contributions to the ministry through their participation in the Animal Loveline Program. This program allows veterinarians to memorialize a client's pet by donating to CVM. These supporters are just as important as the veterinarians who serve on the field.

One part of a successful shuttle is having on-site information. We prefer to have an on-site coordinator. Even with on-the-field facilitators, Murphy's Law can still apply. The best things a person can take on the field are patience and flexibility in large quantities.

An important question for someone contemplating a shuttle is, "How flexible am I?" Some people have been challenged by the situations they encounter; a few have been overwhelmed. It depends on the individual's, perceptions and personality. Obviously, the better someone is prepared for their shuttle, the more likely he or she is to have a positive experience. Most times, the unexpected does have a way of intruding. If we look at a short-term shuttle as a learning experience, and discover what God is teaching us, then I think we profit enormously.

Since the inception of the shuttle program, CVM has facilitated more than 600 shuttles at home and overseas; and that number grows weekly. Shuttles have probably generated more enthusiasm among our constituency than anything else we do. They have been an influential and positive factor in CVM's development.

Some participants in shuttles like to work in one country, then another. Others prefer to return to the same location, because they have developed relationships with people there. Participants feel that this continuity will help them to be more effective. Some make an annual pilgrimage to the same location, to work with the same people.

In the summer of 1980, two vets, Dr. Arthur Moore and Dr. Ted Bullard, from Dothan, Alabama made trips to Haiti. They went to Hospital Albert Schweitzer (HAS), to help with the veterinary clinic that operated under the aegis of HAS.

Arthur said, "Ted volunteered our services and then he sent me first, to act as the guinea pig".

HAS operated the farm to provide the hospital and staff with meat, milk and eggs. Arthur and Ted did Tuberculosis and Brucellosis testing for the dairy. It was a great help to the hospital, and demonstrated what shuttles can do.

Dr. Larry Mellon founded Hospital Albert Schweitzer (HAS) in Haiti in 1956. He had gone back to medical school after being out of school for many years. After he graduated, he wanted to start a hospital in a very needy place. Albert Schweitzer inspired Dr. Mellon, because he had visited his hospital in Africa. Every time I visited Larry, he always showed me a picture of the two of them together. The director of HAS told me that Dr. Mellon was bothered by the Biblical admonition "It is hard for a rich man to enter the Kingdom of Heaven", Luke 18:24.

The first time I visited Haiti, I wanted to meet with Dr. Mellon to discuss placing a veterinarian at the hospital. He declined the meeting, because he had an agreement with someone at Cornell Veterinary School, to provide HAS with its veterinary needs. However, the second time I was in Haiti, it was a different story. I was driving over to Port-au-Prince after visiting up north. I suddenly realized that I was being followed very closely by another car. When the road widened, the driver came alongside and waved me down.

After the driver had stopped the car, a fellow in a large straw hat emerged from it. He walked back to my car, stuck out his hand, and asked if I was Leroy Dorminy. He offered to share his banana and peanut butter sandwich under a palm tree. It was Larry Mellon! I quickly accepted. That was the beginning of a good friendship. Larry and his wife Gwen appreciated the veterinarians and their families that came to live and work at HAS. The feeling was mutual. During the ensuing years, I visited him every time I went to Haiti. These were enjoyable times for me. I was greatly saddened when I discovered his obituary in the New York Times when visiting my son in New York.

Veterinary Missionary positions were opening in other areas of the world. Dr. Tom Wanous confirmed the possibility of one position, working with the Maasai in the Narok area of Kenya. Heed Bangladesh, a consortium of Christian agencies working in that country, requested a worker in Kamalganj. Other countries like Zaire and Algiers were also sending in requests. The biscuits were beginning to pile up, and now we needed some syrup to make things even.

As the word spread through the veterinary profession, people who wanted to serve contacted us. During the long cold winter nights of 1979-1980, Dr. Mark Hinton, from Minnesota, and I had some good telephone conversations. Mark was personally interested in mission service. I, of course, was delighted to explore options with him. He also told me about Dr. Ray Dayton, who was interested in serving. Ray was a veterinarian living in Hastings, Minnesota. My first contact with

Dr. Peter Quesenberry, a veterinarian from California, was in the fall of 1979. This was the pioneer club of CVM long-term workers. What an illustrious group of men and women! What an enviable record they have set. What models of service, for others to follow!

We continued to receive invitations for CVM to be represented at veterinary meetings. In January, we were invited to South Carolina, Indiana, and Louisiana. Unfortunately, I had to decline all of these because of a surgery. I don't think there is any doubt as to where I would rather have been, but the Lord deemed otherwise. It wasn't so much the pain of the surgery, but of missing my first love—talking about CVM.

There was one invitation in February that I was determined to keep—Mississippi State University. My good friend, Dr. James Miller, was the dean of the veterinary school. He had invited me to speak. One hundred people attended the breakfast. It reaffirmed to me that veterinarians were interested in fellowship and missions. The faculty advisors there were Drs. Eleanor and Ashby Green. Later in the fall, they went to a Cheyenne reservation on a shuttle.

In July 1979, the AVMA met in Seattle. Again, this opportunity dovetailed with the development of CVM. It gave us an opportunity to share our vision with Northwest veterinarians. It also was an excellent time to give the board members and others a first hand look at our home office and parent organization. Many supporters joined a tour of King's Garden (later, the name was changed to CRISTA). I think the members of the CVM Board came away more at peace with the merger. They had a greater appreciation for the total ministry, and were happy that CVM was a part of it.

Dr. Clem Fennell of England and his wife, Barbara, attended the AVMA meeting because of his work with the Carnation Co. (Their home office was in the Seattle area). Clem and I had been corresponding for a while. Together, we explored ways to build cooperation between CVM and the veterinary fellowship group in the UK. We talked about developing educational material for use in developing nations. When he asked me about CVM's plans to produce educational material, I told him that we were going to concentrate on single species books. Perhaps later we would look at a single book covering many species. At the present, we have produced 10 books.

The set includes nine in the series <u>Raising Healthy Animals,</u> and <u>Where There Is No Animal Doctor,</u> by Drs. Peter Quesenberry and Maureen Birmingham.

An interesting dynamic was developing in organized veterinary medicine. A few people were apprehensive about a Christian organization participating in conventions and other organized meetings, especially the AVMA. Concerned members cited the separation of church and state. We responded that they were not the state, and we did not claim to be the church. I encouraged everyone to continue with our objective. In time, our detractors would see that we didn't have horns! One or two individuals did try to retaliate against us by threatening a boycott of certain pharmaceutical companies that supported CVM. Fortunately, it didn't get far. Dr. Ed "Bud" Ames was very helpful in walking us through those early mine fields.

We are not in conflict with the profession, nor have we ever been. Rather, we desire to enhance it, by utilizing veterinarians in development work. Through the years, I think members of our profession have gained genuine respect for the work and ministry of CVM. We could participate in the AVMA auto-tutorial program, were provided booth space for our display at no cost, and could participate in the International Veterinary Medicine sessions of the meeting. These were invaluable to us as we made veterinarians aware of opportunities through CVM. We are so very grateful for this relationship with the AVMA and other organizations that have given us this same opportunity.

I really appreciate the things that the Southern Baptist Convention did to help us get involved and to provide information about certain countries and mission work. I would call Richmond, Virginia, the home office of the Foreign Mission Board of Southern Baptists, before going overseas. They would inform me of the Southern Baptist missionaries working there.

For example, in May 1979 we received a request from Dale Beighle. He needed a replacement while he was home on furlough. Dale was teaching in the agricultural school in Taung, Bophuthatswana. I met him when I visited there in March. This was a real benchmark. It allowed us to wade into the mission pool while we learned to swim. Dale wanted someone on the field for one year, beginning December 1, 1979.

For this assignment, we recruited Dr. Ken and Mrs. Ket Weinland. They were a perfect fit. Ken taught clinical medicine at Purdue. Ken and Ket would not have to learn another language, because the courses at Taung were in English. The position was well established. All they had to do was move in and begin working where the Beighles left off. It was our very first long term assignment. There were nine Ag School graduates at the end of the school term. As a gift to the graduates, CVM presented each of them with a Merck Veterinary Manual that the pharmaceutical company had donated.

The students were extremely proud of those manuals. The graduates became livestock inspectors for the various regions of the

Dr. Ken and Ket Weinland. (First vet long-term workers).

country. The transfer of knowledge from people like the Weinlands and Beighles can make such a difference in the lives of people who have had few chances for improvement. Where and how are you depositing your talents for others to use? Remember, your bank account of talents will be inaccessible after you are gone. Share your talents with others while you can.

Later, I visited one of the locations where these inspectors operated. All of the cattle in the country had to be inspected quarterly, and an account was given for any gain or decrease in numbers. The authorities may not know how many people lived in their country, but they sure had a handle on the livestock. Caesar would have been envious of such accounting. I know I was envious of the way the herd owners could control their animals. They literally lined up to go through the chute. I never saw a cow in Georgia that well behaved!

If 1979 was the year of positional identification of veterinarians, then 1980 was the year of assignments. In the fall of 1979, Floyd Votaw and his wife, Doris, went to Haiti. They did an initial survey of the conditions there, and investigated options for service. Miss Faye Goodling, a veterinary technician from Pennsylvania, joined the Votaws. Because Doris could speak French, she was a key player in this effort.

At the time, Doris was battling breast cancer and recuperating from a mastectomy. You can imagine how difficult this was, considering the terrible conditions of the Haitian roads. She showed unusual determination and courage, insisting that she go wherever they went, in order to translate. She succumbed to the cancer a few months after returning to the States.

In addition to the valuable information we learned on that extended shuttle, it set the stage for us to place a long-term worker there. Dr. Bill Baker arrived in 1980.

Mr. Ron Angert, a Heifer Project International representative in Haiti, commented on their efforts, *"I have to tell you that Dr. and Mrs. Votaw and Faye Goodling were just great. I don't think that a better pair could have started the CVM work in Haiti. A trail of improvements remains behind Dr. Votaw, and is very dramatic. Many of the people he visited are doing so much better because of the advice he gave them."*

CHAPTER 7

Moving Out

1980 was a benchmark year for CVM. We began to make progress in placing long-term workers. We broke the barrier in Africa, with the Weinlands; now we were ready to place more long-term workers. Through our African contacts, we developed a proposal to work with the Maasai. The Lord was preparing hearts to fill that need.

Mark Hinton and I continued to discuss missions long distance. Along with Mark and Audrey, Ray and Vicki Dayton of Minnesota, were candidate applicants now. In July, all four of them came to Seattle for formal interviews. We accepted both couples, introduced them to WC/CVM, and gave a brief cross-cultural orientation. We prayed with them and entrusted them to the Lord before seeing them off. They were the first of a large group of people who were called by God to serve through veterinary missions.

One memory of these four will forever be etched in my mind. I walked them to the front of the administration building, and said good-bye as they left for the airport. As I walked back into the building, I was overcome with emotion. I began to sob like a baby. I realized that the Lord had really answered my prayers. CVM was a reality; we had short-term and long-term workers serving on the mission field. The Lord is sovereign and exceedingly good!

Ray and Vicki served their first term with the Maasai. Ray had an unusual knack of working with tribal people. They could see his genuine love for them and their animals. The sights, sounds, and smells of tribal life apparently didn't bother him—at least, it didn't obscure his vision. One of my favorite photographs shows Ray poking his head out of a Maasai dung hut during a visit to give instruction on

Dr. Ray Dayton—Maasai, Kenya.

animal health. Ray and Vicki established themselves as missionaries par excellence. They developed warm relationships with the people.

Ray and Vicki came home on furlough after their first term. Ray told me then that he had no desire to do anything else; he was in the center of the Lord's will for his life.

I was in Florida when I got the call saying that Ray had been in an automobile accident. His motorcycle was hit by a van that was trying

Dr. Mark and Audrey Hinton, Nat, Anne, and Sam.
(First vet showing long-term interest).

to pass on the wrong side. He was taken to the hospital in Nairobi, to no avail. Ray was the first of our long-term workers to die on the field while in the Lord's service through CVM's ministry.

Ray's death was a crushing blow. He was the embodiment of the CVM ministry. His death was so senseless, the result of a foolish error. The Maasai demonstrated their respect and affection for him by holding a 24-hour vigil around his house until his funeral. The services were conducted in three languages: Swahili, Maasai, and English. He is buried in a mission compound near Narok.

My only consolation during that time was to remember what Ray said in 1983; that he was perfectly happy to be in Kenya because that was where the Lord wanted him.

Mark and Audrey lived in Nairobi, where Mark worked with Daystar University, a training institution for national leaders. The Daytons and Hintons seemed to be in ideal positions to use the natural talents God had given them. One of CVM's strengths, I believe, is that it allows each person to maximize his or her talents. The Lord modeled that when He chose a diverse group of men to be His disciples. The truth is that each of us has talents that can be used by God, if we turn them over to Him. Unless we submit, He can do nothing with them.

<hr />

Tina, Bruce, and I headed west from Georgia in early June of 1980. We were traveling in a small Buick Skylark, and pulling a U-Haul trailer. It was enough for that small engine, huffing and puffing, to conquer the Rockies without the trailer; but with it, the trip was almost impossible. The car sputtered, fumed, and ran hot. I found myself saying (like the little engine) "I think I can, I think I can." To the chagrin of our fellow motorists, we were slow, but finally made it to the top.

It is an awesome experience to drive across the U.S. Doing so, affords gorgeous scenes that defy description. It made me appreciate how blessed America really is. We can sing "America the Beautiful," knowing that it is absolutely true. God really gave us a bountiful land. With that gift, goes the responsibility to keep it beautiful. We need to take pride in how we conduct ourselves environmentally, from the smallest discarded paper wrapper to farming practices that conserve the soil, to caring for our National Parks and wildlife. If ever there was a worthy cause, this is one.

I had been coming out to Seattle on occasion, but now the WC staff would have to put up with me on a full time basis. My good friend, Mary Tyree, helped me deal with all of CVM's correspondence. I could not type at that time, and haven't progressed far since. Lawana Norman was a big help with CVM activities. Dave Blackmer has always been a great encourager to me, as well as many other World Concern Workers.

Nadine Court reserved us an apartment in Mountlake Terrace. It was not far from the CRISTA campus, where World Concern and CVM had their offices. Big old cars were sort of a status symbol there, and the little Skylark didn't make the cut (The 1978 Chevrolet Impala I borrowed from WC later would fit just fine). The only unpleasant thing in Mountlake Terrace was the loud music on Friday and Saturday nights. With no air-conditioning, we had to sleep with open windows, and the ten-decibel music blaring made sleep hard!

Shortly after settling into our new home, Dan Martin and I flew to California, to meet with Dr. Peter and Mary Quesenberry. We all were new at candidate selection and preparation. However, I think this caused us to rely more on the Lord than on our own wisdom. Peter and Mary were a newly married couple, who had a sincere desire to serve the Lord. They have proven this with their faithfulness and length of service. The Quesenberrys have served on the mission field continuously since then. They spent the first ten years in Nepal, and have served in Laos and Thailand. They are the deans of the CVM group!

Peter was part of the Intervarsity Christian Fellowship while he was at the University of California at Davis. This helped give him a firm foundation from which to grow. I think that he and Mary, even before marriage, felt the urge to be involved in some kind of ministry. They had a burden to serve people.

Peter and Mary went to Nepal, that strange and exotic place nestled between India and Tibet. It is home to the majestic Himalayas, which extend almost its entire length. Nepal is consid-

54

Dr. Peter and Mary Quesenberry, Nat, Cheri, and Wynn. (Longest
tenure as fieldworkers).

ered the trekking capital of the world. The flight from Kathmandu to
Pokhara reveals God's breathtaking creation. A bus ride between the
two towns offers an economy-class view, with cultural flavor thrown
in—the sights, sounds, and smells.

Pokhara sits near the center of Nepal. Peaks rise majestically up
from the valley. The place, however, reveals poverty, erosion, and difficult living that unfortunately typifies much of Nepal. Cultivating the
denuded hillsides causes severe erosion and reduced production,
making life even harder for the Nepali people.

Peter began working in the Animal Health Improvement Training Project (AHITP) that was started by a British veterinarian,
Dr. Allison Craven. He did elementary training for Animal Health
Workers from that area of Nepal. I remember that one of Peter's
early requests was for a hand-turned centrifuge. We were happy to
locate one for him.

The trainees came in for a two-week course of classroom work
and hands-on training; a very practical curriculum. They walked,
many from great distances! Students came from different castes,

which added another dimension to their relationships. For nearly 3,000 years Hinduism has taught that a stratified social system is a divinely ordained feature of the cosmos. Its backers have given full religious sanction to the four classes (varna) and the innumerable castes (jati). Sometimes this perspective on human relationships can lead to conversations about how God sees each of us as His precious children. Trying to take an obstacle and turn it into something good is a challenge, but our workers do just that.

After the AHITP trainees return to their villages, a trainer visits to see how they are doing. Roads are few and difficult, and follow-up visits must be done on foot. Exercise comes automatically to those living in Pokhara. (I remember that Peter and I once got our cholesterol checked at an AVMA convention. His was 135! No, don't ask about mine. It was a good sales pitch for exercise and lentil diet).

A CVM veterinarian has been involved in the training program at the AHITP since 1980. Many animal health trainers have taken advantage of this opportunity during the seventeen years of CVM conducting training courses there.

❦

We had returned to Georgia when I received a call from Dr. Bill Baker from West Memphis, Arkansas. He was so excited and talked so fast and loud that I didn't know who or exactly what I had on the phone. In fact, I don't think we needed the phone. I was able to catch something about the fact that he was coming to Ocilla to see me and wanted me to meet him at the airport. .

At the airport I picked him up for the two hour drive home. Bill, never at a loss for words, talked non-stop until I deposited him back at the airport the next day. He told us he had just learned about CVM's existence. To say that he was eager to go on the field is an understatement! He assured me that his wife, Mary Jo, and his son Sean would welcome the opportunity as well. Bill got his wish. He and his family went to Haiti as long-term workers in the fall of 1980.

Bill had the best relational skills of anyone I have ever known. This is ideal for Haiti. The Haitians are gracious and lovable people. They have for decades, even centuries, endured some of the most oppressive regimes. How they can still smile and exhibit gentleness

Dr. Bill Baker.

in the face of that is incomprehensible. My prayer continues to be for a just government that will allow the people to develop and thrive; without fear.

Once when Tina and I were visiting Bill and Mary Jo in Haiti, we were driving on the road that connects Hospital Albert Schweitzer at Deschapelles to the main road going to Port-au-Prince. It is a washed out series of immense potholes. Bill was known for his fast driving. In addition, Bill had narcolepsy. He was on Amphetamines, by doctor's orders. That had to make him hyperactive.

Tina asked Bill to slow down several times, but her warnings were lost in the excitement of the day. He sat in the only halfway decent seat. We were in the back bouncing around, bumping our heads, eating dust, trying as best we could to hang on and survive this mobile torture test. We banged on the roof like Haitians using a tap-tap, those mobile carriers of jam packed people. Bill stopped and Tina suggested in no uncertain terms that if he couldn't slow down, would he please let her drive. Bill reluctantly got out but not believing she would try to drive. He was fooled—she did a good job and we were able to make it safely into HAS. Bill never let Tina forget that episode!

Bill served one term with CVM. When the outbreak of African Swine Fever crossed over into Haiti from the Dominican Republic, the Inter-American Institute for Cooperative Agriculture (IICA) began an eradication and repopulation program. Bill accepted a job with them. He managed the large farrowing operation near Port-au-Prince. Bill took CVM workers through his phase of the work several times. He would help brief them on the situation there, which was a valuable orientation for shuttle participants.

Pigs are culturally acceptable in Haiti. During the depopulation phase, when pigs could no longer be raised, CVM started four separate goat projects to help farmers produce income and animal protein. CVM offered farmers three doe and access to one purebred buck, provided they paid back the loan from their goats' offspring. Bill set up these projects and trained the technicians who were supervising them. He made routine visits, monitoring their progress. One of these projects was extremely successful, the others only moderately so. I talked to some of the farmers about how they had been helped. We learned about project development from this effort, and have tried to apply this information to other CVM programs.

Bill was a colorful, wonderful, warm, loving individual with a kind word for everyone. During the latter part of his stay in Haiti, there was a time when anarchy reigned. One day, a mob attacked Bill. A Haitian co-worker who had never driven before grabbed his keys and made a getaway that saved their lives. It was a miracle.

Later, after he had returned to the United States, Bill died following complications from heart surgery.

In the summer of 1980 the AVMA meeting was in Washington, D.C. Dr. Howard Gregory was in charge of CVM's part of the program. Howard was very familiar with CVM's work. He went to Oaxaca, Mexico in March of 1978 to work with an agricultural missionary. Dr. Ed Ruebush, the local CVM representative, was instrumental in getting CVM some exposure through a local radio station talk show. For the auto-tutorial section, we submitted slides of Dr. Weinland's work in Africa.

At the meeting, we met Cameron Purdie from New Zealand. He worked in a practice that his father owned in Christchurch. Through this contact several Christian vets from New Zealand joined our mailing list. It was my good fortune to visit them in the summer of 1983 after I attended the World Veterinary Congress in Australia. CVM's world was expanding!

Another contact that proved to be enormously beneficial was Mr. John D. Velardo of <u>Veterinary Economics</u> magazine. He was interested in CVM's work, and wanted to do a feature article. The December 1982 issue of the <u>Vet Economics</u> had a cover color photograph of two Maasai warriors and their goat, plus an older *grey haired "goat" me!* We received many responses from this article. Publicity from a national veterinary magazine increased CVM's exposure and credibility in the veterinary community.

To gain support for our rural agricultural development efforts, I made contact with several organizations. These included the Soil Conservation Society, American Foresters, American Agronomy Society, and the National Extension Service. Individuals from these groups have served well on shuttles. Other groups that we entered into dialogue with included the International Development Agricultural Group, American International Development, Institute for Food and Development, Pan American Health Organization, and Summer Institute of Linguistics. Churches include Pentecostal of Canada, General Baptist, Southern Baptist, Conservative Baptist, and the Church of God. The net result of these contacts was greater recognition in rural development work, which provided more opportunities and partnerships.

Resources were coming in and aid was going out. Dr. Steve Swaim was a faculty member at Auburn University in Alabama. He called in July to say that he was turning the royalties over to CVM from his book <u>Surgery of Traumatized Skin-Management and Reconstruction in the Dog and Cat,</u> to CVM. His call came during a World Concern staff meeting. It was exciting for the staff to see how people in the veterinary profession were responding. His was quite an example of stewardship.

Around this time we sent a shipment of textbooks and educational materials to Tanzania with the help of Heifer Project

International and Dr. Clarence Mannasmith the veterinarian in charge of this commodities project. During the summer, we sent shuttles to the Navajo, Cheyenne, and Blackfeet people. We also explored possibilities with the Federation of Southern Cooperatives concerning areas of need in Appalachia.

In November Dr. Earle Goodman and I flew to La Paz, Bolivia. Dean and Elaine Kempf, missionaries from Washington, invited us. They were serving in San Borja, El Beni Province, on the edge of the Amazon jungle. It reminded me of what a Texas cow town might have looked 50 or 75 years ago. Some of the people were just as untamed and unpredictable.

The La Paz airport is over 13,000 feet in elevation. As we landed, we saw beautiful snow-capped peaks. The plane crew told us to walk slowly when we got off the plane until we were acclimatized. For people with heart disease, the adjustment is challenging. I was eating nitroglycerin tablets like a chicken pecking corn. Even the city, a thousand feet lower, was still so high that it made sleep impossible

Maasi Kids in Kenya.

for me. Just about the time I was close to falling asleep, I would gasp for air. We were staying at a Lutheran guesthouse in the city. Hotels supplied oxygen for people who needed it.

We went to the airport the next day in an effort to get transportation down to San Borja. We were unable to get a scheduled flight that day. We learned some pilots in the area used old DC-3's to bring meat to La Paz, and that we might catch a ride on one of those on their way back. We should have suspected something when the fellow said that we would need to take out some life insurance before they would let us on one of the flights. This was not exactly a confidence builder!

Only seven people are allowed on a flight; a crew of three and four passengers. When we finally got ready to take off, the crew discovered an eighth person had boarded the plane. For quite some time he refused to get off. When he saw it wasn't going to happen with him aboard, he finally relented. The crew consisted of a pilot and co-pilot who sat at the controls and one young man who looked after the rear of the plane. There were a few sacks of potatoes and onions piled in the center of the cargo hold, which were our seats. The plane had a good-sized hole in its side. Blood from the previous load of beef carcasses was all over the plane. I wasn't sure whether I was shaking from the cold or from fright!

When the young crewman had kicked the inside wall of the plane sufficiently to satisfy him that everything was set to go, we taxied down the runway. It didn't look long enough to allow the pilot to get up speed for takeoff. We finally made it, just barely. The plane had to circle a time or two to gain sufficient altitude to clear the Andes. On the way down, we could see several planes that didn't make it. They were scattered throughout the jungle. In fact, when we arrived at the dirt airstrip in San Borja, there were several airplane carcasses that had been cannibalized to keep others flying. While walking along, we passed one plane that had pancaked in the center of town. We felt sure that the Lord's protective hand was over us.

Dean and Elaine were working with the Chimane Indians and other tribal people in this isolated jungle area. They lived in the center of the town, so to speak, in a house with a thatched roof. The kitchen was set apart from the rest of the house in case the kitchen fire got out of control. Living conditions were primitive, but comfortable.

"Kids in Bolivia"—Their healthy bodies show the good protein diet from a nearby abattoir.

Dean asked us to come because the Indians' cattle were dying inexplicably. Dean and Elaine had heard of CVM through a World Concern worker in Bolivia, Jon Wilson, who was an agronomist from Washington State. Earle and I spent several days with Dean and Elaine, meeting with the Indians and looking at their livestock. The ranchers had us look at their cattle too. We decided that a long-term worker and a laboratory would be useful, if we could secure the person and the funding. We suggested to the cattlemen that they fund half of the cost and we would include them. For various reasons, the project never got off the ground.

About one o'clock on Saturday night, just across the street from Dean's house, a caballero began serenading a senorita. This went on for a while, followed by a heated argument, then a few shots rang out. This drama was repeated several times. Dean mentioned that this was a common occurrence. Finally things got quiet—around 3 am. Then it started to rain. The thatched roof was not leak-proof, and I began to get a few drops in my face. I wondered if we would ever get out of there on a muddy dirt runway. Luckily, we were able to catch a flight back on a turboprop, of all things. The Lord continued to watch over us with His guardian angel.

Back in La Paz, we walked through the center of town. We went by an orphanage run by a Catholic Order. In the front wall there was a turntable. A baby could be deposited there. When it was turned a half turn, a bell would ring. This alerted the attendants to pick up the baby. No questions were asked. It sounds so unbelievable and uncaring in a way, but it is much better than leaving the baby on a trash heap. At least the baby gets cared for..

At the Lutheran guesthouse a worker asked me to vaccinate a dog against rabies. He was the guard dog for the house and usually stayed on the flat roof where he challenged anyone coming to the gate. I pleaded no vaccine and no syringe, whereupon the lady who worked there produced both. Talk about mean as a junkyard dog! I suggested to the lady that she get his front half in the wash room and leave his back end outside and I would perform the feat. Just as I stuck him with the needle, he lunged. I vaccinated myself! Then I learned that the syringe had been used before and was not sterile. I was very concerned about the vaccine, where it was made, and if it was a live vaccine.

A young lady from Minneapolis, who was there trying to adopt a baby, prayed a most welcome prayer for me. I told Earle that I needed to talk with an authority on rabies, so we changed our flight plan and caught a flight back to Miami a day early. My first call was to Dr. Keith Sikes in Georgia, who worked with the Center for Disease Control. I regarded him as the foremost authority on rabies. He wanted to know where the vaccine was made. I told him Brazil. He said not to worry; it was safe. I breathed a sigh of relief, visited a local clinic to get a tetanus booster, and retired for a much needed good night's sleep.

On December 6th, we flew to Port au Prince, Haiti. We wanted to see what our involvement there should be. Bill Baker met us at the airport. Floyd Votaw, from California, who had done the original survey work for CVM came down. So did Fred Gregory, who was the project director for World Concern at that time. We started north.

About halfway to Hospital Albert Schweitzer, we stopped for lunch. After resuming our travels and hitting the dirt road, which was extremely rough, Floyd became very sick. It can happen so easily in these situations. Third world travel is not for the faint-hearted.

Drs. Earl Goodman, Larry Mellon, and Leroy Dorminy—Haiti.

We visited Hospital Albert Schweitzer to see about placing a long-term worker there, and to look at the shuttle program for Haiti. We eventually did place a worker there, much to Larry Mellon's delight. I never visited HAS without Larry showing me the dairy herd, and bragging about the CVM vets that served there. We went on up to Cap Haitien where we met with Kenneth Heneise from the Southern Baptist Mission. Together we explored options for establishing a work in this area.

Some of the most successful programs in Haiti during the early eighties were shuttles that held vaccination and de-worming clinics. At one point, we had eight veterinarians that participated at the same time. Bill Baker was collecting and dropping off shuttles like he was delivering the mail. Many veterinarians had life changing experiences. The work in Haiti was developing very well. As Earle and I returned to the United States and the year ended, we knew that the Lord had blessed CVM mightily!

CHAPTER 8

Consolidating

Fred Gardner was a young man from Kansas, with leanings toward roping and wrangling cattle. In 1980, he applied for long-term service. Fred grew up in a Christian family on a livestock farm in Hartford, Kansas. His faith had been nurtured through Inter-Varsity Christian Fellowship at Kansas State University. He graduated in 1978 with a B.S. in Agriculture and a DVM. After some satisfying veterinary work in Kansas, he considered the great needs in the world, and decided he wanted to serve overseas.

Fred made it through the interview and orientation process and was waiting for a work visa from Bangladesh. Sometimes areas that are more needy can be more difficult places to get permission to work. The months dragged on. I tried to call him and learned that he was in Colorado attending a retreat in the mountains. This allowed him to satisfy some of his spiritual needs along with a little of his cowboy leanings.

Finally touching base with him, I posed the option, *"Fred what about another place to work, one without such a formidable barrier?"* I suggested this in order for him to get on with it.

He declined, saying, *"Leroy, I will just wait it out."*

In so doing, he exhibited a trait that makes for a good worker—patience. Most long-term workers would probably agree with this.

Eventually the visa arrived. Fred was off to work in one of the most heavily populated places in the world, Bangladesh. The country has more than 110 million people on an area the size of Wisconsin. Can you imagine living in such density? Can you imagine the strain on the infrastructure—food production, sanitation, housing, and transportation? If family planning could overcome all the barriers that prevent its implementation, development would have a much better chance and the people a better quality of life.

Because of its topography, Bangladesh is the scene of many natural disasters. Much of the land is at or near sea level. When a typhoon hits (it's location is notorious for them-they are literally in typhoon alley), there is no place to hide from its fury. Some development work has been aimed at creating housing on dirt embankments, to escape lowland flooding.

Bangladesh has many ditches that can be used for aquaculture. In fact, I see this as one of the ways that protein can be supplied through natural habitats and through intensive methods of fish culture. The fish suitable and indigenous to that area of the world have traits that allow for tremendous production per hectare (approx. 2.5 acres). People have made great strides in this area of food production, using integrated techniques that recycle all of the waste products in the process.

Fred served in Bangladesh for almost two years. His fiancée, Jackie, visited and I think he decided that it was time to return from development work overseas, to investigate what might develop at home. They were married soon after he returned. Fred continues to be a good friend of CVM.

At CVM we needed help interviewing and orientating new long-term workers. Fortunately, we had Nadine Court, who worked with the International Personnel Department of World Concern. She taught me to identify the strengths of candidates, especially their personality traits. She was always looking for danger signals that somehow might blur the vision and derail dedicated servants of the Lord. Those on whom He has laid the *"call"* to mission service, can be especially vulnerable. She played a valuable role in implementing many successful mission assignments.

Carolee Boyd was another World Concern worker who nurtured and encouraged many field workers during their terms of service. She was a favorite among the fieldworkers. Whenever I met a worker on the field, the first person they asked about was Carolee. Of course, her job as Deputation Director brought her in close and constant contact with the fieldworkers.

July 25, 1981

Dear CVM Advisory Board Members,

My heart is full and my cup runs over. I have just returned from our first annual CVM seminar. It followed the AVMA meeting in St. Louis, Missouri. I was so encouraged by the fact that veterinarians from all over the country would take time out from their busy schedules to participate in a mission conference!

I have enclosed a copy of the program from that meeting.

Leroy

CVM Annual Seminar
July 1981

Prayer_____	Dr. Felix Smith
What is CVM? _____	Dr. Leroy Dorminy
The Role of the Academic Veterinarian ___	Dr. Ken Weinland
The Role of the Veterinarian in Rural Integrated Development_____	Dr. Floyd Votaw
Heifer Project International_____	Dr. Gordon Hatcher
The Role of a Wife in Missions_____	Dr. Ket Weinland
_____	Dr. Fredda Lois Loafman
Short Term Missions _____	Dr. Earle Goodman
_____	Dr. James Armstrong
_____	Dr. Howard Gregory
_____	Dr. George Grimes
Home Missions_____	Dr. Tom Loafman
_____	Dr. Gerald Mitchum
_____	Dr. David Hunt
Sunday Service _____	Rev. Art Beals.

At the meeting, Dr. Ken Weinland commented, " *I never realized when I retired from teaching at Purdue what the Lord had in store. I attended the AVMA meeting in Seattle in 1979, visited the CVM booth, and subsequently volunteered for service with CVM. That very December, Ket and I were in Taung, Bophuthatswana teaching at the College of Agriculture".*

It can be risky to pray and to make yourself available to the Lord!

This annual meeting became a tradition. CVM staff and friends enjoy good Christian fellowship, while learning about what is taking place in veterinary missions. I cherish the many new friendships I have made and the ones that are renewed during these times. The Bible encourages us to nurture our faith by gathering together with fellow believers. We gain strength when we fellowship with others.

Two new members were elected to the board that year: Dr. Bob Vanderhoof from California, and Dr. Bob Pierson from Colorado. They replaced Dr. Floyd Votaw of California and Dr. Clarence Mannasmith of Arkansas. Other business at the meeting included setting up a system to collect medicines and equipment. We were asked by the Society of Tropical Veterinary Medicine to participate in their poster presentation the following year. Members present were challenged to spread the word about CVM at local, state, and national meetings by using slide and tape programs. We also reminded them that the most effective tool is their personal testimony about CVM. That is true today, and will be tomorrow as well.

On August 5, Tina and I went to Toronto to meet with Henry Freisen, the Director of WC Canada. We wanted to stimulate interest in CVM there, by sharing its story. We were interviewed on a Christian television show called *100 Huntley Street*, hosted by Ron Hembree. I thought it was a strictly Canadian show, until I returned to Ocilla. I received a call from a friend twenty-five miles away, who said he had watched the show.

We had another unusual opportunity while we were in Canada. We visited Tom Roundtree of Brampton. He was involved in shipping semen, embryos, and live animals overseas. His family had been in the dairy business for a number of years and had an impressive operation with fine Holstein cattle. Tom was very helpful to CVM, supplying a tank and semen for artificial insemination in Haiti and Bolivia.

Artificial insemination is appropriate for third world use, because it results in a 50% genetic improvement in breeding stock while retaining the natural immunity offered by the indigenous animals. However, in the vast majority of places and cases, recipient animals are not sufficiently healthy, nor are owners sufficiently knowledgeable to effectively utilize this technology. Training, preparation and time are essential for maximum benefit.

On October 26, Tina and I flew to San Francisco to speak to the fellowship at the California Veterinary Medical Association meeting. Dr. Rick Marshall arranged it, with the help of Ilka Wood, the California Veterinary Medical Association's executive director. Recently Rick was instrumental in providing correspondence courses in Bible studies for our CVM field-workers. He also presently heads up the Christian Foundation for providing funds for Christian workers.

The executive director of the CVMA, Ilka Wood, was a beautiful Christian lady who was not afraid to share her witness with people she met. She arranged for the breakfast time and place to be listed in the meeting program, and she inserted my picture in the program mail-out. Now, that might have been cause for alarm! She had such a lovable personality and was so helpful. I was saddened to learn about her premature death a few months later.

Rick Marshall said, *"She thought veterinarians were the most highly trained people in the world, they could go anywhere to share their training and to teach the Good News."*

Two people who are important to CVM, and to me personally, are Dr. James Rosenberger from Ohio, and Dr. Dan Paulo from Pennsylvania. They both went on shuttles to Haiti in 1981. Dan went to northern Haiti, at Jean Rabel's mission station, and Jim went to the town of Jeremie, in southern Haiti. They loved the program from the start. Both veterinarians have done several shuttles to Haiti, and have served as coordinators for their shuttle sites -Dan at Les Cayes and Jim at Jeremie. Both also served on the CVM Board of Directors.

Jim and Dan attended a shuttle conference in Atlanta in February 1982. It included Dr. Bill Baker, Dr. Tom Gillaspie, Dr. Earle

Goodman, and me. These were the early days, before Bob Otto became shuttle coordinator. We tried to create a way to prepare first-time shuttle participants for a more effective short-term mission. Dan and Jim had gone on shuttles so many times, they could prepare the next people to provide some continuity.

In 1986, Dan went on a shuttle to Ethiopia to take some supplies. This was an arduous trip, he had so much to take, and it was so difficult to get to the work site. Later, he and I made a whirlwind run, through Colombia, Bolivia, Panama, Guatemala, and Honduras. He lugged a battery large enough to run a generator, through all those countries, finally depositing it in the last one. What an ordeal! In addition, it was on this trip, on the flight out of Panama, that Dan got sick. In spite of all the trials of the trip, Dan is a trooper! There is never a dull moment on a shuttle.

❦

In May, I received a letter from Dr. Max and Mrs. Brenda Thornesberry, from Missouri. They wanted an overseas assignment. Dr. Larry Mellon had asked for a resident veterinarian at Hospital Albert Schweitzer. This seemed like a logical fit. Max had large animal experience, and the farm raised cattle, pigs, and chickens.

Generally, it takes a year or more to make long-term field assignments happen, but not this time. Brenda and Max went through the preliminaries in record time. On the Sunday after Thanksgiving, Tina and I met the Thornesberrys in Miami for our trip to Haiti. It was an exciting time.

When we arrived in Haiti, we checked to see that all our baggage had arrived, before we tackled customs. We made it through that maze of organized chaos, and stepped outside. We fell into a sea of faces and hands, all grabbing at our bags and speaking in a mixture of English and Creole.

We yelled *"No, no! We don't need any help"*.

When we got to the waiting vehicle, there were more expectant, outstretched palms than could have possibly touched our bags. An experience like that should come to everyone at least once.

We loaded all of the bags in, on, and around the four-wheel drive Daihatsu truck. Then we began our journey to HAS. Anyplace else, we would have stuck out like a sore thumb; but in Haiti we blended right in. The trip was not all that bad, because the one paved road that runs North and South follows the coast for much of the way. We did the logical thing, and stopped for a picnic lunch by the sea. When we turned onto the road to Deschappelles, the going got rough. The truck could not even average five miles per hour, given the potholes, goats, grain, and other usual or unusual obstructions.

Arriving at HAS, we got a tour of the living quarters, and settled into life on the compound. Someone suggested that Brenda should hire a Haitian lady to help with the house chores. Many of our workers would prefer to do their own housekeeping, but the need for employment is so great in many places. This is one small way of contributing to a local economy.

The needs at the HAS farm were obvious and many. The dairy herd was averaging around 13 pounds of milk per cow per day. The beef herd was showing signs of parasitism, malnutrition, and reproductive problems. What a place this was to utilize the skills of a veterinarian experienced in large animal medicine. Here, another need had come face to face with help, in the form of a CVM veterinarian and spouse—specifically, Max and Brenda.

When I returned home to Ocilla in December, I received a letter from a veterinarian. He did not want to be involved in CVM's work, because of a bad experience on a shuttle. He also criticized the lack of hard numbers in the newsletter, when we described what CVM workers had accomplished on the field. We North Americans want results, now! I must confess that is my bias, too. It is true that we need accountability, but much that goes on can hardly be reduced to numbers and reports. Ministry cannot be weighed and measured like a commodity in the market place.

I responded to his letter, reporting that, in Haiti, CVM had dewormed and treated more than 3,000 animals at a cost of $9,000 that year. As impressive as that was, I was more interested in teaching and training farmers utilizing their own animals. I wrote to him that our ministry was to the whole man—physically and spiritually.

"I know we have made mistakes," I wrote, *" and, unfortunately, will make others, but I assure you they are not of the heart. I intend to keep on working to feed God's people physically and spiritually as long as I am able."*

Through the years, we have sent out a great deal of mail: appeals (in earlier times), newsletters, prayer letters, and general information about various programs. The response has been favorable. We receive numerous encouraging notes, which are so important to us. We like it when you share your ideas with us. When we mail to all veterinarians, not just Christians, we occasionally get a negative response. It reminds me that Christians have a discerning spirit, can identify with the needs, and want to be involved

When veterinarians hear of CVM, many will ask what it costs to join. The answer is nothing. To receive CVM mailings, all a person has to do is sign their name. This caused so much confusion in the early days; we decided to have a membership fee. Anyone making a contribution of 20 dollars in a year would receive membership. By the middle of 1982, we had more than 3,200 people on the mailing list, and six hundred members.

The down side of memberships is that they are a nightmare to maintain. When do members get a membership card, and when do they renew? We decided that was a nice experiment, but it was not the way to go.

Dr. Jim Armstrong, a wonderful friend from Rhode Island, has been involved with CVM since the early days. In 1981, he went to Haiti to help Bill Baker with a goat seminar. This was in conjunction with the four goat projects we had going. Later, he went to Costa Rica with Dr. George Grimes, from Tennessee. They did a community survey in preparation for a long-term worker there. Earlier, Dr. Mike Chesson from Virginia and livestock producer Robert Alphin held a seminar at the veterinary school in San Jose.

Isn't it wonderful and amazing, how God calls people to His service? Dr. Bob Wilmarth, from Florida, had gone to Haiti on a shuttle earlier in the year. When he learned that there was an opening in Costa Rica, he and his wife Janet, answered that call. They began language school in September. After language school, they worked with the rural farmers, running a mobile clinic and returning to San Jose where they lived on the weekends.

Bob, Janet, and their three daughters were a wonderful family, who exemplified the Christian lifestyle. They later adopted a young Costa Rican boy.

At that time, World Concern decided that they would only work in countries with the lowest quality of life index. The index used indicators like literacy, infant mortality, per capita income, caloric intake, life expectancy, and many other factors. A low score on the index means a reduced chance for health, education, and a decent livelihood. Costa Rica did not meet the cutoff for World Concern, but Bob and Janet decided to remain instead of transferring to another country. They have had a wonderful ministry there. We still count them as dear friends.

Costa Rica is the Switzerland of Central America. It is mountainous and very beautiful. Once I visited Bob when he was working on the Panamanian Border. We spent long hours under adverse conditions, vaccinating animals. We had taken some personal supplies, but they were inadequate for the couple of days we were there. We left late in the afternoon, and drove back through the mountains with no food. Bob promised that there was a restaurant on the way. Finally in the dead of night, we discovered a food oasis. I have never eaten so many beans and rice in my whole life!

Our first student shuttle was by Donna Walker of Ohio State. She went to Haiti with Mr. Fred Dieter and Mr. Bill Diehl. They had donated 19 bucks and 6 does. Donna was a hard worker, and she had a good rapport with the Haitians. She and Dr. John Crews, of Florida, blood tested 250 does for Brucellosis. (John later served in Africa with the Southern Baptists.) She recommended the program highly to other students. This was the beginning of an ever-increasing stream of students. Praise God that they get this perspective of service in their early years. Think of all the years to come that will be influenced by these experiences.

Dr. Tom Wanous, from Minnesota, accompanied Mr. Alfred Farris, an agriculturist, on a needs survey in Uganda. They developed a project for a veterinarian, an agriculturist, and an appropriate technology specialist. This later became Hands In Service (HIS). Dr. Brad and Mrs. Angela Frye, of Colorado, worked with them in Soroti, Uganda.

Perhaps the most significant milestone to take place during that year was the assignment of state representatives. It is one thing to send out correspondence from the home office, but it is better to have someone on the local scene who can vouch for an organization. I thank the Lord that men and women of Christian integrity are available and willing to serve in this important capacity. Many have served in this way since the beginning.

State representatives performed many vital functions that could not be effectively dealt with from the home office. They arranged for booth space at state and local meetings, developed promotional mailings to veterinarians in their states, and helped to promote CVM through personal relationships. These people have been crucial to CVM's development.

CHAPTER 9

World Scope

From The Desk of:
Barry Berryman
Executive Director, World Concern Australia

Perth was the venue for the 22nd World Veterinary Congress in August of 1983. It was the first occasion that the Congress had moved to the Southern Hemisphere. It attracted some 1700 delegates from 50 countries. As was to be expected, there was a wide variety of Commercial Exhibitors but, to the surprise of many delegates, Christian Veterinary Mission had its first display at an international congress. Those who registered their inquiry at the CVM booth came from Africa, Asia, Europe, North and South America, as well as delegates from some of the Eastern Bloc countries.

Dr. Jim Martin had set up preliminary plans for the meeting in Perth. Jim was just initiating a Christian Fellowship among the Australian veterinarians. He had a veterinary equipment company "Easy Anesthetics" that also had a booth at the congress. Jim arranged for CVM to share a booth with the budding Australian Christian Veterinary Fellowship. He and I had been corresponding about our efforts here in the States. He was serving as sort of interim President of the Australian Christian Fellowship, trying to get something going.

Since we were spending a couple of days in Sydney before traveling on to Perth, Jim Martin organized a pre-congress meeting. On Saturday, August 20, Tina and I met with 6 veterinarians in St. John's Anglican Church, in Paramatta, a suburb of Sidney. The meeting was scheduled to last for two hours. Instead, it lasted four hours, because of the veterinarians' intense interest in missions, and the excitement of starting their own organization.

Dr. Jim Martin and Dr. Leroy Dorminy.

Dr. Andrew Schactel and Dr. Jonathan Geddes were long-term candidates at that time. Dr. Julie Strauss offered to use her Bible school savings to go to Perth to help with the booth. What Christian commitment these vets exhibited! Some did end up on the mission field. The numbers were small, but the Lord often uses small groups of dedicated people.

Since Jim was busy representing his own company at the congress, I stayed with the booth. Dr. Floyd Votaw, bless his generous and caring heart, flew to Perth from L.A. just to help me with that chore. He was a welcome sight, because I had heart surgery in late March, and I wasn't exactly feeling like the bionic man.

Our plan was to identify as many Christian veterinarians as possible. Of course, we were especially interested in identifying those who had an interest in missions. It is interesting to watch people's reaction to a Christian sign on an exhibit booth. The majority are either repelled, puzzled, or uneasy. A few are attracted to it, as if being drawn by a magnet. Their faces light up as they see that their profession has a Christian presence. They are excited to learn about the organization and opportunities.

Before the Congress closed, we had more than 150 names to add to the mailing list. Half of these came from Australia, and the rest

Dr. Floyd Votaw and Dr. Leroy Dorminy. World Veterinary Congress, Perth, Australia.

from many countries around the world. It was thrilling to meet and share fellowship with Christian veterinarians from many different countries. God had truly blessed our efforts.

On the final morning of the Congress, twenty-two people met for prayer and fellowship over breakfast. The local ACVF was affirmed as a national entity. Dr. Jim Martin of Sydney, New South Wales, was elected President. Serving with him were Dr. Noel Johnston of Mill Park and Victoria and Dr. Ross Buddle of Murdoch, Western Australia. They got off to a jump-start due to Jim alerting us to the opportunity of participating in this world congress.

The following resolution was adopted at the breakfast meeting in Perth:

> *"Be it resolved that a world-wide organization of Christian veterinarians be established, for the ostensible purpose of having fellowship in Jesus Christ, promoting Christian love and ethics, witnessing to the profession and through it to the world community, and encouraging missions both at home and abroad".*

I was given the responsibility of identifying national entities and encouraging them to participate. In addition, I was to coordinate activities of these various groups.

Before leaving Perth, Tina and I enjoyed a dinner with Jim and his wife. With prayerful and humble hearts, we thanked God for the way he had blessed our efforts at the Congress. We talked about co-operating with each other, in organization and mission efforts in Australia and around the world.

The next morning as Tina and I started to leave for the airport, we noticed the headlines on the paper read that someone had run into a motel at Ayers Rock and killed two people. This caught my attention because we were headed for that region. It seems the driver was denied service at the motel bar for boisterous conduct and so he got into his truck and ran into the bar with full force.

On the way to Alice Springs, sort of the middle of the "outback" country, the pilot flew over the rock and then came in low over Alice Springs a couple of times, in order that we might get a bird's eye view of the place. A festival was taking place and Alice Springs was thronged. One special event was a takeoff on the famous regatta, "Henley on the Thames". Instead it was the "Henley on the Todd", a bone dry river bed that hadn't seen a drop of water in months. The makeshift boats built around people, whose sole mobility was through their walking, offered some enthusiastic and vigorous good-natured jousting. It was an unforgettable scene.

We arrived back in Sydney on the 28th, and briefed Barry Berryman on what we thought were the exciting possibilities for a CVM affiliate in Australia. We boarded a bus and went to Canberra. We met Rebecca Gibson Palmer, a good friend of CVM, who was originally from the United States. She lived and practiced there, after marrying an Australian man while serving as a missionary in Papua New Guinea. We enjoyed fellowship and prayer in her home with other Christian veterinarians and their spouses.

The next day we continued to visit other veterinarians in the country. In Adelaide, we met with Dr. Jeremy Rogers, who showed us around the town and shared a good time of fellowship and discussion of the mission. We also met with Dr. David Peek and his wife who had a ministry to drug addicts and alcoholics. We had a very interesting discussion of home and foreign missions.

On Sunday, September 4, we had lunch with Dr. Noel Johnston, his wife, and their four children. Noel worked with the Provincial government. He received his Masters degree at Michigan State.

While there, he attended a veterinary student fellowship group. When he returned home, he started a fellowship group at the University of Melbourne. We met for three hours and discussed the possibilities of ACVF and CVM. It was a most enjoyable meeting.

The next night, we met with other vet students and faculty at the University of Melbourne. About 50 people came. I spoke to them for about 30 minutes, and showed the CVM slide and tape program, followed by a question and answer period. The only problem was the language barrier, with me from South Georgia and they with their strong Aussie brogue. Noel graciously acted as a translator when we were totally incoherent.

September 7 found us in Christchurch, New Zealand, having lunch with Dr. Euan Purdie, his father Cameron, and two other vets. They knew about CVM, having been on the mailing list since I met Euan in New Orleans at an AAHA meeting. I gave them the names of veterinarians on the mailing list from the Northern Island and encouraged them to establish an affiliate in New Zealand, offering the same kind of assistance as we did in Australia.

As we traveled around New Zealand, I tried to contact as many veterinarians as possible, making CVM known to them and determining their interest in joining us. A common bond is, of course, our profession; and if they are Christians then it is a double fit. On the way home, I did this in Honolulu and in Los Angeles. The trip was an effort to take the work of veterinary missions beyond the North American shores and give it a global perspective.

⚜

In January, Dr. Ken and Mrs. Ket Weinland and Dr. Toby and Mrs. Cindy Hoover began language school in Bolivia. Afterwards, Ken began teaching at the veterinary school in Santa Cruz and Toby at the veterinary school in Trinidad. The main emphasis of their work was establishing ambulatory clinics. Many veterinary schools in developing countries do not place much emphasis on clinical work. Graduates feel uncomfortable and inadequate when they are faced with actual practice conditions. In addition to what veterinary students learn at school in the United States, most have to serve an internship as well. We recommend two years of work with another veterinarian in practice before going on the mission field.

Shuttles to Bolivia included Dr. Susan Wilson, Arizona. This was at the request of Toby Hoover. She went to Trinidad to evaluate a laboratory that had been constructed and financed by the Germans but was inoperable. Toby wanted to see what, if anything, could be done to make it usable. It was apparent to her that there were so many things unfinished that it was beyond CVM's capabilities to make it happen. Volumes could be written on unwise and inappropriate projects that have been started in developing countries.

In 1983, the AVMA met in New York. Our third annual seminar included papers by Peter Quesenberry from Nepal, Mark Hinton from Kenya, and Bill Baker from Haiti. Short-term presentations featured our first student shuttle—Donna Walker from Ohio State, technician Maureen Maroney from California, and those captains of shuttles—Dr. Dan Paulo and Dr. James Rosenberger.

He was a red headed veterinarian, fresh out of school from Washington State University (an exception to our normal rule). Dr. Fred Van Gorkom stopped over in New York to attend the meeting. He was on his way to Africa. Later, he took over for Dr. Ed Cushing, from Nevada. Ed worked in Ethiopia for about four months before Fred's arrival. Ed had served a most vital function by quickly filling a need in the interim. He did this even though he had heart problems and recent heart surgery.

Fred did great work with the High Commissioner of the Red Cross (HCRC), working with refugees. The Commissioner honored him for his outstanding work. Dr. Vicki Funkhouser, from Oklahoma, worked with the Southern Baptists in Addis Ababa. She helped in the clinics that Dr. Jerry Bedsole, of Alabama, had initiated. Vicki and Fred discovered each other in the wilds of Africa and decided to begin a joint project of their own; marriage. They went to language school in preparation for working in Alduba, in the remote Gama Gofa region of Southwestern Ethiopia. They are still living and working in this same area today, together with their four children.

In the July 1983 issue of the Journal of the AVMA, there was an article about Dr. Ray and Mrs. Vicki Dayton, and their work with the Maasai in Kenya. It was titled "Blood Brothers, and Brothers in Service". It attracted much attention, because of the unique work and the colorful people. After this national exposure, in an unbiased publication, we received many questions and comments about Ray and Vicki and their work.

Dr. Tom Gillaspie, went to Haiti on the first of his many shuttles. He worked first with Dr. Bill Baker, and later with Dr. Jim Rosenberger in Jeremie. Tom has been the Florida CVM representative for many years. He is very enthusiastic about helping at the Florida State Meeting and the North American Veterinary Conference (NAVC) in Orlando, Florida, each January. He and his wife, Jayma, are truly committed to the Lord's work. Tina and I appreciate their friendship. We are thankful for the opportunity to work with them each year at the NAVC.

Dr. Tom Gillaspie and wife Jayma.

Around this time African Swine Fever (ASF) hit Haiti as it came across from the Dominican Republic. It was devastating, because in Haiti pigs were a mainstay of the people's diet, supplying much needed protein which is often more critical than overall calories. A sad scene for me was to visit the children's ward at Hospital Albert Schweitzer and see the many children suffering from Kwashiorkor (severe malnutrition with protein deficiency). They had swollen bellies, emaciated and dehydrated bodies, reddish hair; a picture of hopelessness. Unfortunately, at that stage it usually is fatal. The ASF outbreak exacerbated it enormously.

You see ASF has no cure or prevention. The only alternative was to slaughter the entire swine population in Haiti, paying indemnity to the owners. This was done under the aegis of IICA (Inter-American Institute for Cooperative Agriculture). Next, there was monitoring for a period of time, with sentinel pigs for detection of any residual virus. When no evidence of the disease was found, restocking began.

CVM, in its effort to overcome this human tragedy and devastation by disease developed a goat project as a substitute protein, to replace the pigs. It worked like this. A farmer would be furnished three native does and access to a purebred Nubian buck. They were to repay the does to the pool for distribution to other farmers. The goats had to be confined for control of breeding and disease. This called for construction of holding pens, watering and feeding troughs, and forage production. We had four such projects, each was in a different locale with a project manager selected by the community.

Dr Bill Baker developed training courses on the care of goats. Project managers participated in this and in turn taught the individual farmers. Bill made regular visits to monitor and advise. Some farmers were more successful than others. This confinement operation was a new concept to them and offered quite a few challenges but could be very rewarding in food and income.

I remember visiting one very successful farmer who had paid back his loan of does and had increased his herd considerably. He was appreciative of his new found prosperity.

In addition to the goat project, Dr. Bill Baker ran a poultry project to help alleviate the devastation caused by the African Swine Fever outbreak in Haiti. Participants learned to manage a 20 layer-hen operation. Initially, for training purposes, production was centralized. Each community had a brooder house to accommodate 300-400 chicks. The brooder house was partitioned according to the number of participants. Each one would house 20 chicks, with each participant responsible for his or her own unit.

The training of animateurs (animal technicians) preceded the project, and they facilitated classes for community participants. These classes covered things like vaccination, confinement principles, sick bird recognition, proper feeding and watering, and general management.

Laying usually starts at around 20 weeks, when each participant took the layers home. Out of the eggs produced, each participant agreed to reimburse the project for the layers they had received. For those who managed their project well, it was enormously successful. The project could be repeated or even enlarged as participants become more adept at managing. Poultry are almost universally accepted as a meat source.

When Haiti was finally declared ASF free, the monumental task of restocking the country with appropriate breeding swine began. A three-way cross of top hybrids (Hampshire, Duroc, and Yorkshire) from the United States from pathogen free herds, was used. Because they differed from the traditional pigs of Haiti, it caused some consternation among the Haitians. The Ministry of Agriculture, based on the large litters and high weaning rates, made this selection of breeds. This shortened the repopulation time. Trainers introduced modern production methods, adapted to the realities of Haiti.

Outside Port au Prince, there was a primary farrowing center with about 500 sows. Secondary centers were established throughout the country. CVM trained recipients in the principles of pig raising. Another encouraging aspect of this was that churches became involved. The church served as a secondary training center, encouraging its people to be involved as a cell group for the distribution. The church also acted as a training center for the recipients.

CVM had several long-term workers and numerous shuttles involved in this project. It was highly successful. Training is CVM's forte. This is true for shuttles as well as long-term personnel. We believe that this is the lasting benefit we can leave. Through the years, CVM workers have trained more than 1150 animal technicians. Now, some of technicians are training new people themselves—a sure sign of good development.

A feed mill was set up in Port au Prince. It processed by-products from the wheat that was shipped in from the states, and rice hulls from local production. Soybeans were shipped from the Midwest. This happened in the initial phase of the program.

The manager of the program for IICA was Mr. Mechel Jacob. His able assistant was Dr. Percy Souix-Akins. They did a tremendous job of making this work. Dr. Frank Mulhern, Director of Animal Health for IICA, helped CVM during our involvement with the swine re-population program in Haiti. We had excellent working relations with everyone involved with the program.

I often think of what this pig-raising project might have meant for the Haitian economy. It could have had a long lasting impact, if it had been followed up with regional feed mills and organized marketing. This may have been possible in the right political environment. It would have been an incredible industry for the Haitian people. I remember Dr. Maureen Birmingham, a CVM long-term worker in Haiti, with tears in her eyes, telling me about how successful the secondary centers had been. Sows were producing healthy litters of 10 pigs or more. She talked about how much the Haitian people wanted and needed this.

After the initial successful phase of the project, due to continued political problems, the Inter-American Development Bank would not release 15 million dollars for the full-scale project. Government officials and those with close connections quickly got involved in the feed industry and the price of wheat bran quadrupled in less than 3 years. Sometimes, if you didn't have connections, you couldn't buy it at any price. The farmers had no alternative but to stop raising pigs. What a tragedy!

An offshoot of the swine repopulation program was CVM's first book. It was written by Dr. Earle Goodman and called <u>Raising Healthy Swine Under Primitive Conditions</u>. It addressed pig farming in developing countries. The book was done in a simple easy to read style. It focused on available resources and feeds. The book had many line drawings that illustrated the text. It was highly successful. This was the beginning of a series of books called <u>Raising Healthy Animals</u>, that now number ten. These books have been sent to more than fifty countries. The demand for them continues to grow.

8 Veterinarians Who Are Making A Difference

Ken Weinland

Ken retired in 1979 and took a CVM assignment in Bophuthatswana, South Africa. He is now serving as a teacher at a university in Bolivia. Ken is from Sebring, Florida, and worked as an extension veterinarian at Purdue University before retirement.

Ray Dayton

Ray has been working with the Maasai of Kenya, East Africa, for three years now. He keeps very busy helping with cattle care in eight villages. He works alongside an evangelist. He received his DVM from Iowa State University in 1966.

Toby Hoover

Toby, from Auburn, Alabama, is in Bolivia where he teaches veterinary science at the University of Trinidad. He graduated from Cornell University and Oklahoma State University.

Peter Quesenberry

Pete is serving in Nepal, that tiny country tucked between China and India. He's involved with animal care on a farm run by the United Mission to Nepal and with helping villagers care for their animals. Pete earned his DVM from the University of California at Davis in 1978.

Bill Baker

Bill, from West Memphis, Arkansas, has been on assignment in Haiti for three years. In addition to a successful goat project, he has started a similar project using poultry. He graduated in 1947 from Texas A & M.

Fred Van Gorkom

Fred is working in drought-stricken Ethiopia. He is a 1983 graduate of Washington State University and is from Yakima, Washington. Fred works under extreme conditions.

Mark Hinton

Mark's assignment is to teach development skills to Africans attending Daystar Communications, a Christian school in Nairobi, Kenya. He is from Golden Valley, Minnesota.

Bob Wilmarth

Bob is from Brooksville, Florida, and is assigned to Costa Rica. He is serving as a teacher, clinician and consultant to the agricultural division of a Christian agency. He works in six rural centers.

These veterinarians are part of the CVM/World Concern team ministering to people in need around the world in the name of Jesus Christ. Their work is possible because of the prayer and financial support of individuals in the United States.

From an old CVM newsletter.

CHAPTER 10

The Cost of Mission Service

A factor in CVM's success is the grassroots effort of volunteers who believe in CVM and have caught the vision. They in their own way, have propagated and nurtured the organization from the start. I cannot overstate that. It doesn't matter what kind of mail we send from the home office, CVM's credibility remains with its local members.

A good example is a state representative like Dr. Clark Vanderhoof. He personally sent a mailing about CVM to all the veterinarians in Utah in 1983. Such local endorsement of CVM reinforces good things people might have heard about the organization. Other representatives have repeated this countless times since. Dr. Harold Landis has done an excellent job over the years, of promoting CVM in Pennsylvania. He makes sure that CVM is always represented at the state meeting. Mike Chesson returned from a shuttle in Costa Rica, and showed slides from his trip to veterinarians in Virginia.

Those small but significant personal contacts, repeated hundreds of times over, build credibility. I regret that I cannot cite some incident or story about each person who has contributed to the success of this ministry, but I have attempted to compile a list of those who served. Many of these volunteers have become close friends, for which I am deeply grateful.

In 1983 Floyd Votaw worked with a mission group in the Philippines helping to develop Sloping Agriculture Land Technology (SALT). It was intended to prevent erosion, while making the land productive. They were using grasses and fast growing trees for forage and grazing. Erosion is a problem as old as the hills, which is exacerbated by pressure from the population explosion and the additional strain on the land to produce more. SALT is a much needed application to prevent soil depletion.

Later, Floyd went to Nepal to explore using this erosion control there. During his stay he was in a very serious motorcycle accident, which caused a comminuted fracture of the tibia that cut an artery. He was fortunate to survive the accident, but spent a long time recuperating at his home in California.

Because of the World Veterinary Congress meeting in Perth, we made contacts in many other countries. In response to their requests, and in an effort to nurture those contacts, Tina and I traveled to England and Europe. In England we visited veterinary schools at Oxford and Cambridge and the Royal Veterinary College in London. English veterinarians had their own fellowship. The fellowship president, Dr. David Fennell, organized a meeting at RVC. There I met student Steven Downes, who later worked with Peter Quesenberry in Nepal. At Cambridge, Dr. John Brown, secretary of the English fellowship, set up a meeting. The group was small, but interested.

The Veterinary Christian Fellowship of the United Kingdom partially supported Dr. Allison Cravens in Nepal and Dr. Julie Mercer in Madagascar. Allison established the project at the Rural Development Center (RDC) in Pokhara, where Peter and Mary Quesenberry later served for many years. The project incorporates training courses for Nepali technicians, in a "hands on", very elementary and practical manner.

In Norway, Dr. Kai-Arne Schie, a practitioner in Eidsvoll, north of Oslo, met us. He and his wife, Ella, were delightful hosts. Kai-Arne was small in stature, but large in heart. Local farmers dubbed him "Mini-Schie." He drove his Saab in a way that would have warmed a race driver's heart. I rode with him for part of a day, making calls. We made 13 visits from 8 am to 4 pm. The farmers would always be waiting in the barn. This was not like some of my experiences in practice, when neither the patient nor the farmer would be visible. He had them trained well—or maybe it was a cultural thing.

I was amazed at the interest that Kai-Arne had generated in the student fellowship group. We met with the fellowship group one night at the vet school in Oslo. Many students, faculty, and practicing veterinarians attended the meeting; so did one very interested drug distributor. It was an inspiring experience. They endorsed the concept of CVM overwhelmingly.

The Navigators organization's interpreter, Ole-Magnus Olafsrud, translated my speech for me. Norwegians have varying English fluency. This caused a rippling effect in response to my remarks. If I said something funny, the ones that were fluent in English laughed right away, then there was a pause, the less fluent ones laughed as they caught on, then when it was translated, the ones who knew no English at all would laugh.

Later, the Schies served on the mission field in Madagascar. They were a lovely family. I remember with great fondness their son playing the violin for us before we left for London. After they returned from the mission field, we learned the sad news that their young daughter had died from cancer. It is hard to understand these things. We can only trust in the Lord.

In Finland we stayed with Dr. Yrjo Grohn and his family. They had two small boys, who were about five and four years old. The family had just returned from three years in the United States doing a research project at the University of California, at Davis. One day I was watching a TV program in their home. The kids, who had picked up some English in the States, started translating for me. Kids pick up language easily, without accents.

I spoke to the Student Union at the veterinary school in Helsinki, following a slide presentation by Eva-Liisa Hintikka, who served in Nigeria. Their fellowship group was not as organized at that point, as the Norwegian one, but they definitely were interested. 75 percent of the veterinary students were female. American veterinary school percentages are now nearing that.

Tina and I went with two Finnish veterinarians, Anna-Maija Lappalainen, and her friend Mardjia, to visit a dairy farm about 120 miles north of Helsinki. The farm was owned by Madjia's father and operated by her brother. Her brother was not married because many of the women do not like to live in rural areas. The women migrate to the city after completing high school and do not return. Pickings are lean.

Dinner included moose that was killed on the farm. It was delicious. In fact, the whole meal was very good-especially the bread. They of necessity had their own oven for making bread.

They had a sauna on a nearby lake where they would sit for a while and then go outside and roll in the snow and then flail themselves with a switch. Strange custom for a Georgia boy!

I was quite interested in the father's story. He was in the Finland-Russian War in the late 1930's. He was justifiably proud. I remembered reading about it when I was in high school. A newspaper article with pictures showed Finnish soldiers taking a steam bath in freezing temperatures. I told him I felt very sorry for them after seeing this picture. He thought my concern was very amusing because of their sauna tradition and being used to the extreme cold. When I congratulated him and the Finnish people for their valiant stand against the Russian Army he became very emotional and thanked me for it.

This trip reinforced my vision for a worldwide fellowship of Christian veterinarians worshipping, witnessing, and promoting missions, international peace, understanding, and goodwill. I sincerely believe that veterinarians can make a tremendous impact globally. After all, the local community is a microcosm of the greater world community.

❧

The World Concern planning meeting in February of 1984 included representatives from Canada, Australia, Korea, and the U.S. I presented a paper entitled "The Rationale For Veterinarians In Mission Work." Veterinarians have unique qualifications for the job. They are practical, problem solving professionals, with compassion for animals and people. They are committed and tenacious. These attributes make a successful missionary. In all my years of practice, I rarely encountered an ideal practice situation. There was always some challenge to overcome.

These unusual qualifications fit perfectly with World Concern's decision to limit the places where they worked. They chose the countries and regions that had the worst "quality of life index." Poor quality of life also makes it difficult to serve in these places. Who is better able to survive or even thrive in this environment? Veterinarians, of course! I myself am amazed at the tenacity of our workers sometimes under extreme circumstances.

There is, of course, another component to the equation—Christian commitment. I have been asked by other organizations how we keep people on the field, doing incredible things, under adverse conditions. CVM workers will be the first to tell you that their strength comes from the Lord. He empowers us in our weakness.

Often, shuttle participants return for long-term service. This was the case with Dr. Rod Frank, from Illinois. In 1984, Rod and Nancy, with their children Eric and Emily, resumed CVM's work at Hospital Albert Schweitzer. Rod was a good student of the Creole language. In a few short months, he spoke Creole like a native. He also had great insights as to the needs of the HAS farm. He returned briefly to his hometown in Illinois, and enlisted friends to help collect supplies. Farrowing crates and a feed mill were among the things they collected and shipped to HAS.

Rod wanted someone with general agricultural expertise to help him develop a plan for the farm. My mind leapt to a long time friend, Jim Collier, who was a retired extension agent. He had worked in Ben Hill County, near where I had practiced veterinary medicine. He volunteered to go and work with Rod. They developed a good friendship.

Jim's knowledge of agriculture is only exceeded by his vast repertoire of humorous stories from his 35 years work as an extension agent. Jim made two trips to Haiti, carrying Bermuda grass stolons for a grazing plot nursery and a bag of peanut seed. You see, the things that work in Georgia usually can be adapted to Haiti. Jim was enormously helpful as a consultant to CVM. He also reviewed the <u>Raising Healthy Animals</u> books from a non-veterinary standpoint.

In September, a couple from Wisconsin, Dr. Brian and Mrs. Karen Kersten, attended orientation in Seattle. During his time at veterinary school Brian attended several Christian Veterinary Fellowship meetings. Dr. Mark Hinton was the speaker at one and told of his work in Kenya. This planted a seed in Brian's mind and it was a point of contact with CVM.

Brian met his future wife, Karen, at a church camp where they both were counselors. After Karen graduated from Nursing School and Brian from veterinary school, they got married that August. Brian had started in a practice. He wrote to CVM for more information and was sent an application. It lay on his desk for a while but finally he responded, after some nudging from Karen. In January 1984 they went to Haiti and were assigned to Les Cayes, Haiti.

They worked with Chevanne Jeune, a young engineer, and a fine Haitian leader. Chevanne had a close association with WC in the early days of their work in Haiti. He headed up the work of Baptist churches in southern Haiti. They too, were involved with the swine re-population program.

In November, Craig Shuck, WC's Latin America Director and I went to Haiti. We met with all of our CVM workers and Haitian partners. While we were there, we visited Jeremie where Dr. Jere Colley from Alabama, and Dr. Dennis Sundbeck from Texas, were on a shuttle. At this time, the local leadership was not very effective. Jere and Dennis could not maximize the use of their time and talents.

Dr. Jere Colley and Dr. Dennis Sunbeck with Haitian children.

Dr. Maureen Birmingham and Dr. Clyde Burns teaching in Haiti. (Maureen first female long-term worker).

These two, not to be deterred, made the best of it. Both have since gone on other shuttles, and they remain big fans of the program.

Things were quite different at Les Cayes, where Chevanne Jeune had assembled Haitian leaders from several communities for a swine seminar. Thirty churches in the area were involved in this program. Dr. Maureen Birmingham, an Illinois graduate, practicing in New York, and Dr. Clyde Burns from North Carolina conducted the training session. On a quiz given the last day, one student answered 20 of 21 questions correctly. Four students scored over 90%! The shuttle program is at its best when participants do the teaching. It was exciting indeed!

I was so impressed by Maureen's ability to communicate in Creole (she knew French) and by her Christian commitment. I asked her if she was interested in returning to Haiti for long-term service. She wanted to think about it for a while. About six months later, she called to tell me that she felt the call of God in her life to serve on the mission field. Maureen returned to Haiti, and worked for four years. During her time there, she wrote and published several practical books in Creole on animal husbandry. They dealt with many of the animals Haitians raised, such as goats, pigs, horses, and chickens.

Maureen was a hard worker and a natural linguist. Later, she worked in Bolivia for a year, and produced some more animal husbandry books in Spanish. Can you believe that she had learned Spanish before arriving? Before leaving Bolivia, she was studying German. She interrupted her career to get a Masters in Public Health at Harvard. Later, she accepted a position with World Health Organization (WHO) and worked in Geneva, Switzerland.

Another veterinarian who began service in the fall of 1984 was Dr. Bob Van Dyke from Arkansas. He responded to an article in the CVM newsletter, advertising for a replacement for Dr. Bill Baker. Bob's swine expertise came at a time when the pig re-population program was gaining momentum. Bob and his wife Doris left what they were doing, and headed to Haiti. His involvement included the goat project that Bill Baker had started in Fond de Blanc. Two brothers, Paul and Jean Thomas were the Haitians heading up this project there. One of Bob's first tasks was helping to build a swine-farrowing house. The Lord provides the right people at the appropriate time.

* * *

April 6, 1984 was a sad day. Ray Dayton was killed while riding his motorcycle in Kenya. This prompted our first prayer chain among the representatives. Often, CVM feels like a family. We held a memorial service for Ray at the annual meeting in New Orleans. We know the scriptures tell us that out of death comes life. In addition to that, it can be a powerful force, which inspires others to serve.

There was a young couple from Florida, Dr. Kit and Mrs. Jan Flowers. They came to the meeting in New Orleans to explore service through CVM, partly because they had read of Ray's death in the CVM newsletter. I can still see them sitting in the back of the room listening intently to the speakers. Later that year, they went on a shuttle to Haiti. Things went wrong at every turn, but the calling was there. They applied for long-term service.

By that time the next year, Kit, Jan, and their two lovely daughters, Molly and Missy, were in Africa. They worked with the Maasai people in Kenya. The Flowers family spent five years in Kenya, and

Dr. Kit and Jan Flowers,
Molly and Missy.

then returned to the United States to work in the CVM office in Seattle. When Kit came to Seattle for orientation before going to the field, I remarked to Carolee Boyd that he had potential to one day lead CVM. How prophetic those words proved to be!

Another couple, Dr. Jere and Mrs. Judy Colley were in Haiti at the same time as the Flowers. They had to lend clothes to the Flowers since their luggage never arrived. However inconvenient and ill fitting those clothes were, enduring friendships resulted. Jere later went to Kenya on a shuttle and worked with Kit after they had begun their ministry there. The Colleys later served in Bangladesh with the Southern Baptists. The Lord guides His work and uses those who lay their lives at His altar, despite temporary setbacks.

The Reverend Art Beals, the World Concern Director, was a special guest at that meeting in New Orleans. The panel also included

Rev. Art Beals and Dr. Leroy Dorminy.

Dr. Floyd Votaw, who had recently returned following his accident in Nepal, and Dr. Howard Jones, from Florida, who led nutrition seminars at the veterinary school in Santa Cruz, Bolivia. Kurt Krusekopf, a veterinary student from Missouri, assisted him on the shuttle. This was a new step up in shuttles—a specialist teaching in a formal setting.

Our Oregon representative, Mr. Andy Parker, spoke about rangeland management. It was the only time a non-veterinarian served as a state representative. Andy had a special love for veterinarians and missions. World Concern's CVM coordinator, Bill Foster, expressed his desire to encourage and facilitate CVM's work in his role at WC.

Mike Chesson helped me at the booth. In a letter to Art Beals, Mike wrote about his appreciation for World Concern's increasing confidence in the effectiveness of CVM field-workers, but cautioned against using emotional appeals to our members. Support, he said, would come as the organization developed a reputation for effective and efficient ministry. Dr. Earle Goodman reiterated these feelings to the leadership also. The wisdom of that approach has served CVM well.

The year 1984 saw leadership changes at World Concern. Art Beals resigned as director, and Ann Sorley resigned as Latin America Director. They had both been true friends of CVM. Art had served nine years as CEO of World Concern. He facilitated the early marriage between World Concern and CVM. Charles Morton, former vice president of Far East Operations for Pepsi Cola International, replaced Art.

Much of CVM's early work was in Latin America. Ann Sorley, a nurse, served well as WC Latin America Director. She could easily identify with veterinarians, and she truly had a heart for ministry. I consider both Ann and Art good friends. I suggested that Ann become an honorary veterinarian, for all her hard work and devotion to CVM.

Two more veterinarians were assigned to long-term service in the fall of 1984. They attended the September orientation. They were Dr. Scott Lubbers, from Oregon, and Dr. Bill and Mrs. Ann Testerman, from Washington. Both Scott and Bill taught at veterinary schools in Bolivia. Scott followed Toby Hoover at Trinidad, and Bill and Anne replaced Ken and Ket Weinland in Santa Cruz. Bill had been a Peace Corps worker, and Scott was fresh out of veterinary school.

<hr />

Veterinarians in Georgia wanted a special project to support. We suggested that they focus on the Navajo Reservation. They collected $4,000 with their first mailing. This allowed us to give a grant to Dr. Bob and Ann Brabrook, from Washington. They started a project on the reservation with help from the Episcopal Church. Part of this project helped the Navajos to improve and preserve a native strain of sheep that seemed particularly well suited for conditions in the Southwestern United States.

We had several successful shuttles during the year, including trips to Haiti by Dr. Joseph Arnoboldi from New York, and student Frank Hooper from Auburn. Dr. Sue Price from Wisconsin, and dairy science major Lorraine Hasse worked with the Weinlands in Bolivia. Scott Griffin from Auburn worked with Dr. Bob Wilmarth in Costa Rica.

We published the book <u>Raising Healthy Swine Under Primitive Conditions</u>. This was quite a milestone. It started out as a book covering all species, but in the end, it was species specific. I think it was a wise choice at that time.

We ended the year with a total of $166,950 income. CVM was not yet self-supporting, but it showed a healthy increase over the previous year. Our income had steadily grown throughout CVM's history. We felt exceedingly blessed.

CHAPTER 11

"Millionaires"

Considering the conditions our fieldworkers struggle under, it is remarkable that they even survive. Even daily chores seem unnecessarily difficult. While reading old prayer letters, I saw again how much field-workers need a sense of humor to get them through the day.

Each worker, at some point during these struggles, wonders, *"why am I here"?*

Two years into his mission, Fred Van Gorkom wrote:

A Prayer Letter

You know the feeling. Sometimes I wonder why the Lord has me here, bumbling through clinics as best I can. Struggling with inexperience, or struggling to explain to a stubborn tribesman that half a dose of medicine is not good enough. Conversely, that if a full dose is good, three times is not really better.

Sometimes I wonder-why I am here, spending weeks in exasperation to get one simple visa entry stamped in my passport. Why not go where I'm welcomed, where I am not constantly called Ferinjee (foreigner) the instant I step out the door. Why not work in a place where medicines are available, where permission to drive to church on Sunday is not a weekly battle, where I don't have to make things like catsup or cottage cheese on my own kitchen stove. Sometimes I wonder.

He answers his own question,

Drs. Fred and Vicki Van Gorkum, Codi, Jessie, Jodi, and Aaron. (Longest service in Africa for male and female fieldworkers).

A Prayer Letter

Other times, I know. Like the day a bright-eyed old woman, her face deep with wrinkles, brought me the last of her life savings— a ewe. It seemed to have a hole in its sternum. She had carefully packed it with the best stuff she knew—cow dung! The hole was two fingers wide, clear through the sternum into the mediastinal space. How that poor, puffing sheep was alive, I dunno.

We usually dispense medicines at break-even prices. Almost everyone can afford that, and free medicine does nothing for their self-respect and has less value to them than medicine they can pay for. But for the poorest, we unobtrusively forget to charge for everything. This was one such time.

I finished cleaning the big black hole in her ewe, doing everything I could, then stood slowly to meet her black eyes. They were no longer pleading, only piercingly grateful. Her ancient wrinkles smiled and she trustingly thrust forward all her coins in one stub-fingered palm. I chose the smallest one. The hope on her face was reward enough. I know why God has me here."

There are lighter sides. Fred wrote,

A Prayer Letter

I was on a farm call one day with Dr. Everett Martin. He is an alumnus and fan of the Texas A & M Aggies. When some kids call out, "feringee" waving as we pass, he leans out the window and tries to teach their untrained Amharic tongues how to say, "Gig 'em Aggies!," an old Texas A&M battle cry. It was only a matter of time until he succeeded.

Several boys gathered around my truck, jabbering cheerfully, talking and commenting, but too rapidly for my comprehension. I just nodded and joined them.

Then in the hubbub, one latecomer said softly in English, "Gig 'em, Aggies".

"Who said that?" I demanded.

My face must have been alarming. All the other boys quickly withdrew from the culprit, who shrank back as small as he could. He could only point speechlessly down the bank. I saw them. They'd been watching from below, where they had taught the boy how to say it and had sent him up after me. Ol' Everrett was doubled up on the ground, about to die laughing. Kifle just cackled, propped like an overcooked noodle against the nearest Eucalyptus tree. Massive entertainment!"

Sometimes the absurdity of what happens causes a smile though the misery it causes is devastating as this cartoon portrays. Dr. Bill and Anne Testerman, Washington, who had served one term in the Peace Corps in Ecuador, write:

A Prayer Letter

After visiting us in Bolivia, our friends Teak and Anne Martin thought we would appreciate this cartoon. We identify thoroughly!

Changing money is such a time consuming activity in our life here. All of our money starts out as dollars from the United States, and needs to be changed to Bolivian Pesos. You might imagine that would be done at a bank, but not so. If you change money in a bank, you would get the official exchange rate of $1 to 75,000 Pesos. No one does that, since the country's economy is based on the "unofficial" rate that is available in "Casa de Cambio" (exchange house) or the street.

When we arrived in Bolivia in August 1984, the dollar brought 7,000 Pesos. To be a "millionaire" you had to cash $143. Now $1.90 will do it. As you can imagine, inflation has run rampant. In 1984, inflation was 2,700%. It has been climbing at a rate of 116,000% this year, which is overwhelming. A newspaper has gone from 700 to 100,000 Pesos. The smallest bill we used to use was 50 Pesos, now it's 5,000 and up to 1,000,000. We've enclosed a 1,000 Peso bill for a souvenir. It is worth .0018 cents."

Audrey Hinton writes,

A Prayer Letter

School is out, and my life seems to be inundated by kids. Last week I had six of them, while Mark took the parents of two of the children to Maasai land where they will be living and working. The major disaster of the week came when one of the girls was leaning against the bathroom sink and it fell off the wall. Gallons of water sprayed forth from the loose pipe. I had just gotten into my nightgown with a sigh of relief at the day being over! We did survive to laugh about it.

Sam made history this week, too. On Friday, he bit the tip of the nipple of his bottle, and I suggested that was the end of his bottle. He got through the night and all of the "sports day," although he was very sad about it. But Sunday was just too much. He was so miserable and crabby that he announced he was "just going to go upstairs and die!" Mother reconsidered, found another nipple, and Sam has been grateful ever since. He is every bit as dramatic as his father!

Our shuttle program got a boost when Dr. Bob Otto came on board as a full time volunteer. He did such a good job, our number of shuttles increased to an all time high—44 in one year. To get a better feel for the job, Bob went to Bolivia and put on a seminar himself. It covered diseases of the eyes, ears, and skin. Part of his time was at Trinidad University where Scott Lubbers, Washington, taught clinics. One of the missing ingredients in many veterinary schools in developing countries is the lack of good clinical experience for students. Scott tried to address those needs. It was not exactly like a mobile clinic in the United States. Scott writes:

A Prayer Letter

This month, I had a student visitor from Alabama, Dan Gentry. That's why I am learning Southern English, Y'all. Dan and I just returned from one of our longest trips, a four-day working trip to Ascension with three students, and our equipment. It took six and one half hours to drive over terrible roads.

The first day, we visited three small family farms to treat their animals: horses skinny from parasites, calves with umbilical infections, and a cow with a retained placenta. Yep, that dreaded smell of retained placentas exists here too! Veterinarians in the states debate how best to treat them, but they have the opportunity to return if needed. We have only the one chance, so we gave her all we had. Even that was limited. On the return trip to Trinidad, we stopped by to see how the cow was doing, but she was nowhere to be found.

But what an experience, and what a witness to the students to have the opportunity to work with missionaries within their project villages!'

Missionaries are sometimes put in unusual situations. Here's one that Bill Testerman shared in a letter:

A Prayer Letter

"An artificial uterus," the carpenter exclaimed, "are you loco?"

This began my introduction to Drs. Jerry and Patricia Olsen, professors at Colorado State University and shuttle veterinarians to Bolivia. Jerry had called a week earlier to say that he would be bringing a plastic bag which would serve as an artificial uterus. With this, we could give practical experience with dystocias and palpation of the reproductive tract.

"Could you please have a structure built to mount the bag in?" he asked.

It sounded like an easy request, since Jerry had sent along a drawing along with the correct dimensions. The carpenter refused to look at the drawing, and insisted on making his own diagram with different measurements.

To my surprise, the project was exactly what Jerry needed. It was even finished five minutes before we were ready to use it. We fitted the artificial uterus in place, and inserted the specimens from the slaughter- house. Everyone was overwhelmed with the practical experience offered by Jerry and his 'homemade cow'.

While Jerry was teaching new methods and new techniques in large animals, Patty was using her skills as a clinician to bring some new ideas to her group of students. Her topics ranged from common diseases in small animals, to laboratory procedures, and artificial insemination. Many of the demonstrations were new to the students, and they were eager to learn all they could from these two specialists. This husband and wife team spent another week in Trinidad, sharing their experiences with students there.

Patty did a wonderful comparison of the struggles of a day in the life of an average Bolivian versus life in the U.S. The things she wrote would apply to most developing countries. There is a great disparity in the *quality of life index*. It really puts things in perspective. She wrote,

"I view my life differently today than I did two weeks ago."

"Jerry and I returned from a two-week mission to Bolivia where we lectured to veterinary students and faculty at two veterinary schools in Santa Cruz and Trinidad. We were referred to as "shuttle veterinarians", self supported but guided and cared for by Christian Veterinary Mission (CVM).

Having acquired some slight illness during the end of my trip, I went to my doctor. I indicated to him that I may have been exposed to brucellosis.

Much of the milk in Bolivia is not pasteurized.

tuberculosis

People in Bolivia die from this disease.

Leaving his office, I was near a grocery store, so I purchased a few groceries. Only a few days ago I commented 'Nothing in the store appeals to me today'.

Our cupboards look very plentiful comparing them to the Bolivian families we stayed with.

Upon returning home I took a nice warm shower.

Very little water in Bolivia is heated. Often some of the water is not suitable for human consumption.

Since I was feeling better, I called the Teaching Hospital that I would be back to work tomorrow. How fortunate I am. I love to teach. Occasionally I feel I have given up a good salary as a private practitioner to teach. However after meeting enthused teachers at the universities in Bolivia who teach but do so for a very small salary, I questioned how much dedication I had.

104

I can't hold a candle to the true educators in Bolivia, who persevere in spite of no funds allocated to their teaching hospital, who scrape to find enough money for used equipment, yet remain excited over treating animals plagued by a variety of infectious diseases, and are enthused to help students become professional veterinarians.

At dinner I set the table, placing glasses on it for milk for my children to drink. We insist that they drink at least 3 to 4 glasses of milk each day.

Many children in Bolivia have no milk.

I knew their diets, although not as good as I'd sometimes like, were wonderful compared to Third World children's diet.

The life expectancy in Bolivia is in the 40's, and anywhere from 160 to 270 children per 1,000 die during the first five years of life.

As we sat down together as a family to eat, we said our prayers to God and then did something that CVM veterinarian Bill and Ann Testerman did with their children each night we stayed with them in Santa Cruz-we told one another about something we were happy about or grateful for, and it seemed real easy to think of things!

I have had a good day today, one that, God gave me. I look upon it much differently than I did prior to our trip to South America. I hope someday all humanity can share in the good life we have and that all children can be fed and happy. Perhaps that is what is meant by. "Thy will be done on earth as it is in heaven."

Thanks Patty, for reminding us of the wonderful blessings we enjoy and also to remind us that all are not so fortunate. We say this not to place a guilt trip, but rather to remind us to share our talents and resources with those who need them. Our fieldworkers, shuttles and the entire CVM constituency, do a marvelous job of this.

Just prior to the Olsons' arrival, two well known poultry specialists, Dr. Conrad Van Dyke from Ontario, Canada, and Dr. Malcolm Reid from Georgia, presented a comprehensive seminar at the veterinary schools in Santa Cruz and Trinidad. It was titled "Management and Disease Prevention in Poultry". Veterinarians and producers attended the seminar. Poultry, both for meat and egg production, is a very important source of protein in Latin America. The demand for it is growing. Dr Reid is the author of the <u>Raising Healthy Poultry</u>, and Dr. Van Dyke now directs CVM Canada.

⸙

May 16, 1985 six CVM supporters met in Miami for the flight to Haiti. This was the first donor tour of CVM overseas projects. The tour included Dr. Mel Swenson , who served as head of the Physiology from Iowa State; Dr. Wayne Sletten, a Practitioner in Faith, South Dakota; Dr. Anita Foote who practiced in Sterling, Virginia; Dr. Donna Harper was manager of a horse farm in Ruidoso, New Mexico; Dr. Max Brand practiced in Ft. Wayne, Indiana; and Dr. L.F. Magnall, a retired practitioner from Tripoli, Iowa; Scott Rodin of World Concern, and me. It was an interesting and educational trip.

The unexpected happened early, Max Brand writes,

> Forest fires in Florida caused a power outage at the Miami International Airport. There were no monitors, loudspeakers or lights. What chaos! A generator made enough to land planes. Candles dimly lit the corridors where people sat around in the humid heat, without air conditioning. Without conveyor belts, it was hectic sorting out luggage by flashlight. Power was restored by 3:30 PM, so by the time we left at 6:30, things were almost back to normal.

The second misfortune happened to Anita. Her checked luggage from Washington D.C. did not arrive on her plane. Somehow the luggage went to New York. It never did catch up with her. The clothes that Anita had on would have to last for eight days. Donna's clothes didn't fit Anita and none of the men could help.

The third mishap involved Jim Grayson. Although Jim lived in New Hampshire for a number of years, he was not an American citizen. He had a New Zealand passport, and a visa from the U.S. He discovered that if he left the U.S., his visa would be revoked and he could not return. So Jim stayed behind, hoping he could join us later, but that wasn't to be.

A comfortable inn is a welcome sight for weary travelers. In Haiti they aren't common, but CVM had one available in Port-au-Prince.

Dr. Jim and Ann Rosenberger, Cecilia and Bill Manness.

Bill Manness met us at the airport and took us to the Methodist Guest House. It was run by his wife, Cecelia. She took care of many CVM shuttle participants as they passed through Port-Au-Prince.

The guest house was such a vital part of the shuttle program and Cecilia did it with such a spirit of love that we later made her an "Honorary Veterinarian". She always requested that the shuttle vet bring Snicker bars. With them, she made the most wickedly rich, best tasting cake imaginable. It was so good you would fight for a piece; and so decadent that you could almost feel the sludge forming in your arteries!

We started our tour by visiting the Swine Multiplication Center (SMC), a central breeding and farrowing center from which weaned pigs were distributed to secondary centers. Dr. Bill Baker managed this operation. CVM was involved in training the recipients of these pigs, farmers and technicians, in pig husbandry.

We traveled to Les Cayes and met with Chavannes Jeune, the IRD Director. He and his wife Mary Lucy, had many skills and a sincere desire to help their fellow Haitians have better lives. They insisted it have a real spiritual dimension. Dr. Brian and Mrs. Karen Kersten of Wisconsin, were working in the south of Haiti. Like all of our field workers there, they were training pig recipients.

From Les Cayes, we traveled north on the only paved road. It was a good road when it was built, but repairs had not kept pace with wear and tear. Our next stop was Fond des Blanc. Dr. Bob and Mrs. Doris Van Dyke from Arkansas, helped a Haitian man named John Thomas with goat, pig, and water development projects. It was interesting to see successful farmers who had been involved with CVM's previous goat project. The most successful were now affluent by Haitian standards.

Next, we went to the Artibonite Valley, the location of Hospital Albert Schweitzer. We met with Bill Jackson, the hospital administrator, and Dr. Larry Mellon, the hospital founder. Dr. and Mrs. Mellon entertained the group with their musical talents. Larry showed us a treasured photo of himself with Dr. Schweitzer. Larry's pride and joy was the farm associated with HAS. It had a beef herd, a dairy herd, chickens, and pigs. It was easy to see why he got along so well with the CVM workers, for the livestock were dear to his heart.

Dr. Rod and Mrs. Nancy Frank worked at HAS during this time. After walking around the beef farm, crawling through barbed wire fences and stopping to eat the abundant mangoes, we returned to the farmhouse that belonged to Venance Dormeus (pronounced Vain-us), the farm manager.

We were treated to some homemade bread, Haitian coffee, and a mixture of milk and soda pop. A young man began to play an accordion and Venance began to sing. Soon other members of his family joined in, followed by the Americans. As Venance sang and danced, the entire group sang and clapped their hands in a happy celebration, transcending language and cultural barriers and creating a wonderful time of fellowship.

Following this, Venance and his wife closed our visit with a prayer. He walked over to Rod Frank and told him how much he loved and appreciated him for all that he had done. With tears streaming down his cheeks, he embraced Rod, calling him his brother. There were few dry eyes in the group.

One of the veterinarians in the tour turned to me and said, "You can show me all the pigs and goats you wish, but this is what it is all about."

The final day of the tour, we visited the Citadel, which is a few miles from Cap Haitien. It is a monument to man's inhumanity to man. The "King of Northern Haiti", Henry Christophe, built it and named it Citadelle Laferriere. Greed and lust for power generates a paranoia that triggers these kinds of acts. As you looked out over the parade ground atop the fortress, it seemed you could hear the screams of the soldiers as they were given the command which sent them over the walls of the Citadel only to demonstrate their complete obedience to the leader! I think our trip to the Citadel sobered us all.

Here are some comments by the group on their experiences during the Haiti tour:

> "I am favorably impressed with what our CVM personnel and their families, by the grace of God, are accomplishing materially and spiritually in Haiti. It was our privilege to be acquainted with them and their work. It makes me more satisfied than ever to be a part of CVM".

> "The Swine Repopulation Program demonstrates man's humanity and concern for his fellowman. It's a great program, and every veterinarian should be proud of the role that the profession is doing through such people as Drs. Van Dyke, Kersten and Frank. They are first class."

> "It opened my eyes to the tremendous size and complexity of the need in Haiti, and to the breadth and the depth of poverty there. It also showed me the strength of the programs that we have down there right now."

Two months later, Tim and Jenny Righetti did a shuttle from California to Haiti. At the CVM convention in Las Vegas, Tim reported on their trip.

"Jenny and I became millionaires this month. Our banker would disagree, but he hasn't been to Haiti. We thank CVM for the opportunity for growth in participating in the shuttle program. After having the experience, we will never be the same.

"I thought I would go to Haiti, help the veterinarians establish the propagation centers, tell Haitians how to raise pigs, and I would have done my bit for a better world. For me it was a humbling experience. I have not affected the problem of world hunger one iota. I don't have the "right stuff"—yet.

"I am so proud of the many Christian veterinarians representing us in Third World countries. They are dedicated, technically excellent, and doing a superlative job under the most difficult conditions imaginable. The people we are trying to help desperately need our help, both spiritual and technical.

"Our CVM veterinarians face real dangers. Your life is in the hands of the Lord whenever you venture into Haitian traffic, both at being hurt or the greater danger of hurting someone else. We ask them to live among disease we don't know how to deal with—TB, Polio, Hepatitis, Rabies, and Amoebic Dysentery. I don't know how they find the strength to do it.

"Are we doing any good? Is it too late? I do not know. For the bloated, pot-bellied children with blank faces and sunken eyes, I'm afraid it's too late. There is extreme poverty, the rich who seem to resist change, and the frustration that results from this. Fortunately, there is more to see.

"If you ask anyone who has been in Haiti for more than 10 years, they will tell you that things are definitely better. The government is sponsoring reforms. The efforts of World Concern and CVM are just now beginning to become evident. Pigs are moving out into the hills. For those who have lost a large part of their means of survival through the loss of their pigs, life will be better.

"Coastal Hybrid Bermuda Grass, which is 16% protein and has the promise of adapting well, is sprouting in propagation plots. Reforestation is under way. Teams of bright-eyed Christian young people are sweating under tropical heat, sticking seedling pines into the soil, and watering them.

"Perhaps the most encouraging evidence of all can be seen on Sunday mornings, along country roads lined with people. From tiny houses with mud walls, thatched roofs, and dirt floors, 6 to 10 people will emerge with clean bodies, pressed clothes, and shining faces. They are carrying Bibles, headed for church. Sometimes it is five miles away, but they go to make a joyful noise unto the Lord!

"There is a fortress near Cap Haitian, called 'The Citadel.' It is sometimes called the eighth wonder of the world. The structure covers 5 acres, and at one point soars 300 feet from its base. A tortuous seven-mile path rises to where 'The Citadel' commands a view of the seaward countryside, for a distance of 20 miles.

"To secure his position of Haiti's first and only king, Henri Christophe built this seemingly impregnable fortress. He was concerned with the return of the French and others who wished to challenge his authority. It took 500,000 workers 14 years to build it. In the process, 20,000 workers died.

"Christophe's empire, like his citadel which never fired a shot, crumbled from within. He lies beneath 30 yards of cement in the center of the parade ground. He beat an assassin's bullet by using one of his own—in suicide.

"I stood on the point where Christophe's sentinels stood, able to see any movement for miles. In this place, I became painfully aware of the citadel I had built within my being. I became aware that I have been preoccupied with the quest for security-storing up material and power beyond my needs, as protection for all threats to my comfort. I saw myself as a small reflection of Christophe's citadel.

"And the nations of the world today, in which at last count 28 separate wars are waging, where the armies of people who want only peace are facing each other in anger, with the equivalent of 100 lbs of TNT under every person inhabiting the earth, is this same citadel. The nations of the world seek security, by placing trust in weapons and technology, rather than addressing the real cause-World Hunger.

"Can we turn the world around? I still don't know. If there is an answer, it will come from Christ-centered people in organizations like CVM and World Concern. We must prevail, because I for one do not want to explain why we took the beautiful garden God gave us to play in, and reduced it to a cinder."

If ever there was an antithesis to the hunger of the Third World, it is the Midwestern United States—the breadbasket of the world. My wife, Tina, and I decided to take a driving trip to visit veterinary schools in Indiana, Michigan, Wisconsin, Iowa, and Illinois.

Each state we drove through had a special attraction of its own. North Georgia, Tennessee, and Kentucky, with their rugged landscapes, were alive with flowers and blooming dogwood trees. Indiana had redbud and lilac in full bloom along the Wabash. Michigan had such a diversity of scenery. Fields of blooming tulips made a beautiful study in color. Wisconsin's green and rolling dairy farms created hillside mosaics. Iowa's black and fertile soil explains its productiveness in corn and pigs. The vast stretches of Illinois farmland underscore how blessed we are to live in the United States.

With each school visit, we spoke to students and discussed CVM, its personnel, and its programs. The CVM representative at each school, in cooperation with the student fellowship groups, set up these sessions. Attendance was good, interest was keen and Christian concern for the less fortunate of the world was genuine. I was impressed with the Christian maturity of these young men and women.

Students were eager to learn about how they could become involved. Many asked how they could prepare themselves for long-term service. I advised them to get a broad educational background, gain some mixed practice experience, acquire a second language, and continue in Bible study.

We came back from our trip greatly encouraged by these young people. We were thankful for them and for the faculty members that work with them. They exhibited a broad perspective, steeped in good values. With them, the future will be bright.

Ken Weinland taught clinics at Purdue before going overseas with CVM. Many people there remembered him for his service at the school. Some of the people with whom we met at the different schools later became involved as follows:

Laurel Logas, Illinois, served on a shuttle following graduation (Tina and I spent the night at her home with her and her husband.)

Stephanie and Doug Lewis, Iowa State-eventually went long term to Cameroon with their church. (Mel Swenson has encouraged many young believers there.)

Michigan State-we visited with Dr. Charlie Coy, who had a history of international involvement, as did the school. Dr Chuck Gibson served as faculty advisor. He and his wife Betty were gracious hosts.

Dr. Sue Price, Avoca, Wisconsin, had made arrangements for our meeting with the students. The school was only in its third year. We had a good visit with the first and second year students.

The Storer family: Mike and Debra, Jason, Kevi, and Jessa.

That night, we visited Dr. Mike and Mrs. Debra Storer, and their three children—Jessa, Jason, and Kevi. The Storers were long-term candidates. Tina and I spent the night. At Mike and Debra's insistence, we slept in their room. During the night, we heard the patter of little feet. It was Kevi, going over to Tina's side of the bed looking for her mother. Not long after, Jason came to my side, looking for his father. Were they ever surprised!

Later that year, The Storers started a project with the Navajo at Hard-Rock, Arizona,. Dr. John Shutz, of New York donated a vehicle for their use. After two years there, they spent four years in Haiti, and then returned to work with the Navajo Gospel Mission where they had started.

In late October, I attended the Latin America planning conference in Port-au-Prince, Haiti. All of the veterinarians and spouses in the Latin American area attended. This included Dr. Rod and Mrs. Nancy Frank, Dr. Brian and Mrs. Karen Kersten, Dr. Maureen Birmingham, Dr. Bill and Mrs. Anne Testerman, Dr. Scott Lubbers, Dr. Bob and Mrs. Janet Wilmarth, and Dr. Mike and Mrs. Debra Storer.

Each veterinarian gave a progress report, along with projections and objectives for the coming year. They shared their frustrations and fulfillments, their successes and failures, and their goals for the future. It was a time of learning, team building, and enjoying Christian fellowship. I think it would be safe to say that each of us was strengthened in our resolve to have the best and most effective ministry possible.

In November, I went to Africa. I needed to visit our veterinarians there, to look for places of service and to attend the World Concern Africa Planning Conference.

I spent one week in Somalia, the easternmost country in Africa. It has a broad desert and semi-desert band extending eastward along the Gulf of Aden. The Somalis are for the most part, a people of nomadic and pastoral traditions. Somalia was at one point divided into French, British and Italian sectors. The economy was largely undeveloped, with little real growth. Much of this was because clan rivalries created civil strife and instability.

I visited the villages around the Leper Hospital staffed by World Concern. It was in Jilib, near the Juba River in Southern Somalia. Mike Madeny, the project director and I, called on local cattle owners to determine their veterinary needs. We wanted to know if CVM shuttles could be effective here. It certainly seemed to be a viable option, but it never happened because the country began to deteriorate politically.

While ferrying across the Juba River, a strange looking object came floating by. Closer inspection revealed a very bloated, dead hippopotamus. I did not know its cause of death but the alligators were taking advantage of it. It kept their minds off the locals as they came to get their daily supply of water for washing and drinking. Obviously, basic sanitation issues come to the forefront when there is a lack of clean water and proper hygiene.

Driving north to Mogadishu presented some interesting challenges. An occasional warthog would run out in front of us. They are extremely ugly; even a mother warthog would agree with that. Nevertheless, they know how to scavenge. They are survivors. Leaving the warthogs behind, we began to pick up speed. We were cruising at 50 miles per hour, when a tremendous pothole appeared, covering the entire road. Night trips can be hazardous to your health.

Then along came a herd of camels that decided to cross the road. None of us wanted to argue with them. It is hard enough to try to examine a camel's mouth or give it a pill; it will bite and spit, and generally act uncooperative. Nomadic herders often accompany camels. Their homes are made of cloth and sticks and can be packed across a camel's back. We saw this pastoral scene many times during our 200-mile trip from Jilib to the capital city.

Visiting the USAID office in Mogadishu, I met two veterinarians, Dr. Pamela Procella, and Dr. Ahmed, who was the Director of Animal Health and Production for the Somali government. We wanted to send some shuttles to initiate a project there. These veterinarians were willing to explore that option. I also visited the veterinary school, but was less successful there. Clan and tribal feuds created obstacles to a promising future there. Later, these disputes developed into civil war. This left no room for meaningful development. It is sad to contemplate, because I think Somalia could have had a future.

Leaving Somalia can be intimidating. We were questioned about why we came and what we were carrying out. Usually you are taken behind a screen and searched. Our declaration of money taken in and out had to balance with the money we spent. I think the axiom applies: "The worse off a country is, the greater the hassle going through customs and immigration." They discourage, rather than encourage people to come and minister.

Stepping onto the Boeing 727, an Ethiopian Airlines plane, I heard a familiar tune coming though the intercom. It was Dolly Parton, singing "Nine to Five". It sounded strange and incongruent with this traditional Muslim world. I don't know if the recording came with the plane, but it was refreshing to hear.

All African countries reflect the power that once controlled them. Coming into Nairobi, you immediately detect its British past. Kenya came under British control in the late nineteenth century. It was organized as a colony (inland) in 1920, and a protectorate (along the coast).

Kenya has one of the highest rates of population increase. This has caused pressure on pastoral people like the Maasai. Land becomes scarce and herders cannot continue their nomadic existence. They have to settle down in one place, which brings a new set of problems.

Mark and Audrey Hinton were thinking about moving to Garissa, in Northeastern Kenya. It is a dry, harsh land on the border of

Somalia—a great place for camels. We rented a small plane because it was a very long, dusty, and time-consuming ride to cover the ground that we needed to. To land, the pilot had to first buzz the runway to drive away the animals. We met with other Garissa missionaries, to ask their opinion about the potential for a veterinarian working in the area. They liked the idea very much.

After viewing the area and evaluating the potential for service, we left for parts west. The salt flats were visible for miles, painting a pretty landscape that was incongruent with this wasted and unproductive part of Kenya. As we neared our next destination, the scene was a bit more benign. Though not lush by any standards, pastoral herders found some grazing for their flocks. One interesting landmark was a well, dubbed Jacob's well, where for many ages flocks and their shepherds came to get that precious commodity—water.

We touched down at Hurri Hills, in a beautiful rolling landscape. Here, Dilly Anderson, a second-generation missionary, had done some excellent development work. Appropriate good yielding crops and some excellent forage was growing, despite less than ideal conditions. The big test in such an endeavor is to develop local ownership for sustainable, reproducible benefits.

It was an enjoyable overnight. Our physical needs had been restored. We could see the potential for this beautiful land. As we took off from Hurri Hills, the hills loomed large and quickly in front of us. The pilot gave all the power our small but overloaded plane could muster and we rose to hit an updraft. It felt like riding a bucking bronco; someone yelled, "Ride 'em cowboy!"

Kenya is a very beautiful and varied country. Below was a wonderful panorama of rolling hills; flocks of sheep-white dots scattered across the landscape. As we neared Nairobi, the picture became even more lush; a wonderful mosaic of coffee and tea plantations. The trip north had been a wonderful experience, but it was good to get back to Nairobi again.

The next day, I flew to Loita to visit Kit and Jan Flowers, who had been in Africa for a year. We made a cow pasture landing and I was greeted by Molly and Missy, holding a hand-made welcome sign. Many Maasai kids, and even some adults joined them. It is a cherished memory.

On Thanksgiving Day, I had dinner with the Flowers. The meal was exceptional. The Maasai had given them a fat ram and wanted us to watch the traditional killing of the ram. It was contrary to all slaughtering methods we would have recommended—they smothered the ram! The Maasai ate the kidneys raw, along with the blood. I failed the test for participating in that. The meat was not cooked thoroughly, just seared on the outside. It was the most unusual Thanksgiving dinner I had ever known. It was also the only time I got sick on this shuttle.

Driving back to Nairobi took more than eight hours, because we had to visit 10,000 potholes along the way. We also stopped off at Narok, for one of the special reasons that I had come. We stopped in a missionary compound and said a prayer at Ray Dayton's grave. He was killed in a motorcycle crash two years earlier. My heart was heavy, but I remembered his remarkable service. I thanked God for that!

CHAPTER 12

Sharing Skills

How do CVM veterinarians do their work? Simply put, they share their skills. However, this is not limited to veterinarians. Each of us can share the special gifts God has given us. I think of Mr. Ray Berry from California. Ray was not a veterinarian but he had a heart for missions. He wrote:

> About a month ago, I visited Costa Rica. We have worked with Heifer Project International off and on for many years. We wanted to see how they were doing in this little democracy.
>
> My wife, Marion, was raised in India where her parents were agricultural missionaries for more than 50 years. Her father headed a goat and chicken station, for improvement of the breeds, and for better milk and egg production in Northern India. We wished to see Latin American people benefit from such a program. By the grace of God and Goodwill Caravans, we were introduced to Dr. Bob Wilmarth.
>
> We spent three days with him on the rocky roads, through streambeds as far south as the Panamanian border. We found Bob to be a most dedicated person. He is not only accepted, but also loved by the rural folks he is assisting. Being with him on his visits was most enlightening and inspiring.

Ray came back from this shuttle and put together a display for our CVM annual meeting in Las Vegas. It said, "A model dairy barn has been designed and constructed by CVM veterinarian, Bob Wilmarth, in San Jose, Costa Rica. It is designed to help teach proper

Dr. Jerry Burch and Dr. Bob Wilmarth.

goat management procedures. Goats are sometimes called the "poor man's milk cow."

As part of his work Bob hosted shuttles by Dr. Chuck Gasaway, Oklahoma, Dr. Jerry Burch, Tennessee and Dr. Bob Sylvestor, Florida. Never did anyone visit Bob and Janet without coming home feeling blessed.

Another non-veterinary worker, Mr. Jim Collier, was important to CVM in the early years. Jim was a Georgia extension agent in adjoining Ben Hill county. Jim combined homespun humor with practical knowledge to convey his points to South Georgia farmers. He was well qualified for Third World development consulting.

Jim once wrote to me in Seattle: *"It's warm in South Georgia—corn is growing, fish are biting. Things look good because it is spring, and no one has had time to mess up the year".*

He wrote about the proposed Watershed Management Project in Haiti:

Leroy, you asked me what I thought about the proposed Watershed Management Project in Haiti. To me, such a project relates

119

specifically to the control, management and utilization of water on a particular watershed to minimize the destructive forces of water, such as floods, erosion, pollution, silting of streams and to fully utilize the water for human, crop, and livestock use.

This is accomplished by structures, such as diversion and storage dams, dikes, drainage ditches, channels, and terraces, to prevent flooding during periods of high rainfall, and to provide needed water during dry spells. Agronomic practices such as permanent sod, contour cultivation, and minimize tillage are also needed to complete the project. But it is important; flying into Haiti on a clear day, erosion is evident in the ocean for miles around.

Jim

Because of Jim's visit to Haiti, combined with his knowledge of farming in the subtropics of South Georgia, he identified some specific objectives. To implement them, he carried down some peanut seed and some Coast Cross-1 grass stolons, a Bermuda Hybrid. World renowned geneticist, Dr. Glenn Burton, of the Georgia Coastal Plains Experiment Station in Tifton, Georgia, developed this grass hybrid. Glenn told me that he had sent grass hybrid stolons to more than sixty countries.

Rod Frank used the grass sprigs to establish a nursery at Hospital Albert Schweitzer. It did well, and helped the cattle-grazing program. From this initial nursery, untold numbers of acres could be established to provide forage and erosion control. One last generous donation Jim made was to send one of his prize purebred bulls to sire cattle to utilize this forage.

Jim spent some time with Dr. Rod Frank at Deschapelles, with Dr. Kent Smith, and finally with Dr. Keith Flanagan. Jim commented on the introduction of Coast Cross-1, a hybrid Bermuda grass for forage production at the HAS farm. He wrote:

Leroy,

I had nothing but my bare eyes to examine the Coast Cross-1, but I could find nothing wrong with it. It looks better at Deschapelles than at Tifton (Georgia Experiment Station). I don't have any reservations about recommending it for general use in Haiti. It has the potential for producing an additional 100 lbs of beef or 1,000 lbs of milk per acre. Consider carefully how much additional food could be provided for Haiti with 1,000—or 10,000 acres of it. And we need to consider this; the CVM vets need a prescription for the single most debilitating disease they encounter in the animals there; 'Lack of Feeditis'.

The Haitian people need help <u>now</u>! With this in mind, it is my opinion that the Hillside Management Project ought to be initiated as soon as possible. You know that I am an old teacher, and I view these challenges in Haiti as teaching opportunities. You cannot teach or change some one unless you start where they are.

Jim

Dear Jim,

I could feel in your letter, your sympathy for the situation. I sense also the feeling, 'the solution is known, why in tarnation don't these people use it'? You have experienced that many times in your professional life, and so have I.

The eighth chapter of Romans speaks of all creation groaning because of the sins of man. That certainly is apparent to me. If such is true, how do we bring about change? First, there must be a change of heart; secondly, an educational process; and then the implementation—all of which is a slow, difficult process.

There is no doubt in my mind that reforestation and grassing of the hillsides is the number one priority in development in Haiti, aside from the spiritual. That is not only true of Haiti but all over the world. Conservation practices in general are necessary, lest all our resources wind up in the sea.

Leroy

Sometimes when long-term workers leave the field, it is not always possible to have another couple take over immediately. The ideal situation is to have an overlap of assignments, so the work does not suffer. Dr. Phil and Mrs. Kathy Schoenborn of Wisconsin, went to work at Hospital Albert Schweitzer for four months following Rod and Nancy Frank's departure from the field. They stayed until Dr. Kent and Mrs. Jo Ann Smith came, to continue the work.

Phil and Kathy wrote, *"It has been very humbling for us to experience life in the Third World. We hope that our work here has facilitated a smoother transition for the Smiths."*

The Schoenborns made a valuable contribution to project continuity in Haiti.

Don Sylvestor was a soil conservationist with the Center For Holistic Resource Management in Albuquerque, New Mexico. Don made a shuttle to the Navajo Reservation to help Dr. Mike Storer with rangeland grazing problems. He later went to Kenya and Somalia to help CVM/WC workers with the same challenges. Part of his time was spent with Dr. Kit and Mrs. Jan Flowers. He commented; *"Kit has the patience of Job and a cast iron stomach. Only a veterinarian could lie down in a cow manure hut and sleep with cowbells clanging, calves grinding their teeth and lambs bleating. I thought about writing a book, 'Sounds in the Night' by 'The Guy Who didn't Sleep'."* He continues, *"Because of my shuttle mission, I have been touched in a powerful way by the hand of the Lord. I will never be the same person as before".*

Don was helpful to us, devising solutions to age-old problems of semi-nomadic grasslands use.

⚜

Our sixth annual meeting took place in Atlanta again, nine years after CVM became a national organization. At the meeting, Dr Q. L. Darbyshire, my classmate and friend, led an exceptional devotion. He challenged attendees to scrutinize their Christian lives, to see if their commitment measured up to Christ's expectations. He suggested that we should not just try to make the cut to get into heaven but live for Christ in the present. Dr. Darbyshire has been a good friend of CVM in many ways.

Rod and Nancy Frank completed a very successful tour of duty in Haiti; so at the meeting they spoke about their work there. Rod was returning to academic life. Bob and Janet Wilmarth were back from Costa Rica. Bob showed a video of his work that he had produced himself. It was factual, but funny. It was Bob's first effort at producing "movies". He wanted perfection, but that was too elusive—even on the third or fourth staged "take". The video left the audience in stitches. I am sure TV's "Funniest Videos" would love to have a copy of it!

Auburn student Scott Truex's description of his shuttle to Nepal got a very different reaction. There was not a dry eye in the group, as he related his experiences on a student shuttle with Dr. Peter Quesenberry. Scott spoke of his good fortune compared to young Nepali boys who had almost nothing. In spite of their lack of even basic necessities, they were eager about life and learning, never lamenting their lack of material things. It made for a very powerful presentation.

We added two more long-term workers during the year; Dr. Ronnie and Mrs. Sue Sarratt, and their children Lee and Courtney; from Ringling, Oklahoma. The Sarratts went to Bolivia to replace the Testermans. Ronnie's lifelong dream was to serve on the mission field.

Ronnie's primary job was to serve as a faculty member at the veterinary school in Santa Cruz. He trained students with "hands on" clinical experience. Later, the Sarratts moved to the rural area of Samipata, offering their services to destitute farmers whose animals suffered from malnutrition and disease. Ronnie wrote:

A Prayer Letter

The farmers and ranchers donated the use of the building. They pay for the water and electricity. They also help introduce us to each community. The farmers use the radio to broadcast two or three days before an upcoming clinic. While I diagnose and treat the sick animals, I teach three senior veterinary students who live in the clinic. The students have a one-month internship program with me in Samipata. It is very rewarding to teach veterinary medicine to the students, and at the same time share Jesus with them".

Dr. Wade and Mrs. Chryse Bradshaw were from Austin Texas. They went to Nepal to take over the work begun there by Dr. Peter Quesenberry and Dr. Allison Cravens, an English veterinarian. I will never forget Wade's remark, "I don't know if I can fill the shoes of such a dedicated worker as Peter."

I answered him, "We can never fill the shoes of another. You should only try to fill your own to the best of your ability. Then you will leave your own indelible mark, as God blesses you." Wade's gifts include writing:

A Prayer Letter

I would not describe it exactly as a 'call'. After becoming a Christian in high school, I soon heard of the planet's gaping needs- both physical and spiritual. Foreign missions of one sort or another seemed the answer, as logical and unavoidable as the multiplication table. It never occurred to me to doubt that one person's efforts could not make an enormous difference and contribution. But the form of my involvement took circuitous years to materialize.

I became interested in agriculture, but as a child of the suburbs, I didn't even know how to start a tractor. One sunny afternoon while camping, the idea of becoming a vet occurred to me. Immediately on the heels of that came another idea. Here, at last, was a manner in which even I could be useful in a poor country and one closed to the more typical missionary.

That discovery was just the beginning. Storms lay ahead. Married just nine months, we learned that Chryse had Hodgkin's disease. It looked as if we should never do something as foolish as leave Western medical care. I found myself dissatisfied with a profession that, to be honest, I might not have chosen had I known that I was to remain in the United States. Don't get me wrong. Poodles are fine and they deserve good care, but spending my days vaccinating them when my desire was to be involved in the Third World left me angry at God and convinced that the Personnel Department in Heaven was making mistakes like any other bureaucracy.

We came to this remote country of Nepal that is perched at the base of the lofty Himalayas, clinging by its callused hands to an environment on the verge of collapse through erosion, deforestation and the growing population's pressure to cultivate even more remote and less fertile land.

Nepal is a country of subsistence farmers, ravaged by disease and infant mortality. Its statistics are full of enough 'mosts' and 'leasts' to numb any idealistic good intentions. A buffalo is considered more valuable than a child, not because of cruelty, but because the child can be readily replaced, while the animal cannot. For that reason, a veterinarian is seen as an important person. He can make an important difference-house by house, family by family. And the doors of those houses are open to his coming.

Nepal is, I suppose, a hard place to live. God's spirit within does not render us immune to giardia, or fevers, or depression, but daily I love this land, this people more.

Wade and Chryse did an outstanding job. Tina and I visited them while he was teaching at the Rural Development Center in Pokhara. I was truly amazed at his command of the Nepali language, and his ability to draw sick and well animals to demonstrate the subject matter and diseases to his students. Students can be brutally truthful. One student told him his Nepali wasn't very good, but a lot better than the year before!

We never know if the seeds we plant will take root, or how they might grow. But sometimes, in faraway places, it happens. Two missions by non-Americans took place in 1986. Louis Kwantes, a student from Canada, went on a shuttle to Haiti during the summer months. He worked with Keith Flanagan and Maureen Birmingham. Louis did an outstanding job helping with epidemiological issues for the region. Later, after graduating from veterinary school, he did another shuttle to Uzbekistan.

Dr. Kai Arne Schie of Norway, along with wife Elle and their children, went to serve in Madagascar. He was invaluable to Tina and me when we visited Norway in 1984 to present the CVM vision to students at Oslo and to practicing veterinarians there.

Dr. Bob Beede got my attention when he said, " I think I know where CVM can get a huge donation of Ivermectin."

An answer to the ever-present problem of chronic and acute parasitism our fieldworkers encounter? I pursued it, pronto. I called a Merck Marketing executive. "I hear you have some Ivermectin you may wish to donate".

"That's possible," he replied. "How much do you need?"

"We could use quite a bit."

"That wasn't my question, how much do you need?" he persisted.

I was feeling hopeful. "Oh, we have several workers overseas, so we could use quite a bit".

He sighed, "That's not what I asked. How much do you need?"

"We need all you can spare," I ventured boldly.

"I am not sure of that, as we have quite a bit".

We came to terms. Soon we were greeted by a truckload of Ivomec Paste. There were several pallets of this precious de-wormer. Merck and Co had graciously sent us several million doses! We shipped it to Haiti, Bolivia, Thailand, Ethiopia, Kenya, Nepal, and Senegal.

Pharmaceutical companies have been generous to CVM throughout the years. They have responded to our requests with some large donations. They are also very generous in donating to individual shuttles going on specific missions. When we are alerted to special needs, we have been able to call on many of the companies, and they have been receptive to our requests. During an outbreak of rabies in Bolivia, several children died. Fort Dodge donated several thousand doses of Rabies vaccine for immediate shipment. The veterinary students in Santa Cruz administered the vaccine under the supervision of one of our fieldworkers.

Dr. Duane Pankratz of Grand Laboratories has been very generous to us through the years. He is supportive of the work of CVM. Mr. Majon Huff and others at Colorado Serum have always been very helpful, as well as Tom Roundtree of Hampton, in Canada. We are also grateful to Pfizer, Lloyd Laboratories, Solvay, Hoechst-Roussel, Salsbury Laboratories, Smith Kline and Beecham, Upjohn, Norden, Coopers, and American Breeders Service. I know there are many others who have helped, and I offer my apologies for not knowing or remembering all those who have contributed.

Our second CVM donor tour included Dr. Robert Hargreaves from California, Dr. Bob Dickerson from California, Dr. Glenn Rogers from Texas, Dr. Donald Heimsoth from Missouri, Dr. James Reif from California, Dr. Jim Armstrong from Rhode Island, Tim Sooter of World Concern, and me. We went in May of 1986 to Haiti. Although we traveled much the same route as the year before, it was another learning experience and a wonderful time of Christian fellowship.

Donald Heimsoth remembers his experiences at the 'Iron Market': *"A mass of humanity and terrible odors, being besieged with vendors of all possible products. People are everywhere, masses of them, standing or sitting with nothing to do and showing a look of great need. Yet despite these horrific conditions, the people are gentle, kind and warm and always had smiles on their faces."*

Haiti is a country about the size of Maryland that is home to 6 million people. That doesn't tell the whole story, because much of the land is mountainous. There is little cultivatable land. Its productivity has been severely compromised through erosion and poor farming methods. Haiti gained its independence in 1804. Since then, it has traded one corrupt regime for another, adding to the misery of its people.

As usual, we enjoyed some of the fine and pleasant miseries. We left the main road, parked our van, and packed into Maureen Birmingham's four-wheel drive vehicle. The roads were awful. We came to a river swollen with recent rains. One pickup was already stuck. We helped her out and then fearlessly proceeded; Maureen was driving and the rest of us were pushing. We made it across and began congratulating ourselves. Minutes later, we were hopelessly stuck in a bog! It took an hour of pushing and digging to free us.

People were sharing skills at home as well as overseas.

Excerpt From CVM Newsletter

From the time that he was a young veterinarian in Seattle in the 1940's, Charles "Bud" Doney was aware of the people whose homes

127

were the streets. He often wondered how those with pets managed to care for them.

But it wasn't until he was fifty years old that Dr. Doney met the Lord. He wanted to "make up for lost time", giving his life and the profession to the service. Bud became an avid supporter of CVM, and served on a shuttle to Kenya in 1982. Then he met some of the staff of the Seattle Union Gospel Mission. He approached them with the idea of a "pet clinic", to be held one Saturday per month at the mission.

The first clinic was held in July, 1983. Two suspicious dog owners arrived, their dogs were examined and vaccinated. Each month, the clinics grew busier. His wife, Nancy, became his enthusiastic assistant. They began to spend evenings at the clinic; Nancy would serve food while Bud listened to the needs and hurts of the people. "They soon learned that we really cared, and it was because of Christ's love that we were doing this", says Nancy.

The local media began stories about the street clinic. Suddenly there were thirty or forty owners for each session. The clinics expanded to twice monthly. Dr. Doney would take seriously ill pets back to his animal hospital for treatment or surgery.

Dr. Doney, wife Nancy, Jack and his dog.

Bud was diagnosed with esophageal cancer in 1985 and died in 1987. Two of the street people attended his service with their dogs. It was one of the most moving events in my life. I was privileged to give the eulogy. The clinics continued through the efforts of veterinarians, the Delta Society, the WSVMA, and the Seattle Gospel Union Mission.

CHAPTER 13

Defining Relationships

1987 began on a sad note, as Dr. Kent Smith continued to deteriorate in his battle with cancer. However, he faithfully remained at his post. He was having a difficult time, with much pain, but he continued to fight against all odds in his effort to stay on the field.

He finally returned to the United States in January, and died three weeks later on February 9, 1987. Kent worked at Hospital Albert Schweitzer beginning in June of the previous year. I attended his memorial service in Eden Prairie, Minnesota.

Kent was a dedicated servant who lived out his wish, "to work in the Lord's Kingdom as long as He wants me to."

Kent and JoAnn Smith, Jared, Benjamin, and Timothy.

Dr. Keith and Jan Flanagan. (Longest fieldworker service this hemisphere).

In May, 1987, Dr. Keith Flanagan, and wife Jan, began work at Hospital Albert Schweitzer (HAS) Deschapelles, Haiti. This was a fit for him, as he spent his childhood and teenage years on a farm in the Oklahoma panhandle where his family raised cattle, sheep, wheat and milo.

He received his DVM from Oklahoma State University college of Veterinary Medicine in 1978. After graduation Keith spent two years in the U.S. Army where he trained Medics. Then he returned to Oklahoma and spent more than six years in a mixed practice in Marlow.

I first met Keith at the AVMA convention in Las Vegas, in 1985. Keith came by the booth to learn about CVM. In a few minutes he volunteered to help with it. I think he spent most of his time there except for an occasional visit to another booth. He never meets a stranger. In Haiti he cannot go half a block without someone calling—*"Dr Keif"*, *"Dr. Keif"*. And he is never too busy to help!

Being on call 24 hours a day leaves him always in need of sleep. When talking on the phone with him in Haiti, it is sometimes necessary to wake him up to end the conversation. It goes uncontested that Keith has more cousins than any other CVM worker!

A couple that was destined to play a major role in CVM went on a shuttle to Bolivia. Dr. John and Mrs. Elaine Fletemeyer went from Colorado Springs, to work with Dr. Ronnie and Mrs. Sue Sarratt. While there, they were involved in a wreck. Although it was not Ronnie's fault, as a foreigner he bore the blame. This so turned off John and Elaine that it took them several years to recover their desire to serve overseas.

I am glad that they reconsidered, because they later served in Vietnam. When they returned to the United States, John worked as the director of the shuttle program. Under John's mentoring, it developed into a significant part of CVM's ministry. A record number of veterinarians, students, and technicians participated. John ministered spiritually to all of these shuttle participants. We still get positive phone calls from people who got to know him during that time.

The Student Chapter of the American Veterinary Medical Association (SCAVMA) invited me to attend their meeting in Fort Collins, Colorado in March. Lisa Molloy was head of the local fellowship group. It was an exciting time, meeting with students who acknowledged Christ in their lives. They were not just from Colorado, but represented most of the veterinary schools in North America. After she graduated, Lisa went on a shuttle to Africa.

While I was attending the meeting, Dr. Brad and Mrs. Angela Frye invited me to dinner. Dr. Gerald Mitchum was another guest. I knew Gerald and Frances when they lived in Galax, Virginia. They worked with the Navajo people in the summer. Later, both families would wind up on the mission field, Gerald and Frances in Mongolia, the Fryes in Uganda.

Traveling through Denver, I visited with Dr. Dennis and Mrs. Beth Smialek in Bennett, Colorado. Dennis had a wheat and beef cattle operation, with a beautiful Hereford herd. Dr. Jim and Mrs. Pat

Carlson from Julesburg, Colorado were attending a meeting of the CVMA in Fort Collins. I had a delightful time of fellowship with the two families. Jim wrote <u>Raising Healthy Beef Cattle</u>. Jim and Dennis served as State Representatives for Colorado. They also went on a shuttle to Haiti together.

Tammy Dodd was the person who coordinated the work of CVM. She worked as an assistant to Tim Sooter. Of the annual meeting she wrote:

CVM NEWS

Summer, 1987

On a warm and windy July day in the heart of Chicago, a special meeting took place - the annual CVM Seminar. It was a day full of blessing.

Tom Wanous led us in devotions and a lovely memorial in honor of Kent Smith who had followed the Lord's calling to serve in Haiti.

There was laughter when Brian Kersten offered slides of a Haitian school lunch program to anyone whose kids complained of their school lunches. There were tears as we heard about Patrick Smith's heartfelt ministry reaching those inside prison walls.

There was much to learn about life in foreign cultures-Peter and Mary Quesenberry's ministry with the Nepalese, Scott Lubber's exciting adventures in Bolivia. On the home front, we learned about Stan and Evelyn Agenbroad's traveling road show in the U.S.

In addition to all this, there was singing and hugging. Hearts were touched. I returned home with a much-strengthened perspective on missions and a greater appreciation for those involved. I realized we are all blessed with gifts God can use.

Tammy Dodd,

CVM Administrative Assistant

The family of CVM was growing in both numbers and projects. More importantly, it was growing in bonding with its constituency.

Our workers, long and short term, our volunteers (region, state and school representatives), and our donors were feeling more like family. It was a very close-knit group, where real bonding was taking place. CVM is different from many organizations!

We had, since February of 1978, operated as part of World Concern, the overseas arm of CRISTA ministries. CRISTA is a Christian non-denominational ministry to the Northwest. We had benefited from this affiliation, but the "family" orientation of CVM began to diverge with the "organizational" orientation of World Concern. At first, I saw that as an irritation; but as time went by, I saw that it was a philosophical point of division. I was becoming frustrated.

I met to discuss these issues with the Vice President of CRISTA, Mr. R. A. Harlan, who was serving as interim president. Later, I met with Mr. Jim Gwinn, the newly appointed President of CRISTA. Both men were sympathetic to my concerns; they genuinely wanted an agreeable solution. They believed in the vision of CVM, and wanted to see that vision grow and prosper.

Fred Gregory, a gentle spirited man and a good friend, was the newly appointed Director of World Concern. He and I sat down together and began to tackle these issues. As a result, I developed a paper on the subject. In it, I outlined our needs. We wanted to foster a healthy environment for the continued growth of CVM, but remain within World Concern, and operate under the umbrella of CRISTA.

Fred and I passed this document back and forth. We both strove to create a workable instrument, while allowing CVM to develop its own identity. We wanted CVM to function effectively but somewhat separately, while continuing to work through World Concern. This understanding was finally signed on May 15, 1989. However, long before that time, Tammy and I had assumed the work of CVM—deputation, prayer letters, donor relations, and constituency correspondence.

CVM – World Concern Statement of Understanding

While working together as one legal organization, World Concern agrees to enable CVM in the development of a worldwide network of Christian Veterinarians working for the poor of the world. CVM commits to provide expertise and vision for animal husbandry programs within World Concern."

"CVM-WC will always reflect, practice, and embody integrity and Biblical stewardship in both developing resources and implementing an efficient and effective ministry overseas. The relationship must be mutually beneficial to CVM and World Concern.

CVM's objectives are to be that vehicle and catalyst, for enabling dedicated and spirit-led veterinarians, students, technicians and those of allied interest in the United States and other countries to minister through their profession to those in need. Short and long term missions will be actively researched and pursued.

Part of CVM's ministry shall be to encourage and promote throughout the world an organization of Christian Veterinarians, for the purpose of having fellowship in Jesus Christ, witnessing to the profession, and through it to the world community, and encouraging missions both at home and abroad."

"It is not in the realm of mortals to anticipate the realities of the future. With that in mind, this agreement shall be reviewed by World Concern and the CVM director, for its relevancy and appropriateness, when conditions in either organization warrant such, by change in size, needs or focus. They shall be guided in this matter by past history, current and future needs, and the Holy Spirit. In the event it is decided that CVM should become an independent legal entity, the CVM mailing list will be retained by CVM with sole ownership."

So many CVM missionaries started by working for Dr. Eric Witherspoon of Carlton, Oregon, that applicants for work there have begun to ask if they are required to go on a mission. That is not the only outstanding thing about his practice, however. He and Dr. Mark Bounds dealt with practice and the Sabbath day in an unusual way. Mark explained:

"How many times have those of us in veterinary medicine wished that we could take this scripture literally, especially those in private practice? No work on Sundays! Unfortunately, animals get sick and injured on Sunday as much as on any other day. We do find in the New Testament several references in which Christ interprets the value and design of the Sabbath, which 'allows' us to work on Sunday in good conscience. Luke 13:15 and Luke 14:5 deal with animals in distress, and concede they must be taken care of.

My partner and I have taken the concept of working on Sundays and turned it into a positive 'Lord's work' situation. When we started our practice six years ago, we decided that all the money earned on Sunday calls would be donated to animal related mission endeavors. Since then, we have given money to CVM and also have begun a herd health project among the Aymara Indians in Peru, along with the Friends Mission.

Knowing this money helps the less fortunate makes it a lot easier to respond to Sunday calls and emergencies.

Our Sunday mission giving has not affected our practice net at all, even when money has been very tight. In fact, several times when we've sent the check for our previous Sunday calls, the next week has been excellent as far as practice income. God obviously takes care of our needs.

On other occasions, when we felt that we should use the Sunday money to pay bills, we found business would inexplicably pick up and all our obligations would be met, including the mission offering. We've also noticed that Sunday clients always pay their bills, and we can't say that about the rest of our accounts receivable.

Our challenge to other veterinarians is to consider this type of arrangement in your own practices. We know that you will be rewarded for your efforts and your giving, and others less fortunate and with greater needs will benefit from your gifts."

CHAPTER 14

On the Road Again

The letters were always postmarked "Somewhere, USA". So began the 'yellow file,' hand written letters on a legal pad. Occasionally, one would come in on some hotel or motel stationery, to break the monotony and color scheme. This was Dr. Stan and Evelyn Agenbroad's way of keeping us posted of their whereabouts, and what was going on in their ministry.

On April 6th, 1987, an important CVM ministry began when Stan and Evelyn left their driveway in Nampa, Idaho. They were driving a pickup truck, pulling a fifth wheel, and heading for parts unknown.

Stan Agenbroad was born on a farm south of Nampa that was homesteaded in 1908. He and Evelyn graduated from Nampa High School. She went to college, while he was in the military. Then they married and farmed south of Nampa for about eight years.

Stan decided there must be a better way to make a living, so he entered veterinary school, graduating in 1962. He worked in Nampa for a while, and then practiced in Twin Falls before moving to Albuquerque, New Mexico, where he owned his own clinic and practiced for 18 years.

Stan and Evelyn approached me in Atlanta, saying that they were ready to go on the mission field. Their hearts were right, but their age wasn't. The odds were against them to successfully learn a language and face three years of tough living in the tropics. I suggested that they that could use their wonderful relationship skills to better advantage here in the United States. Even so, they succeeded beyond my imagination.

Dr. Stan and Evelyn Agenbroad.

Of all the missionaries CVM has sent out, no couple made a greater impact or had a greater ministry than Stan and Evelyn. In every corner of the country, I met people who asked me about them, and said how much they liked them. What good public relations people they were, for CVM and the Lord. Stan and Evelyn usually kept a CVM decal on the door of their truck. This attracted attention, and gave them an opening to tell people about CVM.

Their job description allowed them to do whatever they thought would advance the ministry of CVM. It might be attending meetings, working the CVM booth, arranging prayer breakfasts, meeting with donors, or talking to and encouraging school, state, and regional representatives. They frequently stopped at veterinary clinics to introduce veterinarians to CVM. Sometimes they gave talks at churches along the way. They were roving ambassadors for Christ! Moreover, they raised their own financial support to make it happen.

An example of their ministry exudes from this letter written from St. Louis following the state veterinary meeting for Missouri.

Dear CVM Home Office,

We have just wrapped up the Missouri State Veterinary Association meeting. It is a beautiful morning here in St. Louis. We closed the booth down and Evelyn and I feel very good about the response we had here. We collected 62 names for the mailing list. People didn't just wander by. They were looking for CVM.

We had 42 people at the fellowship breakfast. It reflected an international flavor. We met Dr. Jim Martin from Australia, Dr. David Williams from Cambridge, United Kingdom, two veterinarians from Canada, and a young lady from Vienna, Austria.

Love, Stan and Evelyn

When seeds are planted, they can take root many miles away. They were not only having a ministry here in the U.S., but all over the world!

When Stan and Evelyn retired after three and a half years, they had driven more than one hundred thousand miles!

"These years have resulted in many blessings for us," they wrote. *"We have had the opportunity to travel throughout the continental United States and the three western provinces of Canada. But we traveled with a purpose—to promote Christian Veterinary Mission wherever we could."*

They, along with Bob and Mary Ann Otto, were honored at our annual meeting in Portland in 1988.

Dr. Bob and Mary Ann Otto.

The eighth CVM annual meeting was in Portland, Oregon. We met on Sunday, July 17, 1988, prior to the AVMA conference.

The year before, I first met Drs. Mark Bounds and Susan Stewart in Chicago, at our annual meeting there. Now Mark and Susan were headed for Bolivia to replace Dr. Ronnie and Mrs. Sue Sarratt. It was good for them to have an overlap with the Sarratts at the meeting.

In my mind, I can still see Mark and Susan dancing on the grass, along with hundreds of other people. They were enjoying music by Dr. Eric Witherspoon and his band, there on the banks of the Willamette River.

Mark was a native of Tennessee, and received his DVM from the University of Tennessee at Knoxville in 1981. His previous Third World experience included several months as a Peace Corps worker in the Central African Republic. He was also involved in short-term mission projects in Peru. He was a Co-founder of the Peruvian Friends Herd Health project.

Susan's home state was Colorado. She graduated from Colorado State University in 1982. She recently completed the training manual

Drs. Susan Stewart and Mark Bounds. (Susan longest serving female fieldworker this hemisphere).

"Learning Together". She and Mark had worked on it together. She has conducted seminars in many different countries and to varied groups on participatory training. Her course is now a part of the orientation, for new long-term CVM candidates.

After language study, Susan and Mark moved to Samaipata to begin work where Ronnie and Sue left off. About 2,000 people live in and around Samaipata. Mark supervised veterinary students from Santa Cruz. In addition, he conducted animal seminars for farmers. Susan used her teaching skills in the San Julian project with animators that the community had chosen.

At that time, the Bolivian government was transplanting tin miners, moving them from the Andes to the lowland jungle. They offered 40 hectares to each family who wanted to farm. So, where's the catch? In reality, the land was unbroken jungle. Transplants came with machetes and determination to develop their farms.

Susan chose two women to be part of her team. She hoped to encourage both men and women to attend the health seminars. If the women of San Julian learned better animal health procedures, their families would prosper. How valuable this work has been, for her and for the countless women she has trained.

Dr. Bob Beede led devotions at the meeting. I can remember him saying, *"We come to the meetings and get pumped up, and then we slowly let that enthusiasm die. We need to hold each other accountable."*

Since then, Bob has held us accountable. He has done remarkable work, helping to develop the CVM board and its committees.

At the meeting, Dr. Scott Karper told about his recent shuttle to Haiti. He and his wife, Diane, were destined to later play a significant role in CVM. Kit and Jan Flowers were home on leave from Africa, and took part in the day's events.

Our special guest was Mr. Herb Brussow, a Wycliffe missionary who spent 24 years in South America. He gave an informative, humorous presentation on the need for missionaries to learn how to relate cross-culturally. The inspiring day concluded with an evening fellowship meal at the Reedwood Friends Church.

June 17, 1988
Dear Dr. Dorminy,

To date, the total number of swine produced in the Inter-American Institute of Central America (IICA) Interim Swine Repopulation Project has passed project goals. IICA did not work alone to surpass its project goals. Many organizations collaborated to get pigs back to the peasants.

In particular, Christian Veterinary Mission/World Concern selflessly made large contributions to the Swine Repopulation Project. CVM vets assisted throughout the project. They assisted free of charge at the primary swine reproduction center. They assisted free of charge with technical support at the Secondary Multiplication Centers, many of which were sponsored by World Concern. They conducted countless trainings to farmers who received pigs from the secondary centers. They have kept the project informed of the health status of the project pigs. CVM shuttle vets also assisted at the secondary centers.

The number of hours and the quality of experience that CVM veterinarians and World Concern sponsored staff have contributed to the Swine Repopulation Project are countless. Their enormous contribution is beyond measure

JICA wishes to sincerely thank Christian Veterinary Mission/ World Concern for the dedicated and extensive contribution that they have made to the JICA Swine Repopulation Project over the past five years.

Sincerely,

Dr. Percy Aitken-Sioux
Resident Representative
JICA/Haiti

CVM's effective program in Haiti was again confirmed by another group of supporters touring the work sites. Development people sometimes say that you don't understand development until you have seen it, heard it, smelled it, and gotten it under your fingernails. Seven CVM members had the opportunity to do just that. They included Dr. Irvin and Mrs. Margery Blume from Indiana, Dr. Floyd and Mrs. Jean Votaw from California, Dr. David Smidt from Iowa, Dr. Marvin Meinder from Maryland, Mr. John Briles from Kansas, and Ms. Alice Macy from World Concern.

Together, we learned about the nuts and bolts of veterinary projects. Priscilla Schleigh of World Concern led us in some role-playing about development. We had to be a Haitian farmer, a development worker, or a donor to the supporting agency. It made us think about the different perspectives each person brings to a development project. It also helped us to understand the complexities of doing good development work. We learned the importance of community participation.

We visited all the CVM workers in Haiti, starting with Dr. Mike and Mrs. Debra Storer at Les Cayes. Mike was busy, training Haitian veterinary technicians to treat animals, and teaching farmers how to care for them. Dr. Maureen Birmingham worked at Des Cloches, and in remote Northwest Haiti. Dr. Keith and Mrs. Jan Flanagan worked at Hospital Albert Schweitzer. At the end of the tour, all of the veterinarians expressed a desire to become more involved. They were satisfied that their gifts to CVM were used to make a significant impact for God's Kingdom.

CVM has always emphasized training. This was evident during our time there. One of the highlights of our tour was meeting with the Haitian Veterinary Technicians. As we finished our meal of rice and beans, we listened to several young men, including Feneus Norcius, explain what their veterinary training meant to them. They appreciated having an opportunity to learn, hope for their lives, a chance to improve their lot, and an opportunity to share their faith.

As Keith Flanagan translated their statements to us, I marveled at the positive expressions from men who live in this seemingly hopeless land. That's what our veterinarians and their families strive to do—to live out this message of hope among those in greatest physical and spiritual need.

Keith worked at Hospital Albert Schweitzer. This facility opened in 1956, the result of a vision that Dr. Larry Mellon and his wife, Gwen, had for the health care of the poor in the Artibonite Valley. But his dream was for more than a hospital. It included community development, public health projects, reforestation, and agricultural/animal development.

This expanded vision arose when the Mellons recognized that the poor suffered from many sequelae of poverty—contaminated water, inadequate diets, crowded living conditions, and limited hygiene facilities. When the hospital opened, the life expectancy for people in the valley was 30 years. In 1982, it had increased to 48 years.

When he died, Larry's obituary appeared in the CVM newsletter. "CVM lost a wonderful friend when William Larimer Mellon, founder of Hospital Albert Schweitzer (HAS), in Des Chappelles, Haiti, died of cancer and Parkinson's disease at the age of 79. Many shuttle veterinarians who worked at HAS became acquainted with Larry, as he was affectionately known. He was an excellent example of one who used his life and resources in service to others."

Dr. Dan Paulo teaching Haitian vet techs.

Many people ask how we select sites for service. We continue to make exploratory trips, to see how we can help those areas in need.

From: Dr. Dan Paulo

RE: Latin America Exploratory Trip

Imagine traveling for twelve days through Central and South America with fourteen separate take-offs and landings, a four-hour nail-biting ride across the Andes Mountains, multiple customs and passport inspections, and an eight-hour round-trip bus ride from Tegucigalpa to Catacamas, Honduras.

These are some experiences I shared with Leroy Dorminy as we made a survey trip in early December to Colombia and Honduras. The study trip was undertaken to investigate potential new sites for CVM veterinarians to work either on short-term shuttle or on longer-term assignments. A second objective was to determine availability of housing, transportation, interpreters and to determine if there were political restrictions and other factors, which our veterinarians would encounter if we were to work in these locations. The result of this effort is the exciting possibility of three new sites with a need for shuttle veterinarians.

The first one was Loma Linda, in the central grasslands of Colombia. There, a Wycliffe Bible Translating team has a center, at which they maintain a farm. They also provide training courses and development projects for various Indian tribes from Central Colombia. The second one is at Catamas, Honduras, where World Gospel Mission operates a vocational school for underprivileged boys and a 5,000-acre ranch, with beef and dairy cattle. The third site is Roatan Island, off the coast of Honduras. The island, inhabited by seven distinct cultural groups, has no veterinary services.

CHAPTER 15

Asia Discovered

It was the coldest I had ever seen it in Seattle. It snowed like crazy, melted a little, and then really froze over. Ordinarily, that would not be a problem—I would stay home, read, and watch the misery on TV. Except this time, Tina and I were supposed to leave for Asia and we couldn't even get out of our driveway. Well, it didn't look good. Even the taxis and shuttles were stuck. At the last moment, I called Fred Gregory—he had a four-wheel drive vehicle. He picked us up and took us to the airport. Fred is a great friend!

After a long and tiring trip to Japan, we waited around for several hours to catch the flight to Bangkok. There were problems with the plane, but we finally took off. The plane still wasn't right. There was a leak in one of the lines going along the wall of the plane. The wall next to me seemed as if it was hot enough to catch on fire. The stewardess checked with the pilot, who said it was no problem—but then, he wasn't sitting in my seat. I guess it offset with the freeze in Seattle.

We arrived in Bangkok about midnight. We had been awake for about 24 hours. Thirapong, the World Concern driver, met us. WC Asia Director, Paul Kennel was with him, carrying flowers for Tina! We went to Paul and Mary Kennel's house, where we got a few winks of sleep and began another day. I think by then our bodies were running entirely on adrenaline.

Peter and Mary Quesenberry were in Bangkok. We also met Peter's parents, who were visiting. World Concern was having its Asia Planning Meeting, and most of the country representatives were on hand. We had a wonderful chance to renew friendships. We all went together to visit some World Concern projects. We flew up to the Northern part of Thailand, near the site of an old U.S. Air Force base at Udon. We visited the ISSAN development project near the border with Laos. We saw a small pickup ambling through town, carrying two large hogs in a wire cage on the back. The Thai people seemed to be good hog raisers, and these were fine specimens

Later, we visited an integrated system of pig and fish farming, which used the hog waste for fertilizer. The fish production used a series of ponds, which were created when water was diverted from a river channel. It was a very impressive and productive operation. The grass on the dams was cut and stacked in the water. Decomposing grass, along with manure from the pig houses built over the water, supplied fertilizer. The nutrient content of the water was kept extremely high by this, as revealed by the dark green water.

At this level of fertilization, all the fish would die of oxygen depletion back home in Georgia. The difference is in the species of fish. The ponds contained five different kinds of fish; each kind fed at variable levels in the pond. It made for incredibly high fish production. For an exploding population needing protein, this provided a very efficient supply.

With no refrigeration, the farmers kept the seine handy. When someone wanted to purchase fish, farmers could catch a tub full in one short swing. Kids would go in the pond, swimming along behind the seine, occasionally diving down beneath the water. I suppose their immunity had to be very high against the zillion microbes that surely abounded there.

Nepal was our next stop. Dr. Wade Bradshaw asked me to bring some of the Ivomec paste that Merck had donated. There was a dosing applicator in the box, but the outside of the box called it a "dosage gun." That is not a word that you want to carry around with you when going through customs. I could not explain to the agent that it was not a gun for shooting, but for dosing cattle. Finally, I had to open the box, take out a tube, and demonstrate how it was used.

In Katmandu, we had a rooftop room with no heat. That night, the temperature dropped to 30 degrees. There was plenty of ice on the roof and it wasn't much warmer inside our room. We pushed the two bunk beds together, and shared our blankets. To go to the bathroom, we had to climb down a ladder to the outhouse. This primitive experience helped us identify with the Nepali way of life.

Wade and Chryse Bradshaw lived in Pokhara, near the center of Nepal. To get there, you had two choices. You could either fly on an unreliable airline's prop-plane and arrive in less than an hour, or you could ride all day on the bus. From the plane, there was an incredible view of the Himalayas. Accommodations on our return trip by bus were consistent with the Nepali lifestyle. Pit stops were at established places along the route, and were fraught with danger from previous visitors. The area on one side of the bus was reserved for the men and the opposite side for the women. Basic sanitation did not exist.

I am not sure that we ever really got warm during our entire stay in Nepal. Wade and Chryse's house had no heat, except for a kerosene heater of about 4 BTU's. No heat made it to the third floor where Tina and I slept. The roof had cracks wide enough for visual astronomy. It was more like camping out—inside.

Dr. Patrick Smith, who was serving in Iran Jaya, Indonesia, was visiting the Bradshaws at the same time that we were. We had lots of fun together. There was good-natured bantering about how one or the other might be violating some traditional customs of the country. Patrick lay on the floor and played with Ethan, who was the Bradshaws' only child at the time. Since then, I think they have added one baby for each continent they have lived, with the final count at four!

Patrick wanted very much to find himself a wife. Pickings were lean for missionaries serving in Iran Jaya, where he worked with Missions To Unreached Peoples. Patrick asked for our prayers, and a couple years later he called from Iran Jaya to invite Tina and me to his wedding. The Lord brought him just the right woman. Wendy was teaching English as a Second Language in Iran Jaya.

While in Pokhara, I attended one of Wade's training courses. He started by having each trainee come to the board and write his or her name and address, and the number and kind of animals they had. It was a very revealing exercise. Wade immediately learned the students' literacy skills and how rich or poor according to Nepali standards they were. He illustrated his talk with pictures and drawings of animals. I remembered that, just a few months before, he knew nothing of the language.

Chryse Bradshaw, Ethan, Tina, and Leroy with Nepali Children.

Of his early efforts, Wade wrote, *"Giving God much thanks, I must say it went better than I had allowed myself to hope. Our work has made a difference. Fewer animals die, they are more productive, and in what was a food deficit area, there is now a milk surplus."*

Wade also reported that 14 of his 18 farmer students voluntarily came to a worship service in the local church when he was asked to preach. All this made me feel very proud of his and Chryse's work in Nepal.

The room was crowded. Women, wrapped in shawls to keep out the chill of the day, were huddled against the wall. Children were lying on mats, which covered the floor. A few men sat here and there, scattered throughout the group. We stepped over and around people, and carefully made our way to a small open spot in the back, and sat down.

From the front of the room, a gray-haired man spoke to the group. Everyone listened with rapt attention. People continued to trickle in, alerting the congregation by the squeaking door. Soon, the room was jammed.

The dark-eyed, Navigator trained pastor, stopped talking and led the group in singing to the accompaniment of the guitar. They sang several songs with enthusiasm and hand clapping. Then there was a reading from Psalms, followed by a call to prayer. The pastor had requested several short prayers; instead, two women prayed at length (I considered this profound in this culture).

Since I was not able to understand the preacher, I thought about this opportunity to worship with Nepali Christians. We were in the village of Lamachaur, where Wade and Chryse lived and worked.

I could look out the window and see the towering, austere peak of Fish Tail Mountain in the great Annapurna chain. It reflected the majesty and awesomeness of the One we worshipped. I looked around the room, and though I was unable to understand the language, I could feel our unity in Christian faith. It was a time of fellowship, nurtured by a smile, a handshake, and a knowing nod of the head. This Saturday morning worship service (Saturday is the Sabbath in Nepal) was a heartwarming experience.

Our next stop was Bangladesh. It is a country the size of Wisconsin, with more than 110 million people! Can you imagine that? There are so many people that a person is hard put to find solitude. When you stop on the street in a vehicle, people begin to gather around looking at you. I found out what it felt like to live in a Zoo. If family planning was ever needed, this would be the place. Unfortunately, women's rights are not a reality there. Many women are in bondage to tradition and to the whims of their husbands. They are just beginning to make small inroads into this despicable system.

Bangladesh is always a disaster waiting to happen, with its over-population, low land susceptible to flooding, and the propensity for typhoons in this area.

Mr. Terril Eikenberry met us at the Airport. Terril worked with World Concern and HEED Bangladesh (a development organization). He and Sylvia, his wife, lived in Dakha with their three boys—Toby, Tim, and Ivan. We stayed at the Southern Baptist guesthouse, which was run by Mr. Jim and wife Betty McKinley. Jim and Betty were veteran missionaries in Bangladesh, serving there during the war between Pakistan and Bangladesh. It was interesting to meet the variety of people coming through their large, multistoried guesthouse. It was awesome to learn how high the waters rose in the house during floods from a typhoon. It got to the second floor!

We visited a farm run by the Southern Baptists. It was a model operation, with well-groomed houses, adequate staff, a deep well, irrigated fields, and a man-made integrated pond. The pond housed Khaki Colored Ducks, Tilapia, and Carp. I was impressed. If there was a weakness in all of this, it was the infeasibility of such an operation for the farmers of Bangladesh. It was picture-perfect, in great contrast to the everyday realities of the average Bengali farmer.

Richard Farley directed the model farm operation. He and his wife were scheduled for a furlough, and they were looking for a replacement. The Lord always provides. In this case, He provided a marvelous family, Dr. Jere and Mrs. Judy Colley of Alabama. Being Southern Baptist themselves, it worked out well for them to serve during the interlude. Jere was already a veteran of several CVM short-term missions.

We saw and learned so much in our three-country whirlwind tour of Asia. It was reassuring to see that our veterinarians were performing well, and training others. The World Concern projects we saw were practical and effective. We had lots to think about on the way home.

Dr. Bob Otto, who had been in charge of shuttles for the past four years, decided he needed to retire once more. Having failed at retirement before, he was going to try again. Like so many dedicated servants, he cannot be idle. When he sees a need, he has to respond. He performed an invaluable service as shuttle director, and impacted so many lives with his gentle spirit. It was hard to see him leave, but he had other ministries that he wished to pursue. The good news is that he is still involved with CVM, acts as our chaplain, and occasionally performs commissioning ceremonies for our new field workers.

Our ninth Annual Meeting was in Orlando. Dr. Jere Colley's special time of devotions blessed and challenged us. He shared his impressions of the meeting, " *'Create in me a clean heart, O God, and renew a right spirit within me.' Like so many others, I left a busy practice in peak season where everyday problems overwhelmed me. I came more out of a spirit of obligation than really wanting to attend. But this was short lived. Upon entering the room, the Holy Spirit's presence was clear. We were immediately drawn together as brothers and sisters with one common goal—to bring physical and spiritual hope to the poor in the developing world."*

Dr Gretchen Zarle from Tennessee, and Dr. Karen Studeman from Illinois, talked about their shuttles to Kenya. Dr. Tom and wife, Marcia Van Meter, from Washington, initiated our efforts on Roatan Island, Honduras. They spoke about their experiences. They have been so very generous to the ministry. The manner in which they do it, so quietly and without fanfare, is truly a scriptural model.

Dr. Keith Flanagan, and Dr. Mike Storer, long-term fieldworkers in Haiti, gave an update on their work there. Other speakers included Fred Gregory, the Executive Director of World Concern, and Dave Blackmer, the coordinator of World Concern's Church Relations program. Dr. Tim Blair, representing Christian Veterinary Fellowship, challenged veterinarians to be serious about their spiritual commitments.

Dr. Wayne Sletten from South Dakota gave an update on Steer, Inc. This is a method of fundraising whereby a farmer takes a donated steer, feeds it, and the increase is given to CVM. Following the meeting, Dr. and Mrs. Leland Simmons opened their home to the attendees. We had a lovely barbecue dinner and a wonderful time of fellowship. It was a fitting and relaxing way to end the day.

<hr />

My efforts at recruiting long-term workers for Sudan and Nepal gave me some interesting insights into how we Christians react to God's call on our lives. It was both frustrating and reassuring. I made more than 100 contacts with veterinarians who at one time or another had indicated a desire to serve overseas. I heard many different responses.

First, I found that some highly skilled Christian veterinarians somehow feel they needed more education to be effective on the field. They felt they needed medical training so they could treat humans, or a seminary course so they could plant churches and specialize in evangelism. I do not mean to criticize additional special training in a field or an intense course of Bible study; rather, I am suggesting that we need to be willing to use the specialized skills we already have, in places that need us so badly.

Second, many people felt they had been called to serve in only one country. That country may be India, or possibly China. When I suggested Nepal, which is between those two countries and has similarities to both, I got a negative response. A 'specific country call' may have merit in certain cases, i.e. such as special language. But when it is carried to the extreme, and it ignores needs and opportunities, then I wonder whether the choice of country is the Lord's will or our own.

A third response was, "But the time is not right!" That can be very true. An example of this might be a marital situation that needs healing. Mission service tends to widen cracks that already exist. Another legitimate concern would include children who are at a critical stage in their lives—such as teenagers in high school. It could be that a financial crisis dictates postponement. These can be wise and valid reasons for delaying overseas involvement. However, it may just be that we have failed to prioritize correctly. Maybe we are not sensitive to God's will for our lives.

The most heartwarming response I could hear was when a committed man, woman, couple or family says, "God has called me to mission service. After much prayer, I accept that call. Please help me find that special place where I can be of most benefit in service to Him."

Fortunately, that happened for both Sudan and Nepal. Praise the Lord for that! I hasten to add that Christian service does not have to be overseas. There are many needs right where we live.

Dr. Frank Hooper, from South Carolina, answered the call and went to Sudan. Frank is a "missionary kid", who attended public schools in Israel, where his parents served. Much of the time, he was the only Gentile student. During these years, Frank spent time around animals at an orphanage situated on a large farm. He feels that this time working with dairy cattle, pigs, and chickens may have led him to become a veterinarian.

After some years in Israel, his family moved back to South Carolina, where he completed high school. Later, he attended veterinary college at Auburn. While there, he was a member of the Christian Veterinary Fellowship and subsequently went on a shuttle to Haiti. After graduation, he practiced for a while before applying for mission work.

Frank went to southern Sudan, to manage a huge cattle vaccination program. This part of Sudan was plagued with war and famine. There had been little animal care for several years. Epidemics of Rinderpest had decimated herds, resulting in malnutrition among the people. His job was to train local herdsmen to do the vaccinating. It was a tough assignment for a young man.

CHAPTER 16

Well Done

Dr. Karen Stoufer, her husband Ron, and their daughters Kathryn and Lisa were finally granted visas so that they could live and work in Nepal. Karen carried on the work at Pokhara, which was started by Peter Quesenberry and continued by Wade Bradshaw.

Karen was born in Spokane, Washington, and grew up in California. She did undergraduate work at Washington State University and Cornell University, and received her DVM from Cornell in 1978. She practiced in New York and California for fourteen years.

Dr. Karen and Ron Stoufer, Kathryn, and Lisa. (Longest serving female fieldworker in Asia).

In 1986, Ron, Karen, and Katie, then 14 months old, spent three weeks on the Navajo reservation in Arizona. They worked with, Mike and Debra Storer and their family. Karen and Ron were inspired by the Storers' work, and knew it was something they wanted to do someday. When the opportunity to work in Nepal was presented, they decided this was the time to do mission work.

They left on July 17, 1990 to begin this new adventure. The King of Nepal had recently granted amnesty to all religious prisoners. For the first time, Christians were able to gather in public for worship service. Later Karen writes,

A Prayer Letter

As I stood at our kitchen window, washing dishes and gazing at the view, I thought that we must be the luckiest people in the world to be able to live here. Birds were singing, the blue sky was tinged with streaky pink clouds, and before me was a panorama of the Himalayas. Then I glanced down from our second story flat to see a small, dirty, naked boy urinating into the garden behind us. Ah yes, this **is** Nepal! It is a land of contrasts where unsurpassed beauty goes hand in hand with unsurpassed poverty.

We have the highest mountains in the world and the highest maternal death rate because of lack of education and health care. Beautiful rushing rivers spill down spectacular gorges inviting white water enthusiasts from all over the world to try and navigate their course. These same rivers are conduits of typhoid, cholera, and gastroenteritis, which kill thousands of children every year. And for those who live in the southern flat level jungle land called the Terai, these same waters bring floods and destruction"

"The contrast is also seen in the most important Hindu holiday of the year, Dasain. In its simplest form, Dasain celebrates the triumph of good over evil. Extended families gather together, women get beautiful saris, homes are painted, and special meals are served. Celebrations continue for almost two weeks. Elaborate worship rituals are performed each day, the most important of which involves live animal sacrifice to the goddess Durga (or Kali).

Most sacrifices are by beheading in one swoop of a long curved Nepali knife called a khukuri. As the warm blood spurts out, it is quickly applied to the house and to all forms of transportation. The official government airline applies it to each plane, every taxi driver to his vehicle, and individuals even to their bicycles, to protect against accidents. Strict vegetarian religious sects will sacrifice a pumpkin or cucumber before an idol with the same hacking motions.

To me, who worships a God of love rather than of destruction, it seems terribly sad that these people must repeatedly sacrifice and make offerings in an attempt to obtain that which the Christian God gives as a free gift. The Bible teaches that the death of Jesus Christ was more than sufficient, once and for all, and that no other sacrifice is necessary.

In His Love,
Karen

Karen Stoufer has done outstanding work with women. She writes,

"At first glance, it would seem that women have no status and no rights whatsoever, but of course that is an oversimplification and exaggeration. But the laws that supposedly give women some rights, more often than not merely highlight how terribly unfair the situation is.

"Families arrange 90% of the marriages in Nepal. Often, the bride has either never seen the groom before the wedding day, or has seen him only once. In general, daughters have no property rights. A woman must be married for at least fifteen years and be over 30 years of age to inherit anything from her husband if he should die. The male head of the household can sell up to 50% of jointly owned property without the wife's permission or even knowledge. In practice, it's often 100%.

"Culturally, women are second-class citizens. Few are educated, they eat only what is left over at a meal and the only hope a woman ever has to gain any respect is to be known as a mother of sons."

This illustrates the point well,

A Prayer Letter

Kanchi is a hard working and courageous young woman struggling in a society where the odds are stacked against her as a woman; she is landless and uneducated. As a child, her parents forbade her to attend school, although they sent her brothers to school. She taught herself to read and write. Now at age 26, she has enrolled herself in an evening literacy class so she can help her two sons to learn to read and write properly.

Her mother died when she was young and her father frequently beat her when her housework wasn't good enough. Rather than wait for her father to select a husband, she ran off and married a young man she knew slightly and believed herself to be in love with. Strong and independent, she refused to conform to the pattern of arranged marriages. Soon after their marriage, her husband began to change. His heavy drinking kept them in debt. Kanchi found work with missionary families to pay the bills and feed themselves. Finally, despite her having borne him two sons, he abandoned her 15 days after the second son, Chandra, was born.

Her husband has been gone for six years now, although she occasionally catches a glimpse of him in town. He runs away when he sees her, and it is suspected that he is wanted by the police. She has spent a large part of her earnings for the past six years paying off her absent husband's debts, for which she is legally responsible.

Kanchi now works for us. The salary she earns enables her to pay the rent on a one room, mud walled, dirt floor shack, without a real window. There are no toilets or running water.

In a society that condones petty theft, she is scrupulously honest. In a society where many women in her situation would send the boys out begging for handouts, Kanchi is determined that her sons will go to school and she will work for what she gets. She works for us during the day, cooks for her own boys, then goes to the two-hour literacy class. She and her boys study together at night with only a candle for lighting."

Despite many years of working for missionaries, she has never had much interest in Christianity. However, about two months ago, she asked if she could attend church with us and has even been attending the weeks we are out of town. She wants her boys to come to Sunday School, but is confused and unsure about what she wants for herself. It is a frightening thing for even a strong, independent woman like Kanchi to consider becoming a Christian. She has few ties to her family and friends, but what little she has, she risks losing if she changes her religion from Hinduism. She risks even more isolation and persecution, not only for herself, but for her sons if she should embrace the Christian faith.

Like single parents all over the world, she is plagued with worries. What will happen to my boys if I should get sick or die? Will I be able to feed them and keep them in school? Where will we sleep if the rent is raised? Will I be able to find work when this job ends?

There are no easy answers for Kanchi. Most anything we do for her is short-term. We can only offer the security that comes from our Christian faith, but we cannot say that her immediate troubles will end if she becomes a Christian. Realistically, they will only increase. Helping her with her children's education and medical bills only buys her a little time. In the mission field, we talk a great deal about sustainability. We want to design programs that foster self-help and avoid handouts or the creation of dependence.

Karen and Ron later moved to Okhaldhunga, a remote village in northeastern Nepal. Karen worked with the women there, helping them to organize and complete different development projects. This experience led to another assignment. Karen counseled other NGO's (non governmental organizations), multiplying her influence. The important point is that, unless the Nepali women themselves make development happen, it will not be effective or sustainable.

Ron addressed another issue that plagues all developing countries—water and sanitation.

A Prayer Letter

I was sound asleep when suddenly smoke fumes penetrated my nostrils. 'Fire!' I thought, and jolted awake. Then I remembered where I was. I was sleeping on the mud floor of a house in a village called Masyam. It was 5:30 AM, and the smoke was just the wood fire cooking the water buffalo's porridge for breakfast. I got up and went outside to the outhouse, down the slope behind the house. I was glad there was an outhouse. It was one of the few in the village.

I went to the water tap about 50 feet down the path from the house to wash my hands and face. I turned on the tap. Nothing came out. That was the reason we were there. I was a participant in a training course for water system technicians who assist villagers in building water systems. We discussed in class the best methods to build water tanks and tap stands, then went out and built them.

We also discussed how to get maximum participation from the water users in the village in building their water system. Our class held an evening meeting which about 150 villagers attended. . . .

This was an example of a group of people coming up with the solutions to their own problems—sustainable development.

"Well Done, Thou Good and Faithful Servant" was the theme for our annual meeting, which was held in San Antonio, Texas. We had four workers returning from overseas assignments. Two were leaving CVM, and going on to other things. Dr. Maureen Birmingham, who had last worked in Bolivia, eventually went to work with the World Health Organization. Dr. Wade and Chryse Bradshaw, who had worked in Nepal, went with L' Abri in the United Kingdom and later the Schaeffer Institute in the U.S. Two others were going to different assignments with CVM. Dr. Kit and Jan Flowers were headed to Seattle to work in the home office, and Dr. Peter and Mary Quesenberry were going to another overseas position in Laos.

Long-term workers on the annual meeting program were Dr. Keith and Mrs. Jan Flanagan who talked about their work in Haiti, and Dr Wade and Mrs. Chryse Bradshaw, who described their work in Nepal. Dr. Lisa Molloy talked about her shuttle to Africa and Dr. Floyd Jones and Dr. Sonny Tutt told of their survey in Colombia. Dr. Stan and Mrs. Evelyn Agenbroad enthusiastically described the benefits of volunteering. Dr. Tim Blair updated us on CVF.

This meeting was held on Saturday, because the AVMA was presenting a symposium on World Hunger on Sunday. CVM was invited to be a part of that. Peter, Kit, and I presented "Opportunities and Challenges in Alleviating World Hunger." This was part of the overall topic of "Initiatives of Volunteer Organizations." We were in charge of devotions earlier in the program.

On Sunday evening, CVM members met for a Texas-style barbecue at St. Mark's Episcopal Church. Dr. Dennis Sundbeck, our Texas representative, coordinated the event. It was an evening of good food and warm fellowship.

Dr. Walt Long went to Haiti on a shuttle, working with both Mike Storer and Keith Flanagan. His purpose was two-fold—first, to help with the work, and second, to learn more about the long-term workers and their duties. He was retiring from the Nebraska College of Technical Agriculture for Veterinary Technicians and was planning to travel and promote CVM.

Walt and his wife Judy have traveled for about ten years, attending meetings and promoting CVM, primarily in the high plains area

Dr. Walt and Judy Long.

of the U.S. Walt says, *"If you would like to learn about CVM at your next meeting, contact me. I have a set-up, several programs, and will travel."*

Walt is a graduate of Colorado State University. He operated a solo mixed practice for twelve years. Then for 25 years, he taught and directed one of the country's first veterinary technology programs.

Two national, or indigenous, veterinarians served with CVM Dr. Andres Arana, a Bolivian man, worked under the direction of CVM veterinarians since December 1987, when he graduated from veterinary school in Santa Cruz. While in school, he became acquainted with Dr. Bill Testerman. He attended all of the Bible studies Bill conducted. By the time Andres graduated, Dr. Ronnie Sarratt had taken Bill's place and started a clinic in Samipata, a village nearly 100 miles west of Santa Cruz.

The clinic was meant to be an extension of the veterinary school to provide practical experience for veterinary students. It also became the base for outreach to surrounding villages. Andres began working with Ronnie in the rural clinic right after graduation.

Andres spent three months in the Seattle area, where he attended Edmonds Community College to learn English. He returned to Bolivia to take a leadership role in CVM's project there. He worked with the Aymara Indians near La Paz, teaching farmers basic animal health care.

Dr. John Wambua, a Kenyan veterinarian, heard of the opening at Ilkerin, from his brother. His brother, a lawyer, represented Vicki Dayton in the case involving the accident that led to the death of her husband Ray. Through that relationship, John's brother became acquainted with Howard Berry. Howard told John about CVM's work among the Maasai.

Dr. Wambua said, *"I had always wished to work with the Maasai people since I was in school, so when I heard of the location and the kind of program CVM was involved in, I decided to apply for employment immediately after doing my final examination at the University of Nairobi."*

We learned that Fred Van Gorkom was awarded the "Young Alumnus of the Year" award for 1989 by George Fox College. The award was made for his outstanding service in the missionary field. Fred and his wife, Vicki, continue to work among the Bunna people in southwestern Ethiopia. (It is a long-term commitment they have made to themselves and to the Bunna people.) It is good when others recognize the fine work that our missionaries do.

The year ended on a sad note. Dr. Bill Baker, of Sherwood, Arkansas, died December 28,1990. Complications developed following heart surgery. Bill and wife Mary Jo, and their son, Sean, served the people of Haiti for three and one half years.

CHAPTER 17

Facilitating Others

Since CVM's inception, we have explored ways to enable veterinarians to serve on the mission field. I had been corresponding with Dr. Dave and Mrs. Nikki Bremner of South Africa since 1985.

Dave wrote, *"We are enjoying a super time of fellowship with Mike and Gail Chesson, and are learning lots from their way of life. We are newly married, and I am teaching at the University of Bophuthatswana."*

"In July of 1986, I will be finished with my National Service (Compulsory Army Training) and will be free to take a job. I still have a considerable debt behind my name. When it is paid, we will be free to attend Bible School and then enter the mission field as God leads us. We are available to serve as missionaries after that time."

A Prayer Letter

It was in my third year at vet school that the Lord first spoke to me about missions. I had grown up attending church with my family and had made a personal commitment to Christ at the age of nine. However, I always considered the task of taking the Gospel to strange lands. At a fellowship meeting at vet school, a visiting speaker opened my eyes to the fact that only 50 percent of the world's population is able to hear the message of salvation. This became such a burden to my heart that I decided to be a missionary.

As a South African citizen, I was required to serve two years in the military after completion of my studies, and I was deployed to lecture at a rural university in the country of Bophuthatswana near

South Africa. Here, I had the privilege of working under a missionary veterinarian from the U.S.A. Inspired by this man's dedication, my wife and I decided to make ourselves available to various mission groups working out of South Africa.

Sudanese Interior Missions (SIM) approached us about working with them in South America. After one year of seminary training and a visit to Bolivia and Paraguay, we were accepted as church planters for Paraguay. Our assignment is exciting.

Beginning with their first assignment in Paraguay, CVM has supported the Bremners each year. We did this with a grant, which supplemented the project, while their deputation support comes from South Africa. Dave and Nikki have hosted a number of shuttles from the U.S. and Canada.

❦

Dr. Daniel Karunakaran and his wife Eva lived in Wisconsin. He worked at the Louis Rich Company, as a staff veterinarian specializing in poultry. Their family lived a comfortable life. Nevertheless, something was making them feel uncomfortable! They had a burden to reach the needy. They even had a world map on their living room wall, with pins showing the location of overseas friends and missionaries for whom they prayed regularly.

On a trip to Romania, Daniel felt God calling him to make a leap of faith to go there. He tried to find an agency to share his vision, but he couldn't. He discovered CVM, and presented his vision to serve in Romania. We could not fund his project, but were willing to help where we could with administration, technical advice, and short-term shuttles. The Karunakarans felt so strongly about their calling that they used their own savings, with some donations from friends, and some income from consulting to go. CVM handled administrative needs, like sending prayer letters and channeling donations. In September of 1991, they went to Romania.

Daniel and Eva settled in the north. They discovered people whose spirits had been crushed by poverty brought on by 50 years of communism. They helped 50 families plant 100 acres of wheat. They saw another problem; many churches had poorly qualified teachers, even to the point that some Christians got involved with cults. Daniel and Eva taught Bible studies and spoke at church services on Sunday. They gave out Bibles to Russian tourists who came to the area.

The AVMA met in Seattle again, a dozen years since the last meeting there. One person who had never attended a CVM meeting before said, *"It was like being in a different world"*.

For me, who had worked in relief and development for nearly 15 years, the day was not "different" but pleasantly familiar. What seemed different to one and familiar to the other was the hard reality of the people and conditions of the Third World.

Dr. Bill Testerman, a former field worker and now our Washington representative, started us off with devotions. Mr. Fred Gregory, the CEO of World Concern, welcomed the group and invited them to visit the World Concern/CVM home office. Dr. Bill Lumpkin, a veterinarian in the armed services, introduced Col. Charles Piersee who spoke about the activities of the Military Christian Fellowship.

In their talk called "How the Past Colors the Present", Dan Paulo and Wade Bradshaw told how CVM had impacted their lives. Wade talked about his experiences in Nepal, and Dan described the positive impact shuttles had on his family. They made it a family adventure.

Mike Storer talked about his work in Haiti. It was a reforestation project with an animal care component. Such projects require animals to be confined, which is a concept foreign to Haitian lifestyle.

Shuttle participants included Dr. Don Larson, of Minnesota. He worked in Indonesia with Patrick Smith. Dr. Tom and Mrs. Marcia Van Meter from Oregon served in Haiti and Dr. Bob Vanderhoof from California went on a shuttle to Bolivia.

The afternoon session allowed the audience to listen to one of the most interesting and dynamic speakers today, Tom Sine. My friend Tom and I have shared many great discussions about missions and development work. Tom has always liked the work of CVM, thinking it a model of simplicity, effectiveness, and good stewardship. Tom has written several books, including <u>The Mustard Seed Conspiracy</u>, <u>Wild Hope</u>, and <u>Why Settle For More And Miss The Best.</u>

Tom is a "futurist" by profession, working in future research and planning with major denominations and Christian organizations such as World Concern. He was a staff member and consultant for WC for more than 10 years. A Presbyterian layman, Tom tries to live out his faith each day. He is a proponent of the simple lifestyle. He encourages people to avoid the rat race and "keeping up with the Joneses". Tom says many young people are literally held in bondage to their debt; they are on a treadmill and can't get off.

Tom, speaking on the topic "Anticipating the Future", held the audience spellbound with his amazing speaking skills and his vast knowledge of world conditions and how they relate to mission work. If you don't feel uncomfortable around Tom, then you aren't listening.

Listen to his words, *"The gap between the rich and poor is widening. Population growth is outstripping economic growth and agricultural production in a number of Third World countries. Another factor is the irresponsible use of resources. We see a growing protein deficiency. We are over-fishing the oceans, and the pasture land is shrinking."*

Tom suggested, *"We are waking up to a world in which 'the party is over'! The great consumer society that we Americans have come to take for granted will never be within reach of many of the poor with whom we share the planet. We must remember the stewardship we see modeled in the life of Christ and that earliest community was never a ten percent proposition. It requires a whole-life commitment."*

"There is no right or wrong way to become whole-life disciples or whole life stewards. But if we are going to follow Christ into a very uncertain future, it is essential that we not only have God in our hearts, but place the purposes of God at the very center of our lives; 'sight to the blind, release to the captives and good news to the poor.' Then we have the creative opportunity to reorder how we use our time and resources to put God's purposes first."

It was an outstanding, informative, and thought-provoking presentation. After his lecture, we divided into small groups and tackled the assignments he gave us. Afterwards, we reported to the group. It was a wonderful and productive workshop. The group enjoyed it immensely. We ended a great day with a fellowship meal at the CRISTA Campus.

Jo Anne Whitney chided me a little about closing the annual meeting with my usual remarks, saying, *"This has been the best one ever."*

It's not an insincere or trite phrase, but rather the excitement of the moment. To me it's not difficult to get caught up in the spirit and enthusiasm when I hear others describe how God is working in their lives through CVM. That year, however, I had support for that statement. We asked all those who attended to do an evaluation of the conference. It was unanimous—all the comments were "good", "great", "excellent", "best ever"!

During the year, 26 veterinarians, four veterinary students, one technician, and five spouses served on shuttles. They served from Haiti to Kenya to Indonesia. All came back with exciting testimonies of what their experience had meant to them.

Dr. Arnos Rogers, from Georgia, describes the physical need he witnessed in Haiti, *"Elections were coming up, and a campaigner came through a small village, passing out a few photocopies of campaign material. I watched as a small girl sat quietly and slowly ate the entire sheet of paper. Some children hold rocks or small bits of clay in their mouths to ease the pain of hunger. I saw children seven or eight years old, completely naked. This was not because of immodesty; these children did not have any clothes.*

"However, a veterinarian can learn from these resourceful people. The challenge to the veterinarian is not to perform the service for them, but to learn from the local people about the resources they have and work with them to develop practical and effective applications. I saw this challenge being met by CVM. It gave me a new sense of worth as a veterinarian!"

Dr. Don Larson from Minnesota described his trip to Indonesia to serve with Dr. Patrick Smith. He wrote, *"This shuttle experience could be used by a practicing veterinarian as a glimpse of God's work as a missionary or as a 'Barnabus' act to encourage the missionary. The trip will expose you to more of God's people, God's creation and God's work here on earth."*

Of Dr. and Mrs. David Burrichter's trip from Pennsylvania to Haiti, Linda writes, *"I knew before we left home that this would be a stretching experience for me. I asked the Lord to help me be flexible and to give me the grace that would enable people to see Christ in my life."*

Linda encouraged, *"Just be willing to let God use you, and see what neat things He will do in and through your life."*

Dr. Sonny Tutt from Texas writes, *"My wrist watch broke two days before I was to leave on my shuttle. Needing a short-term replacement, I picked* up a Mickey Mouse watch that plays 'It's a Small World After All,' knowing, my three-year-old grandson would enjoy having it.

"Before I left, my home church made 250 Eternity Bracelets for the children I would meet in the remote villages along the Rio Vichada in eastern Colombia. The bracelets were made of nylon cord and had five beads representing the stages of salvation. Each bracelet came with a sheet of paper explaining in Spanish the significance of the beads.

"I carried them in my backpack through airports, through Bogota, on a small jungle airplane, down miles of hot savanna and jungle trails, and for 50 miles in a dugout canoe.

"Little Guahibo Indian kids are shy. When two giant gringo missionaries walked through their village, they stayed safely behind a parent's knees, their big brown eyes watching our every move. I needed an icebreaker. Remembering my grandson, I said 'Aqui, escuche Mickey. Esta Mundo Pequeno.' When the watch played its tiny tune, the children's eyes lit up. Big smiles pushed away apprehension, and soon the children were crowding in to visit their new friend.

"We gave each child a bracelet. Fabricio, the boatman, read the leaflet explaining the meaning of the beads. Bright yellow and green cords were on every little brown arm. We were invited to the evening culto, a church service. Don Williams, the Wycliffe community development worker, preached and we sang hymns-the Indians in Guahibo, the gringos in English. I think the service was meaningful for the people. I know it was a profound experience for me."

Dr. Victor and Mrs. Riena Kondo, a California veterinarian and his wife, worked with Wycliffe in Loma Linda, Colombia. They helped with translations. They had this advice for those doing shuttles.

"Love can be communicated without words. Everyone laughs in the same language! You wouldn't believe how delighted people are if you learn just one greeting in their language. You can learn many cultural ways by just watching and imitating. When in doubt, ask, people love to help. Non-literate people are often extra observant. Demonstrate your message."

One brother wrote, "In talking with you on the phone, I believe you probably picked up on the fact that while I am very sincere in my Christian beliefs and very dedicated to the mission work that I do, at the same time I find it somewhat difficult to witness to others about my belief. I hope you will be pleased to know that since returning home, I have spoken to a Baptist Youth *group of approximately 50 youth about this work, and will be speaking to a Methodist young adult group soon."*

❦

To supplement our newsletter with a more informal information piece we began publishing the <u>Update</u> in the summer of 1991. We tried to inform the CVM constituency of opportunities for service, and to make them aware of some of the needs, especially relating to shuttles, commodities, and prayer requests from fieldworkers. The new format worked well.

The CVM editor, Jo Anne Whitney, was leaving World Concern. This shocking news meant that she would not be able to write for CVM! That was quite a blow. In addition to her writing skills, which were considerable, she was a dear sister in the Lord. I had known her from my beginning days with World Concern. She was one of the old timers. What would we do without Jo Anne? However, the Lord does provide.

During the AVMA convention of the previous year in Seattle, Tina and I were going over on the ferry to take part in an outing

Tammy Dodd, Dr. Diane Marshall, Dr. Kit Flowers, and Dr. A.L. Dorminy.

hosted by the AVMA. We met a delightful couple from Bellevue, Washington. Both were veterinarians and both were graduates of Washington State University Drs. Gary and Diane Marshall. It was not only our good luck, but providential as well.

It turns out that Diane discovered that she was allergic to animals, not just a few, but all animals. How can that be good news, you say. Well, Diane has writing skills—as you may have discovered by reading the CVM newsletter. She wanted to use those skills in service to the Lord. What a fit! She started by working for us part time. You see, we want to get people hooked first, and then bring on the work!

CHAPTER 18

Christmas

We asked our fieldworkers to share what Christmas was like in the culture where they now lived and worked. Some of their responses were foreign to our traditional thoughts about Christmas.

From Nepal, Ron and Karen Stoufer wrote,

> "Although the Christian church is growing rapidly, less than one percent of the people here are Christians. Therefore, Christmas is not an official holiday. Shops, banks, and government offices are open as usual. Last year, with the coming of the new government, was the first time that Christians were allowed to take the day off.
>
> "There are amazingly few western cultural traditions. Christians don't exchange gifts, decorate homes or trees, send greeting cards, or have any type of Santa Claus traditions. Christmas in the Nepali Christian church is a simple remembrance of Jesus' birth. A worship service is followed by a large outdoor picnic of rice, potatoes and lentils."

From Bolivia, Susan Stewart and Mark Bounds wrote,

> "Christmas is the hottest, steamiest, drippiest time of the year. The middle of the rainy season, it is not uncommon to be slogging around, up to your knees in mud, fighting off swarms of mosquitoes. People don't generally visit us for Christmas."

Keith and Jan Flanagan Describe Christmas in Haiti,

> "Christmas comes with little advance notice. No commercialization, no cold, no snow. However, on a clear, bright, starlit night, with the background noise of the roosters and donkeys, it is easy to

imagine that you are on the hills near Bethlehem. Most of the churches have Christmas Eve services that last most of the night, and a service again Christmas day. Families get together and, if finances allow, a chicken or goat is killed. We have found it easier to focus on God here, than at home."

The Van Gorkoms in Ethiopia wrote,

"In the Ethiopian Calendar, Christmas comes several weeks later—so we get to celebrate twice. They practice for a drama, borrowing a doll for baby Jesus, cutting a star out of foil, taping cotton beards on the wise men. Everyone brings flowers to the church. They sing for several hours, listen to two or three sermons, and perform the story of Jesus outside the church for all who will come. At last, they celebrate with the biggest feast you ever saw, and the food vanishes instantly."

An exciting portrait comes from Patrick Smith in Indonesia,

"A high-pitched rhythmic whooping plays out in the early dawn air. The voice is joined by one after another, until the entire village is astir. It's going to be a great Christmas day, and everyone has a task.

"Groups of young men gather wood for the huge fire that will heat rocks to cook the Christmas feast. Old men bark orders; the women gather sweet potatoes, greens, and vegetables from the garden. Pigs are brought to the cook site, arrowed, singed, and butchered. Young people collect grasses and banana leaves to line the cook pit. They chant and wave their sheaves as they return. The spirit of celebration fills the air. The joy of Jesus is everywhere.

"After the preparations, everyone joins in one crescendo of effort to fill the cook pit. Grasses and leafy branches line the pit. Men and women, armed with split sapling tongs, carry the searing hot rocks to the pit, where they are carefully arranged. Next, sweet potatoes go into the pit, then rocks, greens and vegetables are added until a mound of steaming, baking matter several feet high begins to take shape. Near the top, the splayed-out bodies of the pigs are laid. More rocks and greens are added, until a critical mass is achieved.

"Now it is time to go jump into the stream. Many have been up the whole night, singing, talking, and story telling in anticipation of the big day. A metallic clang rings out the call to worship. Voices join in

songs of praise. God's word is proclaimed in the Dani, language in remembrance of Jesus' birth—God's gift to the world.

"After worship, everyone returns to the cook site. Family and friends gather in groups, patiently waiting while the village elders slice the pork. Young men and women trot back and forth, serving up armloads of sweet potatoes, vegetables, pork, and greens. Having eaten their fill, the crowd disperses for a late afternoon rest. A fitting end to a glorious celebration of the birth of God's son, our Savior Jesus."

Reading the various accounts of Christmas celebration, I see that external circumstances flavor our perceptions of 'normal'. We associate things like the weather, family tradition, and cultural values with proper observance of a holiday. If conditions don't conform to our experiences or expectations, we sometimes say, 'It just doesn't seem like Christmas.'

My earliest Christmas memory involves riding in a wagon to a Christmas party at church. We were well into the automobile era, but this mode of transportation was not unusual for the time. The party was very exciting, until they started handing out gifts. They never did get around to calling my name. Whether my family's Scottish thriftiness dictated this, or depression era economics decided it, I definitely felt left out.

I think of the people around the world, especially in the areas where we work. Many, if not most, are left out—not just for Christmas gifts, but for the essentials of life. The reason gifts are not exchanged is simple. There are just no resources to make it happen.

One worker remembers, *"Wherever we have gone, God has provided us an extended family to share Christmas."* Isn't that a great thing? That is what the Christmas spirit is all about.

The good news is that all can share God's gift to the world, His Son. It is the free and universal gift that does not depend on external circumstances, but only on the hearing and on the heart. Everyone's name can be called at the Party of Life Everlasting.

CVM held its annual meeting in Boston. Dr. Raiford Claxton, our Massachusetts representative, provided a devotional message from the Old Testament. He challenged us to be like Caleb and Joshua, who had faith in God's promise of a land of milk and honey, despite the fearsome Amorites who dwelt in the land.

Dr Marion Hammarlund, our California representative, reminded us, "*The same power that raised Jesus from the dead is at work in my life.*" He spoke on, *'Applying Christian Living at the Community Level.'*

Howard Gobble discussed his work reaching veterinary students through the Student Chapter of the AVMA. After work in Ethiopia, Howard drew a comparison between the unreached peoples of rural Ethiopia and the many unreached veterinary students in the U.S. It is an unsettling thing to contemplate.

Drs. Fred and Vicki Van Gorkom shared their latest videotape and slides, and answered questions about their lives and work amid the Bunna and Tsemai people of Ethiopia. They pointed out how the love of God is opening hearts and changing lives among these hardworking people. "*The Bunna people have traditionally been fierce enemies of the Mursi tribe, shooting on sight. Since coming to know the Lord, some of the Bunna have been willing to go to the Mursi to share the Gospel with them, even though they may risk physical danger.*"

Dr. Jack Eckert of Missouri, Dr. and Mrs. David Burrichter of Pennsylvania, and Dr. Fred Bendick of Missouri all shared their shuttle experiences. They served in Haiti, Belize and Kenya, respectively.

Gary Bekker, Ph.D. presented a workshop entitled "Christ, Culture and Curing." Dr. Bekker was a missionary in the Philippines, and now served as an anthropologist and professor at Gordon Conwell Seminary. He gave an anthropologist's view of culture, and challenged us to evaluate what was important in our own lives in light of our physical surroundings, behaviors, social relationships, and ideologies.

CHAPTER 19

Shifting Gears

Dr. Don Wilson and his wife Marilyn were living in Arnold, Missouri when they felt the Lord's call to long-term missions. Don was raised on a farm in Southern Indiana. He is a 1965 graduate of Purdue Veterinary School. Don went on four shuttles with CVM, and was very committed to the work. He took a leave of absence from his clinic to answer this call. It takes courage and faith to leave a successful practice for the mission field.

Don explained their odyssey,

"About eight years ago, I had the privilege of going to Haiti as a shuttle veterinarian with CVM—going out to work with the poor peasant farmers, teaching them how to better care for their animals. Holding vaccination clinics and de-worming their animals was very exciting, but not nearly as exciting as sharing with them the love of Christ.

"About two years later, Marilyn went back to Haiti with me. She was deeply touched by the people and their needs. Since then, we have traveled to South Africa and Bolivia, each time being more touched and getting a deeper feeling that some day God wanted us to go for an extended time."

"We felt the calling, but we knew there were situations at home that needed to be dealt with first. The most important was our four children. We needed to make sure they were settled and secure. We also have four grandchildren, with another on the way. Leaving the family will be the saddest part of all.

"A final step in the process was going to Seattle for an intense two weeks cross-cultural orientation. We received practical advice about

adjusting to another culture, and how to stay healthy and cope with emotional stress. On the final day, we were commissioned."

The place to which they were going, the Bolivian jungle, is inhospitable. The challenges are formidable, both to the families that live and farm there, and to those who have come to help. It is an area of severe malnutrition and high child mortality.

They worked with residents to select and train community veterinary technicians, improve pastures, and participate in animal loan programs. The diversification, which comes with the introduction of livestock, will allow family farms to move beyond mere survival. The relationships they developed became the basis for sharing their faith, and encouraging and discipling farmers.

Things got off to a rip-roaring start. On the way to language class in Santa Cruz one day, it poured rain. Don and Marilyn decided to call a cab. The cab became stuck in a puddle, and water started pouring in through the floorboards. The water kept rising, until the driver told them to climb out the window and onto the hood. Marilyn reports that this was a real trick, in a skirt. They jumped out into the puddle and walked home, soaked and muddy but laughing.

Other adventures were not so benign. One night, while Don and Marilyn were downtown, they noticed a lot of commotion. What they thought was a celebration turned out to be a student demonstration.

Marilyn writes,

A Prayer Letter

"Suddenly people started screaming and running. Shop owners were closing and locking their doors. People were pushing and shoving, and we didn't have any idea what was happening. Don was hit in the back of his head with a tear-gas bomb. His head was bleeding, and the tear gas had come back into my face. We could not see, and our faces were burning.

"Not knowing what else to do, we ducked under a door as the shop owner was pulling it down.

"Then we heard those wonderful English words, 'I speak English. Follow me, and I will help you.'

"A seventeen year-old boy took us to a sink. He washed the blood from Don's head and got a cold rag for my face. Later, he took us to his home across the street. We stayed there for a couple of hours until the roads were clear enough for him to take us home.

"The young man had just returned from the U.S., where he had been an exchange student in Indiana attending Purdue. Don was wearing a Purdue T-shirt. That's where Don attended veterinary school! It was old home week in Santa Cruz!"

When they finished their term of service, the Wilsons returned to Missouri. They continue to fulfill their mission, however. They do this through periodic shuttles, securing resources, and inviting and encouraging others to participate with them in the projects in Bolivia.

Dr. Dan and Mrs. Gina Grimm were part of Don and Marilyn's "home team". Gina explains how: *"In 1992, Don Wilson, Dan's vet school classmate, told us he was going to do a survey trip to Bolivia. He was, considering a long-term placement there. For months, we had been planning to go to Haiti on a shuttle, but due to political unrest, that trip had been put on hold. We agreed to go with Don and Marilyn to look at Bolivia. When Don and Marilyn decided to go for a two-year term, we told them we would go on regular shuttles to be their support.*

"The Lord has transplanted a chunk of our heart in Bolivia. Over the last seven years, we have developed an on-going relationship with churches in Berlin and San Julian Colonies in the Santa Cruz area of Bolivia. On our first trip to the lowlands, Dan did an equine medicine-training clinic. We met Nicholas Churque, our translator and Don's language tutor. We met Dori Coca, a leader in the animators' animal health workers program. Dori's desire was for Evangelical churches to be encouraged and equipped to meet the needs of the people.

"We brought the desire back to our church, the Christian Fellowship Church. We proposed that, as a congregation, we pray for and encourage the people of these work zones; and that we send short term teams to partner in building up the community of believers through courses, workshops, leadership development, and manpower to build churches.

"Nicholas Churque was called to pastor the pastors in the area. Today, we at CFC continue that partnership by supporting Nicholas to do pastor training, Holistic Christian Community Development, and Theology by Extension, for church leadership development. There are nine churches and three small fellowships with whom we have relationships. We try to do one or two shuttles a year.

"The Lord is doing so much there, we pant to keep up with Him. Recently we have established H.E.A.R.T. Network Mid-America, which will allow us to recruit others in our geographic region to build on this partnership. We praise the Lord for His wisdom in placing the work under the authority of Godly leaders such as Leroy Dorminy, Kit Flowers, Mark Bounds, and Susan Stewart and in such great and rewarding partnerships as Don and Marilyn, Nicolas, Dori Coca, and Phil Bender. Our church mission committee has suggested that this model might be useful in other areas of the world. We told them that we believe CVM/WC is a great door opener for Holistic Christian Community Development ministry."

George and Martha Mixon called me while George was a student in veterinary school at the University of Georgia, in Athens. They were part of the fellowship there, and had heard of CVM. They wanted to know more. They had an interest in missions, but had questions about how should they prepare themselves for such a career.

I was happy to make a few suggestions:

- Take a broad-spectrum approach to the curriculum, but pay special attention to food animal medicine. Practice for two years, preferably in two different practices. This way, the things you were taught in school are quickly assimilated in a practical manner.

- If time permits, learn at least one other language. Two good ones to study are Spanish and/or French. Even if you wind up needing to learn a tribal language, it still is worth it.

- Get a good basic background in the scriptures. Your faith will be assailed from all sides, and the stronger your spiritual life, the more likely you are to be a positive witness. (This is sound advice whether or not you are going overseas).

- Attend a mission-minded church. Find some type of ministry to be involved in. Don't wait until you are overseas to be involved in missions. We frequently ask an applicant, *"Where are you serving now?"*

These contacts with George and Martha continued beyond George's graduation. George took a job in his hometown of Griffin, Georgia. My practice partner, Dr. Dwain Smith was from there. He heard me speak at the University of Georgia about CVM. He came to work with me to allow me to pursue that goal. He is a fine Christian man and a good friend.

George grew up on a hog and cattle farm near Griffin. He accepted Christ at an early age, and had been growing in Him. He had a variety of opportunities for leadership and Christian training through the Inter-Varsity Christian Fellowship. Martha, the daughter of a medical doctor, grew up in a small town in Georgia. There was a Christian atmosphere and a cultured life style, quite unlike the dung huts of Maasai Land.

George went on a shuttle to Kenya with Dr. Dave Garza, from Texas. They worked with the Maasai, in cooperation with Christian Missionary Fellowship.

George observed, *"Missionaries and relief and development workers are really making a difference among the poor and needy of the Third World"*. This was the evidence he needed to tip the scales in favor of long-term service.

"You did not choose me, but I chose you and appointed you to go and bear fruit—fruit that will last" (John 15:16). This verse reflected the way that George and Martha viewed their decision to go on the mission field.

Through the Maasai Mara Veterinary Project, Dr. Mixon trained technicians to educate others in their tribes about disease prevention and veterinary medical treatment. As Kenya becomes more modern, the Maasai's traditional pastoral lifestyle is changing. Increased grazing pressure, livestock overcrowding, and inadequate tick control have compromised animal health.

A Prayer Letter

The rooster crows outside my window at dawn. Wearily, I swing my legs and feet onto the dirt floor, glancing outside at the cows clanking nosily by, on their way to a day of grazing the African plains. I throw on my tennis shoes, grab my bucket, and head to the river to collect water to boil, for a bath and breakfast. When I return, George has the wood stove going and I start heating the water.

For breakfast it's cooked maize meal again, and I'm hoping there will be some fresh goat meat at the market today-I'm planning stew for dinner. While the porridge cooks, I send George to the river again, this time for water to wash our clothes. It's a little brown, but I'm amazed how clean the clothes can get, if you scrub hard enough. Now Beth stumbles sleepily into the room, and I guide her straight to the outhouse, taking with me the nighttime toilet-bucket to empty.

It is difficult to adjust to life in the bush, but it is a time of spiritual growth. George shared his observations on the story of the lost sheep:

A Prayer Letter

Surely our Father in heaven knows each one of us far more than even the Maasai know their sheep. He knows our heart. He knows when we are lost, and He cares very much. The Lord is indeed our Shepherd.

I've thought about why the Maasai knows his animals so well. He lives with each animal. If the animal is not inside the house at night (young calves, kids and lambs), it is just outside the house in the center of the village or in the sheep pen. Most of the Maasai's thought goes into caring for his animals-'Where will I send the cows tomorrow or next month? When will the rains come again?

What will I do about all the East Coast Fever? Every evening he watches the animals enter the village. Every morning he walks among his herd and watches them leave for grazing, possibly shepherding them himself. It reminds me of Psalm 121:8-'The Lord will watch over your coming and going both now and forevermore.

Wendell Cantrell received his DVM in 1978 from Texas A & M. He first made contact with CVM in early 1991 and went on a shuttle to Uganda in 1992. The next summer, Wendell and his wife Jann did a three-month shuttle, living in Nairobi and working in Sudan. Jann decided from the beginning that she didn't think bush life would be for her. No problem.

Jann and Wendell lived in Katy, Texas, an affluent suburb of Houston. Conditions there were nothing like what they were to experience in Africa. Jann was involved in Bible Study Fellowship (BSF). Originally, she had some apprehensions about what her role might be on the field. That was easily solved! Her BSF ministry in Nairobi turned out to be tremendous. In fact, when they considered signing up for a second term, she said her work there was not finished!

Jann wrote, *"Although it still seems like a dream, we are about to board a plane for Nairobi, Kenya to spend the summer as fieldworkers for Christian Veterinary Mission. Our son Tim and I will primarily be providing support for Wendell as he goes over into southern Sudan with ACROSS, a Christian group aiding in agricultural and veterinary relief and development."*

Later, Wendell wrote, *"I am entering my third month in Sudan. The war continues unabated. U.N. security keeps us apprised of which areas are safe to work in. I finished a Community Animal Health Worker training session in the upper Nile yesterday. I was asked to preach in a Presbyterian church. The Sudanese People's Liberation Army commander and his armed guards arrived in mid-service to join us. I hoped this wouldn't be an opportune time for an ambush. I preached on Jonah running away from God. Other than the folks being distracted by our visitors, the service went well."*

After this shuttle, Wendell and Jann made the decision to serve long-term. We commissioned them in February of the following year, and they moved to Nairobi. Wendell was CVM's East Africa coordinator. He traveled to different countries, visiting fieldworkers and looking for prospective sites for service.

At the end of one of those trips, Wendell reflected, *"I am more convinced daily that veterinary medicine is an invaluable tool in East Africa for furthering the cause of Christ."*

Jann invested herself into the ministry through BSF:

A Prayer Letter

I Attended a Maasai ladies circle meeting in one of their homes, a windowless hut made of manure. I experienced two new fears: fear of fainting and of food! I realized that I am definitely not destined to be the next Amy Carmichael, as I can only comply with the first half of her saying, 'Where he leads I will follow, what He feeds I will swallow.'

Our Bible Study Fellowship (BSF) classes have been great sources of joy and means of fruitfulness, as well as places for developing many new relationships. One example- Jane Mwithiga is a middle aged Kenyan woman, who comes in from a village area, where she lives on a farm. It is not easy for her to get to class but she makes it every week. As she began to share with other village women what she was receiving from the Lord through BSF, they asked her to teach them the lesson each week, which she does. Their husbands were so influenced by what the wives were learning that they asked the pastor to get her to share it with the whole church."

Something else was on Wendell's mind—how to balance his life amid all the pulls and tugs of everyday life. He began to put together some thoughts. While home on leave, he developed a program that has been helpful to many people. It is a seminar, also on video, called <u>The Balanced Professional</u>. We have used it at board meetings, regional meetings, and conventions. We think it points to an underlying need in all our lives.

Drs. Steve Hiett and Kim Stender graduated from the Washington State University College of Veterinary Medicine in 1991. Now a husband and wife team they were headed for Cambodia—to the rural province of Prey Veng, where they developed a livestock and poultry project.

They wrote, *"Cambodia may not be the basket case that some countries in Africa are, but when asked, 98% of the people indicated they ran short of rice. 80% had borrowed rice during half the year. For six months out of the year, they did not have sufficient rice to eat. One additional statistic—only two out of a hundred had ever heard of Jesus Christ."*

A Prayer Letter

We are now official homeowners. It is a 5-meter by 6-meter structure (2 meters off the ground) with a bamboo floor, thatch walls, and a clay tile roof. Contained in this expansive abode are a kitchen, a porch and the all purpose living room, dining room, bedroom, study, and office space. Outside to the east is the ever-necessary latrine and shower.

We had a Christian house blessing with Bible readings, prayer, and singing Khmer hymns, followed by fellowship with fruits, cookies, and soft drinks. Things went smoothly until the village leader took the liberty to call in all the other gods that we must have inadvertently forgotten to mention... oh well, we had it pretty well covered before he got to it.

One side of the house is a bit exposed to the community. The 'fish bowl' phenomenon seems to describe it. Being foreigners, we are a bit of a novelty and everyone is interested in the things we do. We were putting our glasses into the food cupboard, when one of our neighbor grannies watched to see how many we put out. There were six. They have six glasses, she hollered out to a woman in the other room, who then proceeded to tell a woman in the other room, who then proceeded to tell another woman, 'they have six glasses', who then yelled to the outside of our house 'they have six glasses." Life may be unusual but not dull!"

Steve and Kim finished out their term, and returned home with plans to eventually return to the mission field.

The not so gentle reminder kept creeping into my mind that in July 1993, I would be 70 years old. I had always said that when someone got that old, they should step aside. One thing I had never taken into account was how young I would feel at that age! Anyway, I had committed to that in my mind, so I carried through with it. There were some special projects I wanted to finish—the CVM Endowment Fund, the educational materials, developing affiliates, and just plain visiting with folks.

And, to tell the truth, I never wanted anyone whispering in my ear, "Leroy don't you think you had better step aside? After all, you are getting pretty old." Lastly, I didn't want the organization to die with me.

The system was in place to select my successor. I asked the CVM Board to assemble in Atlanta. We had a summary of CVM's history, including maps showing the regional representative concept, and the papers I wrote: "Rationale for Veterinarians in Missions" and "The Importance of Veterinarians in Third World Development."

The summary included a list of fieldworkers, CVM publications, shuttles, a financial statement, the organizational structure, and the Statement of Understanding between World Concern and CVM and the Articles and By-laws of the incorporation of the CVM Endowment Fund. We had it all documented for discussion and decision-making.

It was a very successful meeting, one where the Lord's Spirit was evident. We enjoyed two and one half days of work and fellowship. We discussed the direction and focus of CVM, reviewing the past, assessing the present, anticipating, and planning. Since that time, we have met annually.

Dr. Kit Flowers was appointed to the Directorship. He started as a donor to CVM, then participated in a shuttle, and felt called to long-term service. After serving five years in Kenya, he and his family came to Seattle where he worked in the CVM home office. He understood the workings of CVM, but more importantly, Kit has a servant's heart.

Dr. Fred Bendick, from Missouri, was the newly elected Board Chairman. The Board's evolution has been interesting to watch. It is gratifying and reassuring to see new leadership surface with each board meeting. In the beginning of his term, Fred gave each board member a Study Bible, so that all the members could read and study the scriptures together, even though they were scattered across the United States. It promoted spiritual growth and bonding in the board. We were off to a good start.

Board members, in addition to Fred, included Dr. Earle Goodman, South Carolina, Dr. Dan Paulo, Pennsylvania, Dr. Don DeLinks, Massachusetts, Dr. Jerry Burch, Tennessee, Dr. James Rosenberger, Ohio, Dr. Charles Gasaway, Oklahoma, Dr. Walt Long, Nebraska, Dr. Bob Beede, Idaho, Dr. Gary Baker, California, Dr. Floyd Jones, Texas, and Dr. Conrad Van Dijk, Canada. They represented the finest of the Christian community within the profession.

Dr. Mike Staudinger is from Wisconsin. He is one of those people you can call on for a special assignment in short order. We received a call from a church in Ohio that was working in Nicaragua. They were trying to sponsor a dairy there, and needed some advice on setting up the operation. Mike seemed to fit all those qualifications, and he was willing to go at the drop of a hat!

'Matthew 25', of Cincinnati, Ohio, as the overseas ministry was called, planned to fly a load of supplies into the country. Mike agreed to go along. The pastor was overjoyed to have a qualified veterinarian to help with the project on such a short notice. Our ministry amazed him. We, of course, take it for granted that such expertise is flying all over the world at any given time to engage in precisely this sort of activity.

Mr. Dennis Beukelman called me from Sioux Falls, South Dakota. He was part of an organization, AMONG International, that was working in Mongolia. He and four others were going to Mongolia to determine the country's potential for agricultural development. They wanted someone to represent veterinary medicine.

A phone call, and it was settled. However, that person had to cancel just a few days before the trip, too late to recruit someone else. So I went. What a blessing for me!

The delegation included Clancey Genjimatsuda, a retired colonel, Virgil Houtkooper with the Agricultural Soil Conservation Service, Roger Shepherd, a management consultant, Dennis, and me. The purpose of the trip was to learn, explore, and assess Mongolia's situation and to plan appropriate action. From my perspective, the trip was to learn about the veterinary and animal husbandry needs of Mongolia. With this information, CVM could make an assessment and determine what our practical response should be.

Mongolia, as you know, was dominated by the Soviet Union for 70 years. Now they were free of that yoke. They were trying to go from the old communist system to a free market economy. It is a difficult task. The Mongolian Government had just passed a law that would allow veterinarians to practice privately.

Mongolia sits between China and Siberia. In the south is the Gobi Desert, then come the Steppes, and then the colder mountainous region bordering Siberia. The climate is cold and arid; the soil is sandy and dry. Natural grasses do not look that productive for forage. The farmers and herders needed to use the best dry land farming practices available to conserve moisture. AMONG suggested the Concorde (a plow, not a plane), as one way to address the problem. It is excellent, state of the art, no-till equipment, designed with developing countries in mind. It was already being produced in nearby countries.

Even though the growing season is short, Mongolians do some farming. Vegetables are started in greenhouses. For this, farmers needed seeds in the fall. They grow wheat, with some barley and oats. Animal husbandry issues included pasture grasses and the production of forage. Many animals showed evidence of severe malnutrition. The areas that I saw evidenced overgrazing. This was visibly worse nearer the city.

There seemed to be a need for better animal breeding. This has to be done with hardy, resistant strains of basic stock. Introduction of other strains through Artificial Insemination (AI) and Embryo Transfer (ET) is desirable.

L to R; Clancy, Dennis, Leroy, Virgil, Roger, Menyol-Mongolia.

Mongolian herders also needed an extension service for information dissemination. This has had much to do with the tremendous success of American agriculture. One thing making their situation more difficult is the remoteness of the herders with their pastoral lifestyle. However, there still is community among the herders, especially in the winter.

The Minister of Agriculture told us there were 15 million sheep, 5 million goats, 2 million cattle, 2 million horses, and 1/2 million camels. He also said that the herders themselves owned 80% of the livestock.

The veterinarians were mainly trained in Russia. In general, they lacked current knowledge, techniques, and equipment. They recognized this, and were eager to learn. They also recognized that CVM has access to many veterinary specialists who could help them to upgrade their skills. They understood that CVM is a Christian organization, and that men and women of Christian faith did its work.

On Sunday, we went to worship services in a park. It was so encouraging to see young Mongolians worshipping openly with joy in their hearts. I had an opportunity to meet several of them. I had a couple of Bibles, which I gave to them. The freshness and enthusiasm with which these Christians worshipped was wonderful.

I came back from Mongolia very excited about the opportunities. Admittedly, the type of service needed was a departure from the past. However, I thought it offered tremendous potential for CVM to utilize veterinarians that are more specialized. The window of opportunity was open, only the Lord knew when it would close, so we needed to work while the opportunity was still available.

Returning home, I planned the steps to make things happen. I met so many people in the Mongolian veterinary community who were eager for information. I knew we needed many specialists from the United States and other developed countries to help. I began to contact experts that I knew, and suggested short-term shuttles in Mongolia. Since the weather is not very friendly except in the summer months, we decided to schedule a group shuttle for one year later.

⁂

The summer meeting was in Minneapolis. Who was more appropriate to do the devotions than Dr. Tom Wanous, a long time friend of CVM? Dr. Fred Bendick gave an update on the Board's activities. Dr. Mike Staudinger and Dr. John Schneller talked about their shuttle to Bolivia. Dr. Sally Bushhouse, spoke of her work in Kenya. Long-term field-workers who participated were Dr. Karen and Ron Stoufer, of Nepal and Dr. Don and Marilyn Wilson, of Bolivia. Dr. Mark Hinton, a long-time fieldworker in Kenya, presented "Veterinary Missions in Perspective."

Without my knowledge, Kit commissioned John Gilliam, an Idaho artist, to do a limited edition bronze sculpture. It included a Bolivian woman, her goat, and me. We named it "Mission Vet". It is a beautiful piece of art, though I may be a mite prejudiced. Although it is only 13 inches high by 13 inches wide, it is very heavy. Kit lugged it through the airport, to and through the hotel, in order to have it at the meeting. I have it at home in Ocilla, Georgia. Needless to say, I am extremely proud of it. On the cover of this book is a picture of it.

CHAPTER 20

"Gourmet Ministry" or Cleverly Disguised

The CVM Board met in January, in Seattle. Dr. Dan Paulo, from Pennsylvania, was elected incoming chairman. Dan and his wife Kathy were long-time friends of CVM. They participated in the shuttle program as a couple and with their three daughters. It was a family affair.

The Board formed an executive council to handle CVM business between annual board meetings. At this meeting, Christian Veterinary Mission and Christian Veterinary Fellowship became a single entity. Dr. Tim Blair served on the board as a representative-at-large.

Dr. Blair commented, *"The initial vision of CVF was to assist veterinarians to have an effective witness in their practices, to provide prayer support, and to help veterinary students. There was always some confusion in the roles of CVM and CVF and I would like to see continuity in the mission. As we help CVM members to grow spiritually, that in turn will strengthen the overall CVM mission. God sees those who are faithful and gives them more. As we are faithful in this merger, God will bless our efforts."*

The highlight of the meeting was when each board member shared a verse of scripture and explained how it spoke to them about their affiliation with CVM. We followed this with prayer.

Uzbekistan, in Central Asia, is one of fifteen former Soviet republics. Tashkent, the capital city, is home to about 2.5 million of the country's 21.5 million residents. Seventy percent of the people are

Dr. Jeff Bender, Dr. Leroy Dorminy, and Uzbekistan Veterinarians.

Uzbeks; the other 30% represents many ethnic groups. The Muslim religion is the predominant faith.

Like many of its neighbors, Uzbekistan was experiencing economic hardship as it struggled to privatize industry and develop a free market economy. Many things, such as vaccines, were in short supply. They had neither the technology to produce them or the hard currency to purchase them.

Dr. Jeff Bender, from Minnesota, and I went to Uzbekistan to determine how CVM could help during this economic restructuring. We, along with Mr. D. R. Frans of the Netherlands, and Richard Penner, the World Concern country manager, met with government veterinary officials. We visited veterinary clinics, a hog farm, and a dairy farm. The purpose of our trip was to survey rather than assist. We spent time with officials of the State Veterinary Services, Inspectorate Department, and with the Minister of Agriculture. We concluded that there was an unusual opportunity to help veterinarians with this transition. As a result, relationships developed, offering opportunities for spiritual witness and encouragement.

We developed a proposal aimed at the efforts of the Uzbekistan government to privatize certain segments of the agriculture industry. We suggested a project that would provide for the technical assistance in the training and privatization of veterinarians, technicians, and livestock owners. It was step-by-step assistance, beginning with a shuttle program, hopefully to be followed by a long-term worker.

Later in the year, Dr. Cheryl Braswell-Sisson, who is a small animal practitioner in Georgia, and Dr. Louis Kwantes, who is a large animal practitioner in Canada followed with a shuttle visit. They visited veterinary facilities in Tashkent, Bukhara, and Samarkand. They interviewed many veterinary scientists. Cheryl and Louis also gave a series of lectures and demonstrations at Tashkent Agricultural Institute. A number of veterinarians from all regions of Uzbekistan attended.

A year later, another shuttle team put on seminars, lectures, and practical laboratory demonstrations. Dr. Robert Mersch, from Minnesota, addressed large animal concerns, and Dr. Rick Zander, from California, dealt with the small animal aspects. Veterinarians and professors attended these lectures from the school in Tashkent. Drs. Mersch and Zander made some farm visits in the area around Samarkand and held clinics within the city.

Dr. Deron Larson, and Dr. Ronald Terra, both of California, followed the next year. This time, the shuttle evaluated the level of privatization, and added further instructions and assistance. In addition, they wanted to expose students to the principles of a free market economy. It was all geared towards increasing the business acumen of veterinary clinicians. They wanted to educate livestock owners about how to utilize the services of a veterinarian.

Dr. Terra did an outstanding job of summarizing all the previous shuttles to Uzbekistan. I thought this was particularly perceptive on his part, to take the time to really understand CVM's objectives for the country. He was able to lay it all out, to see if we were accomplishing those objectives. It was most helpful.

Finally, a British veterinarian named Dr. David Forster decided to go for long-term service. He began language instruction in Tashkent, and then established himself in the work. He eventually moved to Samarkand, in order to be closer to students at the veterinary school.

Dr. Greg Laurence, a dairy practitioner from Minnesota, participated in several shuttles to Kenya and Honduras. He was impressed by people's enthusiasm for learning more about veterinary medicine. During a severe drought in Kenya, he dewormed and gave vitamin shots to cattle. He believes that the treatments helped the cattle survive until the rains came.

❦

On more than one occasion, veterinarians who are working in a developing country on their own initiative, have contacted CVM. After a while, they are overwhelmed by the magnitude of the needs of the people, and they turn to CVM for help. We are grateful for these resourceful and compassionate veterinarians. Dr. Jim Cornelius, of Arkansas, was one of them.

Jim was working in Pignon, Haiti, helping the best he could through repeated shuttles. He realized that the people needed more than he could offer. He contacted us, and we began to assist with periodic shuttles.

Jim writes, *"The veterinary technician program administered by CVM has inspired the Haitian technicians to assist with procedures, with skill I had not seen before."*

❦

As a follow up to the initial survey in Mongolia, six veterinarians, Dr. Gerald Mitchum from North Carolina, Dr. Paul Kline from Texas, Dr. Richard Houston from Minnesota, Dr. Lloyd Lauerman from Alabama, Dr. Edward Moser from Maryland, and Dr. Bill Ley from Virginia, did a study of needs as they related to their own specific area of expertise. The group visited the veterinary institutions within the country, and spoke with their professional counterparts.

Dr. Lloyd Lauerman had an unusual interaction with Drs. Yondondorj and Tungalag of the Microbiology Department of the veterinary school. *"I spent the entire day discussing problems with the faculty, staff, and graduate students. A subject discussed at length was Brucellosis. It has a high rate of infection in Mongolia. I lectured on "The Risks of Zoonotic Diseases to Veterinarians". I began the lecture saying that I was an Ambassador of Jesus Christ and that I had come to Mongolia to share with them the scientific knowledge He had given me."*

193

Since that time, Lloyd has returned and has kept in close contact with his counterparts at the school. He has served as a valuable resource to their work.

Dr. William Ley wrote, *"I have been involved in the clinical application of Production Management Medicine in livestock systems for the past 8 years. Combined with my specialization in Theriogenology (veterinary reproduction, including AI and ET) and my special interest in small ruminants, I feel suited to respond to their needs. The veterinary research and laboratory personnel expressed interest in training and educational seminars on abortion diseases in small ruminants, lamb mortality, pregnancy diagnosis, embryo transfer and Brucellosis control and eradication."*

Dr. Edward Moser, a nutritionist, observed, *"The main problem from my point of view was a protein/energy deficit. Animals were stressed by major loss in weight during the winter. This results in decreased productivity due to neonatal mortality, lower reproductive efficiency and lower weight gains."*

He recommended better pasture management (rotation/grass selection), strategic culling (decreasing pressure on the pasture), routine parasite control, and strategic use of supplemental nutrients.

Dr. Dick Houston, a dairy specialist, reinforced this. *"Although there are many limiting factors negatively impacting output, I believe the greatest to be nutrition. It was clear to me that their veterinary training and expertise far exceeded livestock production. This tells me veterinarians traditionally have not done a good job of information transfer. The Mongolian vets are capable, but they need to take off their suits and ties, buy a pair of boots, and go to where the animals are!"*

Dr. Paul Kline reported, *"My personal goals for the shuttle were to observe first hand what life in Mongolia was like, and to determine what possible role God would have me fill in terms of long term Christian veterinary service. I was especially interested in meeting the people that I might be working with, in order to establish relationships and communication."*

Apparently, it worked well; Paul and his wife Amanda returned for long-term service in the fall of that same year. Paul and Amanda wrote, *"As the plane approached the runway, we heard the stewardess announce that the temperature outside was -29 degrees. Amanda and I looked at each other and Amanda said, "Did she say 29 degrees below zero?" I just smiled and nodded. As we stepped off the plane onto the runway below, the cold air literally took our breath away. However, things change. Spring is in full swing here, which means wind, snow, cold, heat, sleet, hail and rain."*

Paul and Amanda visited Chandman in the province of Gobi Altai, in western Mongolia. Amanda wrote, *"We had the opportunity on this trip to experience life in the Gobi, and what it will be like to carry water, and go out to the jorlon (outhouse) in the middle of a freezing wind. To have neighbors drop in at all hours of the day and night. Mongolians don't lock their doors, and they don't knock. They simply come in, take their place, and wait for some tea or food and discuss the weather, animals, family, etc."*

Paul and Amanda served in Chandman after completing language school. In addition to the living conditions there were other challenges including:

"What to tell a young believer that is faced with the dilemma of wanting to go to church but having to lie to her Buddhist parents by telling them she is going to study? What to do with street kids that show up regularly at the door wanting something to eat? Always there are many requests for money. How are we to be generous and give freely, while maintaining the proper balance and stewardship?"

Paul and Amanda served in Mongolia with distinction, helping the herders. He later became JCS director, and they moved to Ulaanbaatar, the capital city of Mongolia.

Dr. Gerald Mitchum is another veterinarian who eventually wound up in Mongolia working long-term. He and his wife Frances went the following year.

On the shuttle he observed, *"There is no extension system at the University. This is an area of desperate need for the retraining of the large State operated service to prepare them for privatization."*

It is interesting that he made this observation, because one of Gerald's duties was to organize the shuttle program. He brought in specialists to deal with specific needs. No one had ever taken the shuttle program to such heights before. In addition, he taught some clinics at the veterinary school and Frances taught English as a Second Language.

They became very involved with the students, developing relationships by having them in their home on Sundays for a meal

(Gerald calls Frances the Gourmet Evangelist). This afforded them a wonderful 'one on one' opportunity to share the Gospel. Their results attest to the wisdom of this.

Gerald and Frances reflect on the following event, *"On the flight into Mongolia, we met a young Mongolian man who had been studying in Japan. He said that he does not believe there is a God. However, he is interested to learn more about that possibility. He accepted an invitation to our apartment where we will tell him of this wonderful God who loves him, and we will give him a copy of the Bible."*

A Prayer Letter

We are sitting in a church with nearly a full pew of our young student friends who have decided to follow Jesus. What a joy it is to look at the shining faces, the changed lives, and the smiles filled with hope.

Just over two and one-half years ago, we began to develop relationships with faculty and students of the Mongolian Veterinary Institute. It was a place void of Christian influence. A building crumbling from years of neglect reflected the lives of the inhabitants in a similar state. We would walk down the dark hallways, and teach in rooms spun from another era. How could this ever change? Was there really hope for this archaic system?

Recently a prominent non-believing faculty member approached us with an observation she had made. 'The students you are working with are very different from the others', she said. 'They have high values and they work hard in their studies. These are the leaders in the school and we are so pleased with their fresh attitude.'"

A respected surgeon at the Veterinary Institute recently sent word that he wanted a meeting with us. We always have reservations about this type of request. As I sat around the table with him and other Mongolians, he leaned over and spoke privately. 'I want to go to church with you.' Could they come to our house on Sunday? What a surprise! I had never mentioned the word church to this man. Our lives are often the most important statement that we make in this setting. His children came and now he too is involved in a beginners Bible study and attending our church.

One of our students has just been appointed to the faculty and two others are being groomed to be faculty members after graduation. What an impact they will have on their school. Another is working at the Ministry of Agriculture. Short-term veterinarians are helping to revitalize the school. We see remodeled rooms producing real services with the promise of income production to continue the process. There is a feeling of expectancy that things are getting better."

Shuttles may not result in long-term service, but they always have an impact on the individual. Dr. Bill and Mrs. Carol Deisher served as co-representatives (along with Dr. Bruce Williams) for Illinois. Later, Bill and Carol went on a shuttle to Paraguay.

Dear CVM,

Pinch me! Am I simply having a pleasant dream? Having just returned from a two-week shuttle mission trip to Paraguay and thinking back on what took place, I have that feeling. Did we really:

.....experience that heavy spiritual darkness in places...then fresh winds of the Holy Spirit in the presence of the believers as God's love slipped right past language barriers?

....spay a dog on a kitchen table the first evening for Marciano, an evangelical pastor in a poor section of Asuncion?

....handle those 5 Guarni coins (4 = 1 penny) and think about the widow's mite in Mark 12:42?

....eat all of those different foods with strange sounding names and enjoy it so much?

....repair an umbilical hernia on a heifer and notice she was a little anemic? Blood slides showed the reason why...Babesiosis or Tick Fever.

Lord, thank you so much for what You are doing through CUM and other mission organizations. And for those people who gave up the comforts of home to bring the light of the Good News of Jesus Christ to those living in spiritual darkness."

Bill

Dr. John Fletemeyer of Colorado Springs, Colorado, sold his veterinary practice. He and his wife Elaine sold their home, their cars, and close to half of their belongings and moved to Viet Nam. It was a fulfillment of a lifelong dream by John and Elaine to become missionaries and serve overseas.

John is a 1972 Colorado State University graduate. *"I had always dreamed of helping people through my profession,"* says the soft-spoken redhead. *"I had a solo small animal practice that I really enjoyed for 20 years. I focused on client relations, really listening to the people and taking a genuine interest in their needs. I never advertised, nor were my fees especially low, but I had a very busy, profitable practice."*

During his last six months in practice, John studied with professors at CSU to become current on the latest methods in sheep production. He also attended a small ruminant reproduction seminar in late August of 1994. This was in preparation for working in Bhutan. World Concern had been invited by the Bhutanese government to help start a wool production program as part of a sheep development project. John would be working with them.

Several weeks after John and Elaine moved to temporary quarters and transferred ownership of their practice, the Bhutanese government changed agricultural ministers and they withdrew the offer! John and Elaine, of course, were very disappointed, but after exploring their goals and areas of interest, a new assignment surfaced in Vietnam.

John reflects, *"I have always been intrigued by Asia and Buddhist cultures. We were thrilled with the opportunity to go to Vietnam."*

In Vietnam, World Concern and USAID were involved in a project for displaced children.

"Families are all broken up after a war," explains John. *"Even though the war ended over 20 years before, children were displaced because of the death of a parent, divorce, and abandonment."*

World Concern helped sponsor youths aged 12 to 20 with scholarships to attend vocational school. The school was limited in the topics that were available to study; basic carpentry and motorcycle repair for the boys, and sewing for the girls.

John introduced a new subject—animal husbandry. *"Most families had a pig or water buffalo at home, but they were ignorant as to nutritional requirements, disease prevention and parasite control, as well as how to raise animals for sale."*

John's duties largely involved negotiating with partners in the Vietnamese government to facilitate the hiring of local veterinarians to teach classes and run demonstration laboratories at the school. He also facilitated the development of a school cattle herd, which the students tended. The herd generated income, which was returned to the scholarship program. Eventually, agricultural practices such as basic gardening and reforestation were incorporated into the curriculum.

After returning to Colorado Springs following his year of service in Vietnam, John became Director of Short Term Shuttles for CVM. He recruited and trained veterinarians for trips overseas and here in the US. The length of these shuttles range from two weeks to three months. Some shuttle participants come back and decide to serve long-term.

Does John believe he really helped the people of Vietnam?

"It is relationship building, becoming a friend, communication," he says. *"Getting the people to talk with each other, identify their own needs, build their self-esteem. For many years, they thought there was no hope. We are helping people with sustainable development."*

For John, his religious faith is of paramount importance. *"We are commanded to love our neighbor as ourselves, so we look on their things as just as important as our things,"* he says earnestly. *"We don't just go out and tell people about Jesus Christ, that's only half of it. We also must do something for the people. The service is the message."* He continues with growing passion, *"We have trained ourselves (as veterinarians) to be workaholics, often to the detriment of our own personal lives. It's almost as if we are on autopilot! Someone needs to grab the steering wheel, put a little crack in the window, and say, 'Hey, there is something else!' We are blessed to have this profession as a way to serve God."*

Deborah Storie is an Australian veterinarian who worked in Afghanistan. Though she was primarily funded by TEAR Fund (Australia), CVM provided some of her support. She was considered a CVM affiliate. She lived in the remote village of Qeshlawqe Bekh. She trained two Afghan co-workers, Ehsan and Sabera, to help her. They helped her to identify the needs of the villagers. All worked together to meet those needs.

Deborah describes a revealing interview:

"Why do you think so many children die here?"

"Not many children die. It is the chickens that die. You should stop our chickens from dying."

"You say not many children die. Last Thursday Chindah died, the day before Khasa's son died, then there was that small baby down at the end of the village, and the representative's daughter who had diarrhea, and little Abdul, and what about Zerabai's grandchild they fed goat's milk?"

"I did not say no children died. Of course they die. They are sick all the time."

"Do you know, that in all my life in my country I only knew four children who died, and two of those died before they were born."

(No answer)

"Why do you think children get sick in this village?"

"We have no good medicine."

"Do you need medicine if you don't get sick?"

"No, but all children get sick. If the doctor is intelligent, and the injections good, they get better. Pakistani medicine is no good. You have good medicine you bought overseas."

"I buy medicine in the bazaar, just like you do. Do you know that, apart from vaccines, I cannot remember myself, my brothers or my sister ever being injected."

"Don't you have doctors in your country? Don't you have medicine?"

"Yes, we have doctors, we have medicine. My mother was a doctor. She knew we did not need injections when we got sick so she did not give them to us. She vaccinated us so we would be sick less often."

"We do not vaccinate our children."

"Why not?"

"It makes them cry."

"Do you know what measles are?"

"Oh yes! Two of my children died of measles, one son and one daughter."

You can see what a frustrating process this can be.

In addition to dealing with situations like the one in her letter, it actually was dangerous serving in Afghanistan, because of the continuing civil war raging there. Deborah amazed me with her patience, perseverance, and courage. She, like many others, gives of herself no matter what the cost!

A supporter once paraphrased his pastor, saying that we can be "Disciples of Christ, skillfully disguised as veterinarians."

CVM 1994 Annual Meeting
San Francisco, California

This meeting is dedicated to all those who, through the veterinary profession and their personal lives, function as 'Disciples of Christ;' those who see their entire lives as opportunities for ministry.

–There are people who leave behind the familiar and for several weeks or months or years, show Christ's love to people far away.

–There are people who, through diligent prayer, fight the spiritual battles of this ministry.

–Academicians who take valuable time to support and encourage students so that they can be disciples now and in the future.

–Employers and employees who follow God's principles in a take-all-you-can business climate.

–Volunteers who haul and set up displays, smile, and shake hundreds of hands so that CVM's story can be told.
–Friends and family members whose letters, packages, and prayers bring cheer to fieldworkers.
–People who have seen the need of the elderly, sick, and homeless and have worked to make a difference in their lives.
–Christian veterinarians, students, technicians and many others contribute to this dynamic ministry which is CVM."

Dr. Gary Baker opened the meeting with devotions. Dr. Susan Stewart and Dr. Mark Bounds told of the work in Bolivia. Dr. Keith Flanagan described the work in Haiti. Dr. Patrick and Mrs. Wendy Smith related their upcoming plans for Myanmar. Shuttle talk included Dr. Lloyd Lauerman, about Mongolia; Hailu Kinde, about Ethiopia; and the group shuttle by Dr. Gerry and Mrs. Myrna Walker to Bolivia. Dr. Rick Marshall gave an interesting and informative talk—'Sharing Christ Through His Creation.'

CHAPTER 21

A Time to Weep
and a Time to Laugh

Tina and I drove down from Ocilla, on Sunday morning, to Tallahassee, FL. We were going to attend the commissioning service of Dr. Ivan and Mary Barineau, who were going to work in Haiti. We were delighted to see them again, and to participate in the service. Ivan is a University of Georgia graduate. We had come to know and appreciate them since they stayed with us in Seattle while in orientation for overseas service. They are a delightful Christian couple. After the service, we had an opportunity to have lunch with their family and friends.

During the Barineaus' first term, they were involved with an ECHO project in Southern Haiti. They supervised the implementation of health classes in 80 churches and the building of latrines and water cisterns in 20 schools. Haiti has never been an easy place to travel, but with Ivan's description you can feel the aches.

A Prayer Letter

"We drove the 'machine rouge' (Ivan's red truck) as far as we could, parked it under a Mango tree and tackled the slope on foot. Our destination lay across a steep ravine and up the patchwork hillside that stretched in front of us. The walk was long and tiring. We took a few shortcuts through people's backyards-permitted as long as you are courteous and deliver the proper greeting. We had to cross a stream but we made a bridge of stones. My companions

Saintales and Ludger hopped across-no problem. Not only did I fall in the stream but I sprawled out like I was going for a swim. My companions rushed back to rescue me but to lessen the embarrassment just a little, I managed to struggle out on my own!"

During their second term, Ivan and Mary worked in the north of Haiti but still with one foot in the south. One of the projects was Improved Goat Production. Ivan explains,

A Prayer Letter

"Last week, Mary and I returned to Les Cayes along with a tank of liquid nitrogen, thirty straws of goat semen and related insemination equipment, to fulfill an earlier promise. We had been unable to obtain enough breeding bucks to meet all the needs. I envisioned that deficiency to be met by the importation of AI (artificial insemination) technology."

"The theory seemed practical enough, after the Lord provided such money for basic equipment, a start up supply of semen, and a system to import the all-important refrigerant-liquid nitrogen from the States. The most important training for me was to learn the technique so that I could teach it to Haitian vet techs. My nagging doubts were answered, I was able to find enough non-pregnant goats locally to enable me to do this. The process described to synchronize the breedings worked to a 't' and we had an enthusiastic group of students awaiting us. The only fly in the ointment was rain."

At first it sprinkled. The first inseminations went well. Then the sprinkle demanded more respect. We pulled out the tarp and huddled under it-goats, students, teacher, and equipment, all seeking that little dry spot. Then it rained! I don't mean it rained, I mean IT RAINED!

I could not make myself heard over it. It ran down all the secret dry places on my partially dry body. It was miserable. It was hopeless to continue. People were more interested in closing toward the center of the tarp than learning the technique, and I couldn't blame them. There was no other shelter in sight so we closed up shop, loaded both front and back of the truck with students and headed back to town, all of us drenched to the bone.

In spite of the rain-shortened practice, all considered the seminar a resounding success. The technology is fresh, but alive in the hands of a small Haitian group. Others will learn from them. People who had never before had access to improved genetics will now have that access. It's a start!"

We cannot depart without a comment from Mary.

"We've not had much time to do 'porch-sitting' lately-one of our favorite activities in Haiti. Our little apartment has a very narrow balcony facing the National Road. We are about 75 yards off the road, close enough to watch but not so close that we have to smile or wave. It is great fun sitting with my best friend, Ivan, in the late afternoon (before mosquitoes arrive in armed battalion) and watching Haiti go by. I never tire of the sights, noises, laughter, bleating of animals, back firing of very old and out-of-shape trucks and cars, the 'unusual' sights in front of us and for wondering what's happening at home! We would love to show you how to 'porch-sit' in Haiti."

On January 5th, a truly great lady-Jo Anne Whitney went to be with the Lord. She was married to Clyde. They had three sons, John, Jim and Joel, and one daughter, Kathy. She was organist for the Maplewood Presbyterian Church and had served in that capacity for 37 years.

Jo Anne was a very talented Christian lady, having great musical and writing skills. She used these God-given talents in service to the Lord's work, in her job, church and home. The thing that impressed me most about Jo Anne was that she never compromised her principles either in her writing or in her personal conduct.

For several years she was the writer for the CVM newsletter. She really believed in the work of CVM. Her writings revealed that love. Jo Anne made a trip to visit project sites in Haiti when the pig re-population program was in high gear. She really seemed to get a kick out of donning coveralls and visiting inside farrowing houses to get a first hand look at the baby pigs that later would be distributed to the peasant farmers of Haiti. She made a very significant contribution to the ministry.

On January 14th, 1995, Canada held its first board meeting of the newly formed CVMC, with a teleconference. Those participating were Dr. Conrad Van Dijk, Dr. Ron Downey, Dr. Gary Partlow, Dr. Don Barnum, Dr. Ed Neufeld, Dr. Wally Kononoff, Dr. Murray Gordon, Dr. Laslo De Roth, Dr. Patty Sharko and student Angie Bosman. A vision and mission statement was adopted that parallels that of CVM U.S. Registration was filed for with the Council for Charitable Contributions. In addition, the Board made plans to have a presence at both the Ontario meeting in February and the CVMA meeting in July.

The U.S.-CVM Board met in Seattle, January 26-28, 1995. All board members were in attendance but one. Also, Fred Gregory, the Director of World Concern attended but announced his retirement. Dan Paulo, chairman, presided. The status of the board was upgraded to be an active Board of Directors of CVM. There was affirmation by World Concern and CVM to the agreement known as the Memorandum of Understanding (MOU) concerning that relationship. It was also agreed that CVM would have the freedom to look for partnerships outside the WC relationship. Both groups came away from the meeting feeling that it was a mutually beneficial agreement.

Dr. Jerry Burch, Tennessee, was the incoming board chairman. Jerry knows better than anyone I have ever seen, how to cut through the maze and get to the nitty gritty. He is an individual who gives very generously of his time, talents and resources to the Lord's ministry whether it be with CVM, his church or his community. Jerry, when serving as state representative, divided the state into districts and identified a chairman in each. Later, as region representative, he developed a routine for visiting the state and school representatives by phone or mail. He was a very effective regional representative.

Jerry has a wonderful help meet Judy, and two children Emily and Wade, who honor their parents with their own Christian witness. This family has demonstrated to me that amid the hustle and bustle of life a person can be a witness through their living and their giving. I am reminded of that saying "I would rather see a sermon than to hear one."

Dr. Janice Fuquay, a 1989 graduate of Oregon State, began her service by attending language school in Bolivia, prior to going to the Altiplana area of Peru. Her focus of work was with local communities at the grass roots level, assisting them in identifying and solving their own problems. One objective was the improved production and marketing of livestock products that would in turn improve family nutrition and income. One built in challenge was to get women to be active participants in the program.

Janice also took on a commendable second challenge, to make a joint working project with both the Catholic and Protestant groups. It was a first in the community. Added to this, was the fact, that Peru had been devastated, by the Maoist terrorists. The people had suffered greatly at the hands of the terrorists. Only a deteriorating economic and political situation remained. Alpacas had been replaced by sheep and cattle, which proved to be inappropriate for the harsh climate. The Aymara Indians that occupied this area were estranged from the mainstream of society.

Janice writes of working with two Aymara men, Eosebio and Teodora.

A Prayer Letter

"They both volunteer their time to work with the Agricultural/ Animal committee of their church. They are called animal health promoters, and make themselves available to help others in their communities with technical advice about raising animals. They give vaccines, vitamin injections, and de-wormers, only charging the cost of the medicine. They give advice on better management practices to improve production and raise healthier animals. Why have they made this commitment to serving others and bettering their communities? They respond, that it is the love of Christ in their lives that enables them to do this."

Of a specific member of the ALPACA project, named Reuben, Janice writes,

A Prayer Letter

"He is about 5 feet tall, very thin, and has an infectious smile that never fails to brighten my day. I've often thought that the strong altiplano winds would just pick him up and carry him away. At Easter time, a medical team from the Pacific Northwest came to Peru. When asked by one of the tall and husky built translators why he wanted a consultation with one of the doctors, Reuben replied, 'I want to be tall and fat like you'."

Reuben is a husband and father of three young children living on the Llave Peninsula. (The peninsula is a large section of land that juts into Lake Titicaca, a large lake, with an elevation of 12,500 feet on the high plains of the Peruvian Andes Mountains). He is a subsistence farmer, who makes his living from the crops and animals that he can raise on his land. The family lives in an adobe house, with access to well water. Just recently electricity arrived in their village. Reuben raises cattle, sheep, pigs, burros, barley, potatoes and beans.

As a member of the training team, Reuben learns how to better raise animals. He also teaches people in remote areas. To enable him to do this, he has to learn other things involving social issues, like; how to work together, how to communicate, resolve conflicts and solve problems, and to encourage others. Reuben describes his wife's response when he first came home and began teaching some of the new ideas to the family. 'She was wary at first about the new way to look at things, but when she realized how much it could help their family, she was enthusiastic about learning more'. Reuben is teaching his family about how to communicate better among themselves. He is teaching them how to use constructive criticism and positive feedback to help each other improve themselves in all aspects of their lives. This is unusual in the Aymara culture, where destructive criticism behind one's back is more the norm. Especially remarkable, is the fact that in the traditionally male dominated culture, is the permission Reuben has asked his wife to speak and communicate freely, and offer him feedback and constructive advice on how his actions are affecting his own personal development, his relationship with God, and the lives of his family.

Four people who have played an enormous role in the success of CVM but who are not widely known, are the mailroom ladies. Betty Ellis, Lucille Jones and Dolly Hansen began working for World Concern as switchboard operators in 1981. Three years later they moved to the mailroom and began to handle CVM's mail. Gwen Murray was looking for a part-time job after her retirement. On the recommendation of her friend Betty, she joined the team in September of 1994. Since that time June Anderson has joined the group.

What makes these ladies so special is their commitment to their work as service to the Lord. Others may see that they stuff envelopes, but may not recognize the dedication and personal interest that they bring to their work. All of them take prayer letters home so that they can read about the field workers and the work of their ministries. Prayer is an important part of their ministry. The mailroom ladies pray over each mailing as it goes out. They pray for the writers, the deliverers and the recipients of their mail. Isn't CVM blessed to have such dedicated workers for the Lord?

Dr. Brad Frye, a graduate of Colorado State in 1989 and his wife Angela arrived in Uganda with their family, Zeb, Josiah, and Rayni, in April, of 1995. They began their work in Soroti, working on an oxen-restocking project with the Teso people. Years of civil strife and cattle rustling had removed as much as 95% of the oxen from that region of Uganda. These oxen were critical to the people for plowing the fields to produce their crops. Over 600,000 people in this region are dependent on agriculture for their livelihood.

Karamoja is the region where Brad worked. His description of the situation follows,

---

A Prayer Letter

"It is inhabited by the Karamajong, the nomadic tribe that are kin to the Teso but have not gotten along well. The tribal wars had devastated the oxen. The land is vast and rolling with bushes and trees spread across the landscape. In some areas the land is dotted with gardens of 2-3 acres. However, where there is no garden, the grass stands taller than your head. This vast cattle land is drastically underutilized. Soon the area will start to see thousands of cattle though, as the Karamajong start to move south in search of water and feed as the dry season approaches. Most of the tall grass will disappear, but not from grazing but from fire! If, it could be harvested by animals, the people would be better off, the soil would be better off, and so would the wildlife."

The Fryes had shuttles visit them while they were in Soroti. One such student shuttle comments,

---

"My name is Jessica Englund, and I have been with the Fryes and Val Shean through CVM for almost six months. I graduated from college last May. I had long ago decided that I would take some time off, and from a brief trip to Kenya, I felt a strong pull to actually live and work here. Being in the bush without many of the material comforts of home seems to make our human weaknesses more visible. Consequently we are forced to turn to God for strength, mercy, insight and yes, patience, with a culture that is not our own. I realize more each day that true home does not indicate a geographical area but is rather in His presence. And through that wonderful gift I have relished the chance to be at home in Africa."

Angela's parents from New Zealand visited. Her dad wrote,

A Prayer Letter

"It is really an education to see how the simple things in life mean so much to the people of Uganda. They are poor. The wage for a day's work is about $1 dollar U.S. Their work is hard, they have to work their land by hand and plant their crops. The soil is very fertile and grows things well. Before Amin's reign of terror they had cattle for plowing and milking and some meat. One pair of oxen can help four families. The work that Brad is doing to help these people with their oxen is really worthwhile."

Perhaps Brad and Angela's greatest work is with kids. Let them explain,

A Prayer Letter

"There are about 45 boys (aged 10-16) that have attended Bible club over the last 6 months. The number has grown from 6 in our first meeting to an average of about 25 regular attendees. It has been encouraging to see the dedication of some of the boys in completing their lessons and memorizing their verses. A number of them have prayed to receive the Lord as their Savior. One young seventeen year old wrote on his lesson 'after I read the lesson I found I was following the broad road so I went to a silent place and took Jesus as my Savior. From now and forever I am saved.'"

The 15th annual meeting was in Pittsburgh. Dr. Dan Paulo opened with devotions. It was a special time as the dean of our overseas delegation, Dr. Peter and Mary Quesenberry, gave the program. This young, committed, and dedicated couple began their work in 1980 at the Rural Development Training Center (RDTC) living in the village of Lamachur, on the edge of Pokhara, Nepal.

Dr Wendel Koenig and wife, Sandi, told of the group shuttle to Nepal, consisting of Dr. Frank Jordan, Dr. Keith Stewart and Dr. Jerry Walker and his wife Myrna.

"The group saw many aspects of development work in Nepal, including animal healthcare, human health care and education. Though it was a busy schedule no one complained. They were trying to keep pace with 82 year old Dr. Jordan!"

They attended a worship service at Lamachur. Dr. Koenig wrote,

"We had a special reason for being there. Our church members of St. James U.C.C. in Limerick, Pennsylvania, had formed a bond with this church, because we helped with their building fund."

The day seemed to concentrate on work in Nepal. Dr. Karen and Ron Stoufer spoke of their work at Pokhara at the Rural Development Training Center (RDTC). Later, they moved to the very remote region of Okhalhunga, where Karen would work with Non Governmental Organizations (NGO's) in rural villages. Ron would help with the water systems. Workers to be, Dr. Bob and Karen Hott, Michigan, revealed their plans to begin work in Nepal soon. Dr John Gunther talked about his shuttle to Bolivia. Afterwards, a fellowship meal was enjoyed by all at the First Presbyterian Church.

<hr />

Dr. John Schneller, Wisconsin, went on his second shuttle to Bolivia. He since has completed a couple of them taking his daughter, Claire, with him the last time. John's expertise is in embryo transfer and artificial insemination. He has done some outstanding work in this area. His repeated shuttles to Bolivia have allowed him to gain knowledge about the people and the conditions to make his short-term work more effective. He especially enjoyed working with Jim Nash, who has expertise in this type of work also. Jim was able to arrange things before John arrived, enabling them to accomplish more.

<hr />

In late June, Dr. Glenn Hurley and his wife Lois, from Iowa, traveled to Kenya for a three-month shuttle. They were not new to service overseas, having served in Guatemala and Morocco. Kenya had suffered a severe drought, which devastated many of the animals that the tribes people depended on for their living. Famine was becoming widespread. World Concern/CVM began a project to purchase and distribute 2,500 young female goats to 500 destitute Maasai families. It was a large undertaking, covering an area that extended over 14,400 square miles. It was to be achieved in three months. They exceeded this goal by distributing 3,288 goats to 633 recipients.

One significant milestone was reached this fiscal year. The total CVM budget reached a million dollars for the first time. It was the growth in deputation giving (individuals or churches supporting specific fieldworkers) that produced this increase. Giving to the CVM general fund continued to increase at a modest rate, as it has done since the inception of CVM. It was the giving to individual workers that accounted for much of the budget. This is healthy because this type of giving is usually very consistent and faithful. The downside is when the CVM worker comes off the field. Gifts normally given in support of that individual usually dissipate. Thus, a long-term support base is not being built.

1992 graduates of the University of Missouri Veterinary School, Drs. Chuck and Lisa Dodd, along with their children, Caleb and Hannah, arrived in the strife torn country of Rwanda. It is a scene of great desolation Chuck describes:

A Prayer Letter

"Sheltered in solemn orphanages in Rwanda are children who mourn. Their dark eyes are dull and tired. Their spirits lie broken. They seldom play, their smiles and laughter have been forgotten and replaced by blank stares. They were forced to play a role they did not want—witnesses to the worst of human nature, a nightmare of ruthless slaughter that is beyond our comprehension."

"Last year, on the eve of power sharing between the Hutus and the Tutsis in the Rwandan government, the Hutus brutally began a planned extermination of Rwandans who were Tutsi, of mixed Tutsi-Hutu descent, or who sympathized with the Tutis. Men, women and children were gathered into schools, churches, and other buildings and murdered. Of an original 7 million people in Rwanda, more than 1 million people were killed, 2.2 million people became refugees, and more than 130,000 children were orphaned."

Chuck and Lisa were following up on a shuttle effort by Dr. James Eubanks, Kansas, to help with a poultry shuttle that needed to be extended into long-term project. They began to lead a project to restock laying poultry, milk goats, and rabbits. The animals and training associated with this, was for the benefit of the Unaccompanied Children Centers, to improve nutrition for the children.

The Dodds served in Rwanda until it became an unsafe place for their family to live. After a furlough, the Dodds relocated in Tanzania to work with the Maasai people. They settled in Gelai Meru-Goi, in the northern part of Tanzania. They wrote,

A Prayer Letter

"We now contemplate our role in helping the Maasai. We realize our work is not the end, but only the means. Even though we have an unexplainable quenching in our hearts by returning here, we know that in each and every moment we have to ask God to break our hearts for the Maasai. We cannot give them hope of tall grass and sufficient water throughout the year but we can share what will last......Jesus. That is our burden and we thank God for letting us all be a part of it.

It's not often that Tina and I have taken a vacation apart from a CVM function, but this year we did. After all, I had been promising her for a long time. We had never been to Alaska, so we booked a combination tour of land and cruise. We flew to Anchorage, took the train and then the bus, working our way around to the Yukon Territory and then to Juneau to pick up the cruise ship.

Alaska in early September is very beautiful. The hills were alive with a yellow landscape. Even Mount McKinley showed itself in its entirety, an event that occurs a bare 5% of the time or less. We considered ourselves lucky to witness God's wonderful creation in all its splendor. The frosting on the cake was to see a giant bear cavorting around between times of berry picking.

When we arrived in Whitehorse, Yukon Territory, I had a message to call Kit. He gave me the unthinkable news-Mark Bounds' had tragically died in Bolivia, from an apparent allergic reaction. Needless to say, I was shocked, stunned and in a state of unbelief. It was so sudden, and so unexpected. After coming to the true realization of what I was hearing, I began to try and make some plans. I could not change from Whitehorse very well but was able to call the airline and make reservations to fly from Juneau.

It was a sad flight to Seattle, as I thought about Mark. He was so young, and so involved in ministry; a large gentle guy with a heart bigger than his enormous size. He was forty. It is at a time like this that you have to reach way down to find that bedrock of faith, or else it all crumbles. As I look back on my personal relationship with Mark, I would have to say my own faith was definitely bolstered by just knowing him. He exemplified so much of what the Christian faith is about. He did it in such a quiet and unassuming way-the way it should be done. Kit and I attended memorial services for him in Knoxville, Tennessee.

Within a week, we received word that Mike Storer had died. This was not unexpected, because we knew that he had terminal cancer. He had suffered a great deal in his battle against Multiple Myeloma. Even though we knew that his time was limited, it still did not erase the hurt or the realization that the Lord has called him home and we would not fellowship with him again in this world. Once again Kit and I were off, this time to La Jolla, New Mexico where Mike and Debra and family had lived since coming back from Haiti. They had moved there, to begin anew their work with the Navajo people.

The Storer home sat on a ridge on the outskirts of La Jolla, over-looking a beautiful valley. The memorial service took place in the pasture behind the house. It was quite touching, as the Navajos and Mike's family held a loving service for him. Afterwards Debra, Jason, Kevi and Jessica scattered his ashes in the valley.

Debra wrote,

> *"Mike has been my faithful friend for the past 29 years. he has taught me much about God, life, veterinary medicine, steadfastness and endurance. These last two years of suffering made these attributes even more evident. The Lord blessed us with precious, hilarious and even deeply sad moments-we treasure them all. His love for Kevi, Jason, Jessa and me never faltered. May we carry such a rich heritage."*

CHAPTER 22

Milestones

The CVM Board meeting was hosted by Dr.Floyd Jones and his wife Delores, in Bryan, Texas, January 25-29, 1996. Members stepping down from Board duties were Dr. Floyd Jones, Texas, Dr. Fred Bendick, Missouri, and Dr. Tim Blair, Wisconsin. New members welcomed to the board were Dr.George Moore, Texas, Dr. Karen Studemann, Illinois and Dr. Gerald Walker, California.

The board spent a busy three days working on issues related to CVM structure and organization, finances and budget. They discussed the shuttle program and CVM's presence at professional meetings. Several workshops were held. One was conducted by, Dr. Wendell Cantrell, who was CVM's East Africa Coordinator. Dr. Dean Gauge of Texas A&M presented a special leadership seminar.

Since we know that all work and no play makes Jack a dull boy, the board took full advantage of the hospitality of Dr. and Mrs. Bobby Cargyle, who hosted an authentic Texas barbecue. In addition, there was a fish fry and concert by the Senior Men's class of the Central Baptist Church. This class had been supporting CVM for many months through the encouragement of Dr. Floyd Jones.

Dr. Bob Beede was the incoming chairman of the board. Bob committed an unusual amount of time to that job. One of the major contributions he made during his term was the establishment of the various committees of the board. He encouraged members to read and learn about the function of the board and how they could best fill their role as a board member. Bob spent a great deal of time in Seattle helping Kit and me with that.

I first met Bob and his wife Susan in Portland in 1989 at the AVMA meeting there. He has been a great encouragement to me.

Bob also served on a shuttle to Peru and has been very supportive of Janice Fuquay in her work there. Bob is writing the book, <u>Raising Healthy Horses,</u> for CVM. He has meant much to the success of CVM's ministry.

❧

Shuttles have a habit of breaking records in many different ways but Diane wrote of one,

---

"If tag-team deworming ever becomes an Olympic event, CVM will send Drs. Lee Bregitzer and Tom Yost. On a recent trip to Kenya, these two veterinarians set a new CVM shuttle record. In just five days, they treated more than 13,000 animals! Over 9,000 sheep and goats and more than 3,000 cattle were dewormed and treated for disease, malnutrition, and drought stress.

A runner went from village to village, notifying everyone of the upcoming clinics. The Maasai set up five treatment points over five days. They built holding pens from thorny bushes and stanchions for restraint. Then, each morning, herders came with their animals until the air was filled with the dust of thousands of cattle, sheep and goats."

This was Lee and Tom's third shuttle to Maasailand. He comments,

"The Maasai know us, they trust us, and they look forward to our coming." He encourages other veterinarians to have the shuttle experience. "You just need to do it. You'll meet some wonderful people with a tremendous need for what we have to offer. Your business will be there when you get back. And should you think that only large-animal practitioners can be effective in Africa, Lee reminds us, 'I've been a dog doctor for 27 years.'"

❧

Dr Bob Hott is a 1984 graduate of the University of Illinois. He and his wife Karen and three children Genevieve, Christopher and Elsbeth live in Plymouth, Michigan. Bob had conducted a mixed practice for a while, later bowing to the demographics of the times, and going over to a small animal clinic. His wife Karen came from missionary parents and grew up in Nigeria.

When they came through orientation I thought; Bob has come from a fairly sophisticated practice, he relies on laboratory procedures, he is going to a most unsophisticated area of the world, to teach the very basics to those with little formal education. He will have a tough time adjusting. And Karen will have no problem. It turned out to be the opposite. It is difficult to predict the individual reaction to culture shock.

As I listened to them give their presentation at the AVMA meeting in Baltimore, I have never been more proud than when Karen gave a candid view of her struggles to live in Nepal. It was most heartwarming and most reassuring. It dealt with how God had seen her and the family through this time. There were few dry eyes in the audience. I know mine were not.

The Hotts served at the Rural Development Center in Pokhara. Dr. Hott served as a technical advisor to the Animal Health Worker Training Program. Bob made significant contributions through his work to develop testing models to register village animal health workers with the government of Nepal. The Hott family also served in the local Nepali church in ministry and outreach.

I quote Bob about this thought-provoking incident that happened in Nepal. *"I was asked by a Hindu co-worker, 'What advantages would there be for me if I became a Christian?' We talked for a long time, but it bothered me that I had no quick answer for him. Shortly afterwards my dad sent me a letter that contained four gifts that are ours as members of God's family through Jesus Christ. I committed them to memory so I can always have a ready answer to my friend's question. Maybe you could memorize them too!*

1. We're delivered from Satan's kingdom. Colossians 1:13-14.
2. The debt for our sin is paid in full. Colossians 2:13-14.
3. We have peace with God. Romans 5:1.
4. We have a home in heaven. John 14:1-3.

Bob and Karen came back after their first term to resettle in Plymouth. Bob still wanted to be involved with CVM. Thus was born the idea of an area representative. Bob serves in that role in the midwestern United States. His personality fits this role well, as he is outgoing and relates well to people, especially the students at the veterinary schools. He is very competent in computer skills and has earned the respected title of 'Techno Bob.' I frequently use him as my computer consultant. He is always obliging.

Dr. Val Shean, was an Oregon State graduate in 1988. She had worked in Uganda, at the village level, with Mission Moving Mountains (MMM) for a term. She had originally considered service with CVM, and since being on the field she'd had contact with some of our field workers. She felt that in professional missions CVM might be more relevant to what she was doing in the field. So at the end of her first term with MMM she asked to go with CVM.

Over the years I have really enjoyed interviewing candidates. When I see these dedicated men and women offering their talents in service to the Lord, it makes me want to do more. Too, I have learned much more about myself as they tell of their pilgrimage in faith. To tell you the truth, I think I would have had a hard time making the cut. I told Val after the interview that my only problem with her was she seemed to me to be a "too perfect" candidate. She had demonstrated exemplary service.

She describes her feelings after returning to the field.

A Prayer Letter

"Since I've been back and observed the phasing out of MMM projects, I've seen some really exciting things happen in the lives and hearts of local leaders. They are more attentive to our teachings and much more reliant on God to work in and through them. The African ladies were so excited about baking bread in their own homes (over an open fire) that they kept mixing and stirring and baking from 1:00 PM to 10:00PM that night! One of the ladies stood up and gave a spontaneous message that she felt God was saying to them. She explained how Jesus was actually the true Bread of Life. The loaves they were cooking would be gone the next day but only by partaking of the true bread would we be satisfied forever.

When I think of leaving Kapchorwa, my heart cries out to God. Only because I have seen His love pour out all over me and sensed an ocean of His peace surrounding me, have I been able to turn and face a new direction. I love the people and the work of Kapchorwa, but the work is God's work and through Him it will thrive. Meanwhile, I'm transitioning into a new ministry in Soroti. Although the dusty bombed-out town doesn't have much aesthetic appeal, the people are very energetic and are really seeking to see how God can uplift their poverty-stricken lives. I am praying for flowers to bloom in their desert."

We worry about all our workers, for their health and for their safety, but our single women serving on the mission field seem particularly vulnerable. However, by the grace of God, they have come through with flying colors. Let Val tell you of one such incident, but I must warn you; read at your own risk!

A Prayer Letter

"It was a sunny, peaceful day on the brushy rolling hills of Karamoja. Four in the afternoon. Our veterinary seminar for the non-literate herders had been a big success, despite our fears that these warrior-herdsmen may not want to learn how to draw pictures of cows and chickens! (They cannot write, therefore all teaching is done pictorially, with each person drawing a diagnostic picture book for themselves, for future reference.) The Karamojong tribe are in neighboring Soroti, where I live, but there has been aggressive cattle rustling throughout the region. I have felt that the Lord may some day use veterinary medicine as a way to reconcile the Karamojong herders to the other tribes, as well as to Himself.

As we were driving back from the seminar, many thoughts and prayers were going through my mind. I asked the Lord to help me understand the situation better, to help me know how to identify with the people in the area so that I could be more useful to Him.

We came around a corner and over a crest in the road. I was shortly to experience what life is like, living with the Karamojong as neighbors.

At first, I only saw two of them, as they walked across the road. They often carry machine guns, so the sight of the AK 47's didn't really alarm me that much. Then the first one pivoted towards the truck. The man in the passenger's seat shouted, 'NO, NO, Stop, Stop!!!' He opened the door as if to jump out. I was still going 40 mph, and stopping on a loose gravel road takes some distance. Suddenly, I heard the shots, Te,te-te-te-te! Smoke and flashes of light could be seen as we all stared down the barrel of his machine gun, pointed at our windshield. Slamming on the brakes, I skidded to within 30 yards of the two, armed warriors. All of us were crouched down below the level of the dashboard.

From the back seat, one passenger shouted frantically 'Reverse, Reverse, they are coming from all sides, there are many of them!' Peeking out the side window, the full impact of the ambush hit me when I saw 10 more crouched warriors jumping up from their hiding places in the tall grass, running towards our pickup, swinging their AK 47's from side to side as they bounded over the bushes. The two men in front were also jogging towards us. Both were wearing Khaki brown shirts and a blanket draped over their shoulders. Nobody really likes to wear pants in Karamoja villages.

Milliseconds later, after shooting a desperate flare of prayer up to God, I crammed the gears into reverse and spun out backwards as fast as that little truck would go. The spitting gravel caused the two warriors to hesitate just long enough for the truck to get going, but that made them even madder. Firing wildly at us, the whole group began chasing us with their blankets flying away in the wind. High speed reverse down a gravel road has never been a common means of travel for me, but I knew that was our only escape route.

Huddling down between the steering wheel and the rear view mirror, I just kept praying for God to rescue us. But the warriors were getting closer; they wanted to jump onto the side of the vehicle. Just then, we came to a slight incline in the road. As our reverse squealed up the hill, the ambushers slowly started to run out of gas. Their running decreased to an exhausted jog, then they began walking. The hill was making them too tired. As the distance slowly increased, we crested the hill, backed around another corner, then another straight stretch, 'til we knew we were far enough away. I turned the pickup around and zoomed off to the police barracks a few miles away.

Driving along, we all started praising God and thanking Him for His might and protection. Getting out at the police barracks, we checked out the truck. Amazingly, not a single bullet had hit it. Not a single person was injured. We all gathered for a group prayer of thanksgiving, then went off to the barracks with the police."

There are always important milestones in the lives of individuals and organizations. An important one for me was my second heart by-pass operation in April, of 1996. You see, I had four by-passes in 1983. They don't usually last more than 10 years, so I had been having some plaque buildup. Periodic angioplasty and even stents had put off the inevitable. Returning from Seattle, I had an anginal attack on the plane. I wound up at Emory University for my second operation, to redo the four by-passes.

It is most reassuring to have friends praying for us in times like this. I thank the Lord for His provision that gives us intercessory prayer. I thank all my friends for participating in that exercise of love and concern. May the Lord bless you always.

A milestone for CVM occurred when we celebrated the 20th anniversary of its inception. At the suggestion of our able newsletter editor, Diane Marshall, we developed an Anniversary Poster that showed "Christian Veterinary Mission" in 20 languages. We discovered during our research that CVM fieldworkers had actually worked in more than 20 languages.

We acknowledged this in the annual meeting bulletin for July 21, 1996, in Louisville, Kentucky. I wrote,

"We celebrate 20 years of the Lord's work through CVM. It was a step of faith then and it continues to be a walk in faith now. A group of veterinarians gathered to acknowledge Him in meeting the needs of His children. Since that time, there has been an ever increasing stream of veterinarians, students, and technicians, each one using his or her own special gifts and professional skills in a unique way, bringing encouragement, hope and love as revealed through our Lord and Savior Jesus Christ.

Only when we are willing to let Him lead us through His Spirit are we able to discern His will for our lives, grasp the vision for service, and access His power in our witness. My prayer is that CVM will continue to be an instrument of His love and grace, and that more and more veterinarians will accept the challenge to serve Him through their profession—one that offers unique opportunities in meeting the needs of the poor. I thank you for your part in that ministry."

Dr. Jim Rosenberger, Ohio, opened the session with praise, worship and devotions. Dr. John Kruckeberg, Tennessee, sometimes called "Dr Shuttle" because he has participated in so many, spoke of his most recent shuttle. He must have been inspired by his own talk as he went to the Navajo reservation in September, and to Mongolia in October!

Regina Maddox, a student from Mississippi, gave an unusual presentation of her time in Kenya. I was so impressed, not only with her commitment and her video, but the fact that she had invited her parents to attend. I know they had to be extremely proud of her.

A long-term worker, Dr. Don Wilson, challenged the group to discuss the difficult issues fieldworkers face. They include; appropriate training methods, projects that take workers away from their families for long periods, and what to do when one spouse feels called to overseas missions and the other does not.

Dr. Fred Van Gorkom told of his family's long term commitment to the Bunna people in Southwestern Ethiopia. *"Don't think I am anybody special. If God calls you to missions, you could do this too."* (We at CVM think he and all the rest of our workers are pretty special)

Dr. Wendell Cantrell gave a presentation called "The Balanced Professional." It has been used many times since, in presentations to veterinarians, students, and technicians. It seems to strike a sensitive chord in the profession.

Since the AVMA family night fell on Sunday night we did not have a special fellowship meal for CVM but rather participated with the national group.

Dr Bob Beede, Idaho, Board Chairman, presided over the CVM Executive Committee meeting. He began with a devotion quoting an Olympics coach when interviewed who stated, 'I did not look so much for ability but for those who are coach-able.' Each of us, have gifts to use in His work and we have a training manual in His Word.

Bob began to encourage the board to learn more about what the role of a CVM Board Member should be. He bought and gave to each board member one of the books from the Non Profit Board Series. He encouraged them to read and to learn what a non-profit board should look like. He challenged them to learn what their specific tasks were, and how they could contribute to the success of the ministry. He emphasized the fact that CVM was a relationship based organization and that needed to continue.

Dr Conrad Van Dijk, wrote,

"Praise the Lord for the good news. On March 26, 1996, Christian Veterinary Mission of Canada was officially notified by Revenue Canada that we are registered as a charitable organization because CVMC meets the requirements of subsection q49.1 (1) of the Income Tax Act."

Dr. Patrick M. Smith, Michigan State University, 1982, accepted an invitation to be a child of God and follower of Jesus Christ from a Ugandan Bishop when he attended a 'Renewal in Missions' conference in 1984. Patrick's faith was strengthened by reading Christy Wilson's book 'Tentmakers'. Responding to this personal challenge, Patrick attended "Urbana 1984". This added nurture to a seedling that had sprouted in Patrick's heart for overseas service.

After two years of prayer, Patrick opened his church bulletin to read from an insert called, "Have a Good Day", introducing Leroy Dorminy and CVM. It was the fleece he had been searching for. Patrick attended the annual AVMA meeting. There he met CVM missionary, Rod Frank and I, and a student who had made a shuttle to see Peter Quesenberry and his work in Nepal. All of these events whetted his appetite for mission service.

In the fall of 1986, Patrick went on a shuttle trip with Dr. Bill Hager to Haiti. He spent time there with Dr. Brian and Mrs. Karen Kerstin. During this shuttle, he received confirmation for long-term service. At that time CVM had no funded positions for long term. We introduced him to, 'Missions to Unreached Peoples,' also based in Seattle. He went to Irian Jaya, Indonesia in 1988. It was there that he met Wendy, his future wife.

In Irian Jaya, Patrick trained village animal health workers and did community development. He continued to receive supplies and support from CVM. He hosted two CVM shuttle vets, Dr. Don Larson, Minnesota and Dr. Roger Chong, Australia. After five years in Indonesia, Patrick and Wendy took a furlough in 1993. They were invited to join the CVM team.

When his term of service was up, Patrick and Wendy returned to the United States, where he made application to serve with CVM. In the meantime, Patrick enrolled at University of California at Davis, and pursued a Master's Degree in Preventive Veterinary Medicine. As part of his Master's program, Patrick designed and developed a comic book style instructional manual. The book taught fundamental lessons on germ theory, calf husbandry, and calf health care. Illustrations are by Dr. Todd Cooney, Indiana, and as usual, they are terrific. The booklet was translated into Spanish. I thought it was outstanding.

Since World Concern was not working in Indonesia at the time, Patrick and CVM made a decision to go to Myanmar (formerly Burma). The Smith family had now grown to four, Michael-Patrick was 2, and Timmy was 8 months. After a few departure dates and some difficulty, including illness, Patrick and his family finally arrived in Myanmar in Aug 1996. Their mission was short lived. The difficulties and lack of support there became too much. After 5 months, they returned home. They describe it as follows,

"It was like being in a battle and getting shot. When you are wounded, you return home to recover. Praise God for the excellent 'first aid' we received at Link Care. The couple of months we spent in the restoration and personal growth for pastors and missionaries was a soothing balm and invigorating tonic.

'Forget the former things, we do not dwell on the past'. Isaiah 43:18-19. We made the decision to settle down in Fresno. Our resettlement proceeded rapidly and marvelously. The changes, adjustments, and decision making, seemed overwhelming at times. Through all the

tumult of transition we have experienced the love of God in the body of Christ. We know the love of our family, church, and CVM." Patrick has just begun a house-call practice in Fresno.

None of us escape difficult times. It is then, that we grow. Some of us can't quite face up to it. Patrick and Wendy used it as a wake-up call to adjust their course, and sail full steam ahead, on the right course God has called them to. Experience is a painful teacher and sometimes the tuition is quite high but it can be a life changing experience for good! We thank Patrick and Wendy for the ministry they have had through CVM. We thank the Lord that they are doing well and are still excited about being involved in future ministry.

<hr/>

It was in San Antonio at the 1990 AVMA meeting that I first met Dr. Jim Nash, Virginia. He was relatively new in his Christian walk and, as is typical, was showing the excitement that sometimes we "older Christians" lose. He was eager to be involved in ministry and was well qualified professionally. His pastor said that Jim was probably one of the most spiritual members of his church. Jim had struggled with a problem prior to accepting Christ. During this time he lost his family and lucrative practice. Now things were different! He had made that crucial decision that would head him in the right direction.

Jim had a support group of Christian men who were mentoring him. Overseas ministry had to be put off for a while. His time was used for 'growing in the Lord' He distanced himself from those things of the past. Jim eventually did go to Zaire, with CVM, on a shuttle. The tides of civil strife there thwarted his efforts.

Jim wound up in Kenya, working with World Vision. He became sick but decided to stay in Kenya, only to became very ill, even close to death. After emergency surgery he was able to return to the U.S. and live with his mother in Florida while recuperating. Eventually he returned to veterinary practice in Alabama.

Jim met a lovely Christian lady, Randy Friese, and the two later married. They jointly began to other explore avenues of service with CVM. Soon a decision was made for them to serve in Bolivia. Jim picks it up from there.

"We are in our final days of Spanish school here in Guatemala and are awaiting the next step. Are we fluent in Spanish? No. Are we able to speak Spanish? Yes. Now we know more study will be necessary for us if we want to be able to communicate on the speaking level in order to be effective communicators in our work."

Jim and Randy had a rather unusual working arrangement. In order to care for their aging parents, Jim sometimes worked a few weeks in Bolivia by himself and then sometimes Randy joined him for a while. He was helping to develop dairy cooperatives and cheese factories.

Jim continued,

A Prayer Letter

"It has been an interesting day for me, a day of reflection. I write from here in Bolivia now, but in a few weeks I will be returning to the States for a while. Today, though, I have been thinking about what has happened here, what God's work is here, and what our work is here. It is a day of joy and a day of loneliness for us, since it is our wedding anniversary and we are on two different continents as we celebrate our marriage.

As we serve Him and serve one another we see that He changes lives. This has been true in our marriage. At times we have struggled because of our stubborn insistence that our own individual needs be met first. When we remember that our Lord calls us to serve one another, our marriage changes. The joy we feel then is almost indescribable. It is a pity that we are such slow learners and that we so often need to be re-educated.

Today we celebrate the joy of our marriage because Jesus has changed our lives. And He is changing lives here in Bolivia, too. Six years ago, Benito was a struggling small farmer in the San Julian area. He took some courses on animal care offered by CVM in his village, got excited by them and took more courses to become a veterinary technician in his area. His integrity and his commitment were recognized, by his villagers, and he was elected Area Director of his agricultural cooperative. He is now taking courses in administration and management in the city, a five-hour bus ride away that he makes twice a month. He has become a committed Christian leader in his community. His life has been changed."

Isn't it marvelous how one life changed can have that same impact on another? God always chooses us, the imperfect beings, to represent Him. That indeed is profound. It is an example of perfect love toward us. I thank the Lord for that.

⬥

The World Small Animal Veterinary Association (WSAVA) was meeting in Jerusalem the latter part of October. Several months prior to it, Ray Markus, DVM, from Tel Aviv, Israel called me. He requested CVM make known to its constituency of this meeting. He asked if CVM would sponsor a tour to the Holy Land in conjunction with the meeting. Tina and I had only visited Jerusalem for a day, and to be quite truthful, did not have a burning desire to return. But his call did pique my interest, because it afforded a forum to expose more of the veterinary profession to the opportunities of service through CVM. So, I accepted his request, but more in a perfunctory mode than with conviction. And, as many times in the past, I was proven wrong.

The Middle East has never lacked for controversy and there seemed to be an inordinate amount of conflict during the 18 months preceding the meeting. So, as you can imagine, many people were reluctant to make the trip with the newspapers daily screaming of some new crisis. However, a few brave souls took the plunge and signed on for the trip. They included; Dr.Amy Krell, from Illinois, Dr. Gerald Walker and wife, Myrna, from California, Dr. Booker Alford and wife Juanita, from New Jersey, Dr. John Schutz and wife Donna from New York, Dr. Charles Graham and wife Brenda, from Georgia, Dr. Clyde Burns, North Carolina, Dr. Mike Chesson and wife Gail, from Virginia, Dr. Cameron Shaul, Tennessee, Dr. John Haberlein and wife Mary, from Michigan, and Dr. Rick Reed, Australia.

To handle the arrangements and logistics of the trip we selected World Mission Tours, Miami Springs, Florida. It was a good choice. Herb McComas, a retired preacher, was our contact. He had made the trip many times. Herb could offer good solid advice and wise counseling, concerning our itinerary and accommodations. It turned out to be one fantastic trip. Doors opened and short windows of opportunity presented themselves throughout our travels. The Lord really watched over us and blessed our time in so many ways.

For Tina and me it was the trip of our lives. It was so interesting, educational, motivational, and inspiring; a never-to-be-forgotten experience. Bible names became real places, something tangible that I could deal with. I think, without a doubt, that it was the most nearly perfect trip that I have ever taken with a group. It exceeded my expectations in almost every way. Surely the Lord was in it.

Myrna Walker summarized,

"Our trip began and ended in Jordan. There we saw the ancient ruins of Petra carved by the Nabataneans. We traveled the King's Highway, spoken of in the Old Testament. It had been a major trade route. We also went to the top of Mount Nebo to look over the Promised Land, just as Moses had done.

Our first stop in Israel was in Jericho. We then went up the productive Jordan River Valley. We stopped for lunch at a Kibbutz, and visited their ultra-modern dairy facility. We proceeded to Tiberias, on the shores of the Sea of Galilee. This area provided opportunities to visit the Mount of the Beatitudes, Capernum, Caesarea Philippi, and the Golan Heights. Our day ended with a peaceful boat ride across the Sea of Galilee.

As we traveled across the country to Nazareth, Mount Carmel, Caesarea-by-the-Sea, and finally up to Jerusalem, we were awestruck by the beauty of the land. Development seemed to be taking place in every area of the country.

It was overwhelming, trying to process information on so many different levels-from Old Testament History to present-day political situations. Our guide, a Palestinian Christian, added immeasurably to the richness of our experience.

Jerusalem was the culmination of the Holy sites we visited. Here we saw the wailing- wall, the Dome of the Rock, and the Church of the Holy Sepulcher. We visited Gethsemane, and Old City of David. It was an emotional experience when we attended services at the Garden Tomb. We also saw the Museum of the Dead Sea Scrolls."

An extra bonus was being able to visit inside the Palestinian area of Jerusalem, because our driver was from there and because we were a small group. This allowed us to visit the famous Spring of Gihon. It flows through the original tunnel, dug during King Hezikiah's reign through the Hill of Zion. The Spring provided water when this area was under siege thus, making it more difficult to capture. It may have been the reason David had to live in Hebron for seven years.

Myrna summarizes,

"At the WSAVA meetings in Jerusalem, CVM hosted a booth, explaining the work and purpose of the organization. Many people, vets and students, showed interest in the work, and the booth was enthusiastically received. Bruce Christie, President of the Australian Christian Veterinary Fellowship (ACVF) presented a check to Dr. Dorminy, to further the work of CVM projects.

As we returned to Amman, we traveled along the Dead Sea to tour the ruins at Masada and the caves at Qumran where the Dead Sea Scrolls were found. Our trip was nearly over, but the memories that each of us held would last a lifetime. The Lord surely had walked with us each and every step of the way. I believe that, through our trip to the Holy Land, each one of us saw Him more clearly than ever before."

CHAPTER 23

Comings and Goings

One of CVM's major success stories has been its development of the educational material targeting those people and countries that lack resources of this kind. When we began working in those difficult places, we discovered there just weren't any appropriate practical books available. In addition, the audience we were trying to reach had little or no formal training.

As a solution to this, we began to develop a series of books called Raising Healthy Animals. The authors have done a marvelous job of putting these books together. CVM made known the need and volunteers with special expertise and a desire to write have come forth to produce these books. The authors and the publishing dates are listed in the back of this book.

Taking this to the next level, Dr. Earl Goodman came up with the idea of an International Animal Health Newsletter (IAHN). It would be a quarterly newsletter for passing along practical, up-to-date information on livestock and veterinary subjects. Many times ideas conceived go through an evolutionary process. This one was no exception. This time our target audience was a bit more advanced in technical knowledge than the target audience for the original book series. Those receiving the IAHN included agricultural colleges, research workers and some agricultural missionary specialists.

After our first edition of assorted material on swine and poultry subjects, we decided that we would concentrate on public health issues. Each article was written by a person, known to be a leading authority, on the particular subject we chose. The result has been outstanding. We have had very good feedback and our plan now is to take these twelve public health issues and make a small book of them. And so our educational resources continue to grow.

CVM Board.

Seattle was the site of the 1997 board meeting. Dr. Dennis Sundbeck, Texas, served as board chairman. Dennis and his wife Rebecca, a charming and vivacious southern lady, have been faithful and generous supporters of CVM for many years. They tend to specialize, having four daughters.

Dennis first went to Haiti on a shuttle in 1984. We had a wonderful picture on the CVM office wall of Dennis and Dr. Jere Colley playing with Haitian kids. I don't know who was smiling the widest and having the most fun, them or the kids. Ironically, someone took it down and apparently was going to discard it. This happened just before the meeting, but luckily, Dennis was able to retrieve it. I assume it graces the reception area of his office. I must get down to Round Rock and check.

Dr. Laurie Wallace, Missouri, took the position of Dr. Jerry Burch on the board. She was doing some outstanding work with a fellowship group at the veterinary school in Columbia. Board members Dr. Fred Bendick, Missouri, Dr. Tim Blair, Wisconsin, and Dr. Floyd Jones, Texas were stepping down. They were replaced by Dr. Don Wilson, Missouri, Dr. Rod Frank, Michigan, Dr. Mary Ballenger, Oklahoma. Much of the work of the board that year was affirming the key objectives in light of the CVM Vision and Mission Statement. They evaluated the Strategic Objectives in meeting them.

Mary Ballenger has served as state representative for Oklahoma and has been a special friend of the Flanagans and Van Gorkoms. She lives in Tulsa with her wonderful family; her husband Richard, sons John and George, and daughter Sally. It is so encouraging to see how they live out their Christian faith as a family. Mary's contribution to the meeting in Manhattan, Kansas, was called "Witnessing in Practice." I wish you could have seen the students gathered about her and listening with great intensity. It so vividly demonstrated their hunger for a meaningful faith and their need for a solid foundation for a successful life.

Dr. Tom Sine facilitated a workshop to help the board members and leadership think through what CVM's role is in the future of missions. His creative, well-informed, high-energy approach piqued the interest of the board and encouraged them to be enthusiastic about their role.

Drs. Paul and Margaret Brand attended the fellowship meal. Dr Paul shared some of their lifetime experiences on the mission field. They had a tremendous mission ministry to lepers in India and other places. They served on the World Concern Board of Directors.

CVM Canada began to publish its own newsletter. Some of the shuttles listed here, include those who were destined to play a significant role in CVMC's development. Dr. Devin Hunt went on a shuttle to Uganda, working with Dr. Brad and Mrs. Angela Frye and Dr. Valery Shean. Devin later became executive director of the CVMC. Dr. Wally Kononoff, Saskatoon, went to Romania and serves on the board. Dr. Louis Kwantes, Alberta, who had previous mission experience to Haiti, went to Uzbekistan, along with Dr. Cheryl Braswell-Sisson, Georgia.

Sometimes shuttles deal with the lowly and abused, Dr. John Fletemeyer wrote this description,

> *"In many countries, the horse (or its cousin, the donkey) does not represent a status symbol of power (to pull chariots or to ride into battle) but rather serves as an humble tool for survival."*

Susan Waller, veterinary technician and shuttle participant to Haiti, says,

Dr. Devin and Sarah Hunt, Mark, Rebecca, Matthew, and Rachel. (First Canadian executive director).

"The donkey in Haiti is more like a utility truck. People can't afford non-essential items. If their animals aren't healthy, the people are going to starve. Since many people can't grow gardens (there is not enough water during the dry season), they must go to market to get their basic supplies and to sell their wares. The markets are in a different village each week, so traders must rise in the middle of the night and load their donkeys for the long journeys ahead."

Susan and Dr. Lisa Demumbrum have twice done shuttles together to the same community in Pignon, Haiti. Before they left, they contacted two groups of church women who were motivated to share with the people of Haiti. Susan communicated a need: Terrible saddle sores are often produced by the weight and friction of wicker saddles on the backs of these beasts of burden. The church ladies sewed saddle blankets and shipped them to the mission in Haiti. Susan and Lisa brought medications for the saddle sores and gave instructions on how to treat and prevent them. She says,

"Our God cares about every one of His creatures. On His triumphal entry into Jerusalem, He chose to be identified with that animal,

the donkey. The people laid their coats down for the donkey to step on, to honor their King. Through the CVM shuttle program to Haiti, the beasts of burden have been given coats on their backs, to bring honor to our King."

Dr. Janet Varhus, Colorado, reflects on her shuttle experiences.

"The shuttle program has been a way for me to use my talents, find my faith renewed and find strength in my walk with God. My children have shared these experiences and hopefully they have a lasting impression."

"In 1992, Dr. Sally Bushhouse, Minnesota, and I went to Kenya to work with the Maasai. While there, we went to a women's retreat, spending two weeks in the bush, treating cattle and goats in the villages and teaching as well. The final day was spent in summation of what we had done. One village killed a goat in our honor, while another gave us their last 'chai'. I was humbled by their giving from the little they had.

My two children and I made three trips to the Four Corners area to work on the Navajo Reservation. Most of our time was spent holding vaccination clinics. Several students were helping and I found myself witnessing to them also. I learned the true power of prayer and I experienced complete trust in God. Basic necessities took on a much simpler meaning. Bible lessons became real experiences. Now when I find my faith weakening, I remember my time in Kenya or Shiprock, New Mexico."

Dr. Don Thayer, Wisconsin, is another one of those who really believes in the shuttle program. He has participated several times, and in more than one country. His daughter Debbie, following in her dad's footsteps in profession and in his zest for missions, has participated in one herself. In fact they did one together! Later he took his other daughters. What a wonderful heritage to pass on to one's offspring!

In April, Tina and I traveled to Birmingham, England for the World Small Animal Veterinary Association (WSAVA) meeting. It was

L to R—Dr. Peter Brown, Dr. David Watson, Tina, and Dr. Leroy Dorminy—WSAVA and BSAVA meeting.

held in conjunction with the British Small Animal Veterinary Association (BSAVA). We shared a booth with the Veterinary Christian Fellowship (VCF) of the United Kingdom. Dr. David Watson, of Sleaford, who worked with Pedigree at the time, made the arrangements and set things up. His company had done some murals for the booth. They were very attractive and depicted the story of missions by the VCF.

We had an excellent location. The booth was given complimentary by the WSAVA. The booth was small but the location gave us tremendous exposure, as this was the major artery and only passageway to many of the lectures. Dr. Peter Brown, of Huntingdon, and Dr. Alice Hall, of Chippenham, helped Tina and me work the booth. Alice had gone on a shuttle to Uzbekistan where Dr. David Forster, of Tonbridge was a long-term worker at Samarkand.

The VCF hosted a fellowship worship service in the evening. The speaker was Dr. David Soldan, from Huntingdon. Tina and I had met him when we were in the United Kingdom in 1984. It was a great time of fellowship. We were able to visit with others whom we had met before. They included Dr. John Aspley Davis, of Holt, Australian Capital Territory, Australia, whom we had met in 1983 in Canberra. Veterinarians from other countries were represented at the meeting.

A lovely Scottish lady, Dr. Catherine Botcherby, from Dundonald, Ayrshire, had been corresponding with CVM. She came down for a day. She was very interested in going long-term but complications involved her boyfriend, Alastair, who didn't share an overseas call to missions. I feel for those couples, who, despite their love for each other, must choose between missions or marriage.

Catherine was able to fulfill part of her dream for mission work by going to South Africa to work during the summer. She came back through Kenya and worked with Drs. Brad Frye and Val Shean for a while. She served there later as a furlough replacement for Brad and Angela. Catherine writes,

✝
■

A Prayer Letter

"I can hardly believe it's been four weeks since I set foot on African soil. I feel quite at home here, though I doubt I will ever get used to being constantly exposed to hardships so many people have to endure here.

Something I have noticed is the people's amazing capacity for joy, despite the sorrows and hardships they have endured. Take Pastor Calvin, for example. He lost his father and three brothers during the insurgency and is left with 18 children to raise-six of his own and twelve nieces and nephews. His smile is one of the most heart-warming I have ever seen. Then there is James, who was lined up with 67 others to be shot. He was fourth in line of seven men. By a miracle, the gun refused to fire on him and after three attempts, the soldiers gave up and set him free along with two others. All the rest were killed."

Catherine really pitched in and worked during her few months there. She describes it,

"On the veterinary side of things, I had a rewarding session last week with some folks who recently received heifers. We did some training and treatments. People know a lot about their animals and seem to enjoy getting involved, sharing their ideas and knowledge freely. The Bible club is flourishing. More kids come each week"

Catherine's term ended a bit differently from most. She explains,

"Suddenly nine months have passed-it is almost time for me to go home. And get married! On top of Kilimanjaro, Alastair got down on bended knee, produced a beautiful ring and said, 'Will you marry me?' So we are hoping to get married in July or August. I am so excited and thankful to God for giving me such a wonderful man for a husband. Leaving here is going to be hard but the prospect of our life together makes it so much easier."

Team shuttles can be exciting and challenging. Dr Jerry and Mrs. Myrna Walker were leaders for a student shuttle to Africa. This was their second time at hosting a group shuttle. Their previous one was to Bolivia. The benefits must outweigh the negatives. Participating students were Andrea Alfred, of Guelph, Lena Gutberlet, of Virginia, Allison Mahoney, Kansas, Barry Schwenk, Kansas, Wendi Solis, Florida, and Jennifer Lee, Oklahoma. Isn't it wonderful that students involve themselves in missions!

Christmas Gift Catalog was an inspiration of Diane Marshall. It featured "Wild and Wooly". It was an effort to raise money for special projects that included; Animal Health Training, Endowment Fund, Veterinary Pharmacy and Animal Loan program. The idea was to give a gift to CVM and designate it in honor of a friend. This was in lieu of a traditional Christmas gift.

Dr. Todd Cooney, Indiana, did the drawings. They were outstanding. Todd is so generous with his talents, which are tremendous. He is an excellent artist but, more importantly, he shares his God given talent with others.

As part of a home ministries outreach, CVM worked in partnership with Dr. Leroy Roemer, and Dogs for the Disabled. CVM provided partial funding to raise, train, and place Shelby, a Labrador Retreiver.

An excerpt from Dr. Roemer's report follows.

"Please join me in giving thanks to the Lord for the successful completion of this service dog project that you made possible. On December 20th, Shelby, now a trained service dog, was placed with Kevin, a sixteen year old high school senior with cardiomyopathy and Fredreich's Ataxia. Shelby was one of two dogs donated by a North Carolina breeder. A foster home was established, and Shelby went through four months of professional training as a service dog.

Kevin says that he has been teased in school, because he is the only handicapped person there. He has a motorized scooter, which sometimes gets off the sidewalk or into corners. When that happens Shelby can pull him out. She is trained to pick up things he drops, turn light switches on and off, carry a backpack, and pull a wheelchair."

Dr Roemer says,

"This process created joy in the Lord. It was done by Him and through Him. It was not done by might or power, but by His Spirit. And so we can say the project was sucessfully completed. The spiritual impact, however, is not complete. We hope it will continue for a long time as we tell others about it, as Kevin tells others about CVM's role and the role of Christian veterinarians."

CVM is forever indebted to our volunteers. The ministry could not exist, let alone thrive, without their help. We certainly would never be able to hire help for all the things we need to accomplish. A case in point is Dr. Pam Broussard who faithfully comes by the office and logs into the computer, the names of veterinarians and their contributions to the Animal Loveline Program. Pam married since she started working with CVM and now an extra bonus is getting to play with Tyler, her adorable little girl. She will even let an old gray head hold her!

A part time worker for CVM, was Nikki Stevenson-Bonilla. Nikki met her husband in Honduras, while serving there as a missionary. He worked as the Community Pastor with Project Global Village in an urban slum outside of Tegucigalpa. The focus was reaching out to youths. Nikki worked in the PAG central office, and in the slums with a women's micro-enterprise. They had come to the U.S. temporarily for Luis to learn English. She was a great asset to CVM.

Reno, Nevada was the site of 17th Annual Meeting. My good friends, Dr. Ed Cushing and wife Norma, from nearby Sparks, have been the only CVM representative we have ever had in Nevada. I had to kid them during introductions, by saying, "Reno is so close to hell you can see Sparks!

Dr. Gary Baker, California, opened the annual meeting with devotions. Dr. Andrea Mikolon, California, gave a summary of her shuttle to Mongolia, where she worked on Brucellosis disease in cattle and yak. Susan Waller, California, talked about her shuttle to Haiti. She showed her usual high energy and boundless enthusiasm, working for the Lord. Susan has a prayer warrior ministry on E-mail. Literally hundreds of people pray for those with special needs.

Editor, Dr. Diane Marshall, held a workshop on the CVM newsletter. She threw out some ideas and received feedback from the participants, about what they would like to see the newsletter become.

Long-term workers Dr. Karen Stoufer and husband Ron, talked about their work in Nepal. Dr. Wendell Cantrell and wife, Jan, told of their involvement in East Africa.

The executive committee focused on helping CVM Canada to jump-start their "stand alone" efforts. It was given quite a push forward when, Dr. Devin Hunt was designated the new Executive Director. Devin had gone on a shuttle to Uganda previously. He and his wife, Sarah, had a mutual desire to serve the Lord in missions. This would afford a wonderful opportunity to do that, out of their home in Sarnia. It has proven to be a wise and timely move.

Devin wrote,

"Participation on this mission trip has impacted my family tremendously. Even though Sarah did not physically go to Africa, she

241

realized that the Lord had a calling for us as a family through CVMC. After praying together for the Lord's direction and guidance, I have taken a position as a domestic field worker with Christian Veterinary Mission of Canada (CVMC).

It is my responsibility to coordinate the domestic and overseas activities. Sarah and I are very excited about this ministry. The Lord will present us with many opportunities to challenge other veterinarians to work in ministry through their profession here at home and abroad. The global impact of this ministry will have eternal significance."

As happens many times, the initial contact from people who want information on CVM and opportunities for service, translates into service months or even years later. My first contact with Dr. Kevin Hasch, Nebraska, was in the 1980's. Now, he had offered to serve in Kenya, while Dr. George and Martha Mixon came home on a year-long furlough.

On getting ready, Kevin voiced what many have experienced,

"Do any of us have our ducks in a row? So many to do lists— passports, visas, international drivers license, immunizations, physicals/check-ups, work permits, reading about the culture, language—an absolutely seemingly endless list of preparations. As I consider this before the Lord, He has been reminding me that preparation truly is important, but that I must prioritize, with Him first. As I prepare, I remember a quote 'prayer is not so much preparation for the battle, as it is the battle itself.' In other words, the battles are won or lost long before we step out the door. Walls have either been prayed down, or they have not."

Right on!
Kevin's on-the-field indoctrination started quickly,

"My first welcome to the bush revealed that this was not a place you'd likely find Paul of the New Testament praying to be sent, You guessed it...too many thorns. In fact my claim is, an accurate way to measure distance traveled is by the number of flat tires and by counting the bumps. Things are changing. Since El Nino, it is 'How many times have you been stuck?'

But it is more serious than that at times,

A Prayer Letter

"Ololdikany, one of Dr. Mixon's and now my co-worker, came to me the first thing in the morning, face swollen and in much pain. He said he had been 'spit' on -by a Cobra. Their primary defense and offensive method of dealing with an intruder is to blind them, so they spit their venom into the eyes rendering the person or animal helpless and vulnerable to attack. It was tall grass and he did not actually see the Cobra but there was no doubt as to what it was. Fortunately Ololdikany recovered fully."

Ironically enough, later on a disease we can identify with more easily, affected Ololdikany's brother, Brucellosis, an all too common disease in Maasailand. He came to me one day with a swollen leg and joints, fever and headache. So we loaded up to go to Olkoroi where we confirmed what I suspected: Undulant Fever (human Brucellosis). This required days of shots and pills. Did it have to be? No. They know that you can't drink fresh milk and be safe unless it is boiled or soured first. And they know that by handling the aborted fetus, placenta and sometimes just by milking an infected cow or goat they may acquire the disease. They have the knowledge but it takes discipline to make it work."

Kevin served out his term of substituting for the Mixons with distinction. It was a test for him to see if God was calling him to mission work full time. He updates us,

"Currently, I am in Phillipsburg, Kansas, working on big cows and little cows (cats, dogs, turkeys, etc.) I believe God led me back here for a purpose and for a time. Until November of last year I believed I would be headed back to Ethiopia later this year. Instead, I believe His plans for me now entail further education in seminary or Bible college. I am still praying about overseas service to follow."

Dr. Glenn and Lisa Craft, California, were in the first orientation class for overseas service that used the participatory training method. The course was developed by Dr. Susan Stewart, while she was working in Bolivia. Several of us in the CVM office attended the sessions to learn more about it. We wanted to see if it would help to prepare candidates for overseas service. It not only does that, but it helps in our relationships with family, friends and co-workers. I needed this course many years earlier.

It was interesting to learn more about each candidate and to see the different skills they brought. Glenn had good computer skills, which really helps to communicate both with supporters and with the home office. These are needed, whether in preparation for going or after arriving on the field. Lisa, being Thai, would help in the adjustment to culture, since they were going to serve in Thailand. The Lord can always use whatever we bring.

After selling their house and cars, and a few garage sales later, they left for Thailand in October. Living in Lopburi, they began language school. During their stay they had an interesting but sad and profound experience. They explain,

A Prayer Letter

"A small group of us, mostly OMF language students and one teacher, visited the 'AIDS Temple'. When we first walked in, (AIDS infects young girls brought into the city for prostitution) I felt absolutely helpless at first. What could we possibly do to help these people, especially with our limited Thai? We began to mingle among the beds, and speak to those who seemed to yearn for a true visitor, and not a tourist.

One of the first men I spoke to seemed especially bitter, but began to chat with me. He asked for money, as we were told they all would. When I asked him if he knew about God, he reached in his shirt and pulled out a gold medal of Mary. I rejoiced with him but when I gently encouraged him to put his total trust in Jesus, he turned away.

I turned around to find a very thin young girl sitting on the edge of her bed. She was 22, had a pretty smile, but she was very, very thin. She was quick to converse with me and accepted the special tract for AIDS patients (in Thai). She suddenly brightened as a girl friend, Bun, approached who was able to speak English fairly well. Bun was talkative, and helped translate for her friend as I spoke about Jesus to them.

We left deeply touched and constrained to much prayer in the days ahead. You see it is estimated by the year 2000, Thailand will have over 100,000 children orphaned by AIDS."

Later, Glenn and Lisa moved from Lopburi to Chiangkham, to begin their ministry. They would be splitting their time between overseeing and monitoring livestock projects under World Concern, both in Chiangrai and Chiangkham. They would be conducting AIDS counseling and training for local groups, churches and soldiers. They would oversee the establishment of an orphanage for children orphaned by AIDS, and help to guide and encourage a new Thai church. Quite an ambitious program, but relying on God's help and under the guidance of His Holy Spirit, it is amazing what can be accomplished.

CHAPTER 24

Encouragement Post-Communism

The CVM Board meeting was in Manhattan, Kansas in January, 1998. The reason for choosing this setting was the emphasis CVM was now placing on student ministry. We had always included students in our ministry plans but now we were trying to be a bit more proactive. It proved to be an immensely successful meeting from our perspective, with students not only from K-State but Iowa and Oklahoma as well. Barry Schwenk, along with other K-State students, helped set it up. Barry had been on a shuttle to Africa.

The students came on Friday night for a time of getting acquainted, fellowship and learning about CVM. Saturday sessions included seminars on Student Debt Load, Witnessing in Practice, Shuttles, Making Choices and Long-term Service. Since the sessions were repeated, each student was able to attend two of them. This time was followed by panel discussions on such things as gender issues, veterinary fellowship groups, and opportunities for employment after graduation. The day ended with a banquet for the students and board.

Our regular board session began on Wednesday night with Susan Stewart using a get acquainted hour to start us on the CVM Values session she was conducting. (You have to watch Susan. She will have you working when you are supposed to be having fun!) This was followed Thursday morning with another session. I thought I had enrolled in K-State by mistake. Susan is quite a good facilitator for audience participation. She earned her wings through experience in the field. She is very knowledgeable on the subject, and has now compiled this material into a manual. We were breaking new ground.

The challenge now is to bring all the fieldworkers into a working knowledge of this concept.

General business matters focused on the By-Laws and the Memorandum-of-Understanding (MOU). Pros and cons of the agreement we have with World Concern/CRISTA were discussed.It was concluded that this was a good arrangement for both parties, at that time.

Dr. Jim Rosenberger was the incoming chairman of the board. He has been a faithful supporter of CVM for many years. He and his wife, Anne, exemplify a Christian lifestyle. It is demonstrated in their family and church, and in their professional and civic responsibilities. In the past couple of years I have come to appreciate them more than ever.

Jim asked me if I would be interested in coming to the Ohio VMA meeting in February. This was an opportunity to visit with the students, and help Judy and Walt Long work the booth. An added incentive was the opportunity to speak at an ecumenical worship service. You know about how long it took me to say yes. When it's talking about missions, and more particularly veterinary missions, I am ready! This proved to be an exceptionally gratifying experience.

Never have CVM or myself, been given a more royal welcome at a veterinary meeting. Much of this was because of the esteem with which Jim and Anne are held in their state. Barbara Madison, OVMA Executive Secretary, has been so gracious and helpful as well. She came by CVM's booth in Toronto to give us a special invitation.

Our first stop was at the Ohio Veterinary School. We were able to meet with the fellowship group during lunch. They are extremely lucky to have Dr. Richard Slemons as their faculty advisor. He has a 'low key' manner about him that the students like and is available when the students ask for his input. I was fortunate enough to visit with Richard and his family while I was there. He and Elizabeth exhibit those same good parental traits when dealing with their own kids.

The Sunday morning service was held in the Atrium of the Hyatt Regency Hotel. It is an excellent venue for such a meeting. People can visit casually without someone pointing a finger and saying you went to the Ecumenical Worship Service! Jim's daughter, Beth Miller, and her friend Nancy Heath brought the music, with two beautiful songs. It was wonderful. We really didn't need any service after that but I spoke anyway! The frosting on the cake was that we were invited back the next year!

Tuskegee Veterinary Fellowship. L to R Tommy Asinga, Trey Wofford, Dr. Leroy Dorminy, Michelle Mitchell, Dr. Fredrick Tippett.

Through the years, one thing that Tina and I look forward to is visiting with students at the veterinary schools. It may not keep you young but it really livens up the aging process. During the spring of 1998 I visited and in 1999 together Tina and I visited some schools in the Southeast. Our first stop was with the students at Auburn University.

They have a large fellowship group that meets every Wednesday. A local Baptist church brings in lunch. Remembering my lean school years, that has to be an extra incentive to attend. Steve Thompson heads up the Baptist Student Union there at Auburn. He does a good job of encouraging the students. Student Kelly Wilkerson went on a shuttle to Honduras and spoke about this at our annual meeting at the AVMA in New Orleans.

Our next visit took us to Tuskegee Institute. It is only a few miles from the Auburn campus. My good friend, Fred Tippets, serves as faculty advisor. Fred was a member of the original fellowship group at Tuskegee. They are fortunate to have a man of Fred's integrity and character to mentor them.

Student Trey Wofford was the one who invited me. He and his wife Melanie and their daughters lived in Montgomery. It was a delight to visit with them. I had the pleasure of reading the children's book Barney to their youngest daughter a few dozen times! She never tired of it.

Student, Kelly Crowdis, went on a shuttle to Tanzania and did an excellent job of evaluating the needs at the school's clinic while there. Kelly desires to serve full time with CVM following graduation.

We arrived at Mississippi State on the day that Dr. Dwight Mercer was stepping down as dean of the school. Later, Dr John Thompson, who went to Mongolia on two shuttles, was appointed dean to replace Dr. Mercer. Dr. Richard Hopper, faculty advisor to the fellowship group managed a meeting with some of the students and faculty. We had a good discussion of CVM activity and how to be involved. This was my fourth visit to the Mississippi State.

***

This interesting vignette comes from Dr. Gerald Mitchum as a result of CVM's work in Mongolia.

"This is our favorite time of the year (Thanksgiving) and we sure miss being around the table with you folks. We don't get turkey over here but the wonderful friends God has given us go a long way toward filling that void. Anyway, I don't want to talk about turkey... it is pork that is on my mind.

She just wouldn't go away. Remember the widow who kept coming to the judge in Luke 18. 'Finally, he said to himself, even though I don't fear God or care about men, yet because this widow keeps bothering me I will see that she gets justice, so that she won't eventually wear me out with her coming!' This is the exact picture of the 'Pig Lady'.

She started coming to our organization seeking help to expand her pig operation. She worried them so constantly that they were happy to pass her on to me. She wanted help and she wanted it right now. Explanations of how slowly things often work with mission organizations made no impact on her. She knocked, called, and generally made a nuisance of herself.

But, there was a quality about Setegmaa that I really liked. She could not be stopped until she found help and accomplished her goals. I thought, this woman is going to succeed and I want to be able to take a little bit of the credit.

We had several shuttle veterinarians who were able to give good advice on swine production. A swine consulting company in the U.S. is considering a loan to this family and at this time it appears it will materialize. Veterinarians from Iowa State University and Virginia Polytechnic Institute are here and they will visit the farm and develop a good plan for investing these funds. I get the feeling that we will be eating 'country ham' in Mongolia soon.

It was quiet and our pastor was in the middle of his sermon. The little room where we met was already packed. The door cracked and there she was with her entourage. 'The Pig Lady', coming to hear about Jesus. That's been a few weeks ago and this past Sunday she told me she now believes in One God. She says she has thrown away their idols and she repeats the sermons to her husband who must stay with the pigs. She told me she had a pregnant sow that could not have her pigs. She knew the sow was going to die so she began to pray to her new-found God. Well, the sow gave birth to twelve healthy pigs and mom and babies are all fine.

"Poor Mongolia...this lady will not rest until everyone hears of Jesus. She will knock, call and pester until they cry out for peace and turn to her Lord."

Dr. Jean Grade, Wisconsin, is an unforgettable lady. She is a tall, slim, highly mobile bundle of energy. She may have set a record for a shuttle in both time and distance. It started from Wisconsin, with a flight to Paris for a short time of sight seeing,

"We mimicked the hunchback and crawled to the top of Notre Dame for a beautiful view of the city."
"Four days, 7,000 miles and seven time zones later we made it to Cameroon."

There she worked with Dr. Doug and Stephanie Lewis. Jean always tries her very best to relate to those she meets,

"Today I met the head chief of the local tribe and gave him a gift of palm oil-with help of two interpreters. I was careful not to shake his hand, cross my legs or to hand the oil to his interpreter with my left hand."

A few weeks later she writes from the other side of the continent,

"I'm in Karamoja, Uganda, delving into the ethno-veterinary project with the local villages with the help of Dr. Valery Shean."
Things didn't go all that smoothly,
"There wasn't much time to react after the African green monkey bit my hand. Time was suspended as I watched the frightened Mount Elgon vervet grab my right calf with her soft human-like hands and sink her sharp canines deep into the muscle-spurting my blood on her face and the ground."

"Those few seconds of pandemonium resulted in weeks of pain and frustration, and moments of anxiety. Mount Elgon is the site of early Ebola virus outbreaks and the vervet monkey was the carrier. The wounds couldn't be sutured and therefore, had to be scrubbed harshly twice daily. My fever persisted and at one point, I was diagnosed with Brucellosis and Malaria."

She toughed it out,

"Well, it's October and I'm still in Uganda. As the Neilsville, Wisconsin signpost once welcomed me-'Stay a day, a week, a lifetime.' I've had this dream of Africa, this calling since high school. The first time I drove into the dry savannah of Karamoja, with its occasional lonely thorny acacia tree, I felt an incredible sense of belonging and a desire to serve. I am making arrangements to wrap up my work by the end of the year when I will return to the States to prepare for long-term service in Africa."

This she did, coming to orientation in February and returning to Africa in June.

<hr />

Dr. John Schneller, Wisconsin, started his shuttle experience in Haiti in 1991. He really found his niche in Bolivia, however, participating in four different shuttles there. He comments, *"Several of us have had the opportunity to participate in an Embryo Transfer (ET) program for the needy in rural areas of Bolivia. Cooperation among the various ministries helped make it a success.*

The measurable results of the project are dairy breeding bulls available to the villages. Many families can share in this. In addition, long-term workers have been supported in the process. The improved cattle that follow will reward the farmers and the livestock management training classes.

The benefit I have received from participating in shuttles can be summarized by; a better understanding of the work and an appreciation for the program. My daughter, Claire, and I have gained a better perspective of the developing world. We now have a greater appreciation of those who live the test of poverty and those who commit their lives in service to them in obedience to His will."

<hr />

Drs. Monty and Shelly Mathis, Washington, and their children, Ashley and Morgan, learned they had been accepted to serve in Jumla, Nepal. Monty's position would be Vocational Training and Extension Specialist. They would be working through United Missions to Nepal. It had been a long, tortuous road getting there, but I think it is during these times that God really prepares us for service. Jumla is up in the mountains of western Nepal, elevation 8000 feet. The largest lake in Nepal, Rara Lake, is close by.

Shelly and Monty had previously gone on a shuttle to Africa and later Monty took a shuttle to Mongolia with hopes for long-term service there, but it was not to be. So now, they found themselves finally going to Nepal. They claimed Psalm 40 that begins, *"I waited patiently for the Lord; He turned to me and heard my cry."* and *"He put a new song in my mouth, a hymn to praise our God."* It is easy to see how their thoughts turned to this Psalm.

Of their new assignment they wrote,

"Our role in Jumla is to work alongside Nepali instructors developing practical veterinary teaching for the training of students in Community Animal Health. We will be working with the local communities in identifying animal health needs and putting together classes that address those needs, and train people for the task at hand."

After arriving at their new home in Jumla an event happened that very nearly turned their mission into disaster. In their words,

A Prayer Letter

"I write this from our future house in Jumla. It has been a beautiful, warm, sunny day here, though it is now threatening thunderstorms and cloudbursts. We traveled the surrounding areas hoping to see all the future sites of the work. We had been out three days already and were leaving the area Patrasi, a day's walk east of the village of Jumla. We had rented horses for the children due to the distance we needed to travel daily.

One hour on our way Morgan fell off his horse. He was a little banged up but OK. We kept him in second with Ashley riding the lead. All of a sudden Ashley's horse spooked. She pulled the horse in and it began to turn. At the same time Ashley started to go over sideways. Her cinch tore and she hit the ground trying to get her foot out of the stirrup. She cried out 'Daddy, help!' but I could do nothing since I was behind Morgan's horse and the path was narrow and walled in by rock and thorn bushes.

The horse began to trot. She screamed and the horse bolted into a canter. Ashley was drug alongside the horse over the rocks. I found myself off the path and in a side field, hoping somehow to get in front of the horse. I ran so hard. My pack came off, as if the Lord had undone all the straps and I was freed to run through the brush and fields. A Mugali (Tibetan) man was coming up the trail and diverted the horse into a cornfield but not before the horse jumped over a stone-wall. The horse now began trotting around in circles with Ashley in the middle.

I arrived shortly at the scene to find our princess stripped of her clothes and lying in the mud with her foot still stuck in the stirrup. She was conscious and did her best to smile and say 'Daddy, I am OK.' Her leg did not appear to be broken and I removed her shoe to free her from the horse. To the Praise of our Father, her body had no obvious broken bones or deep lacerations. Her body was none-the-less a mass of abrasions and cuts. She had fortunately lost consciousness during most of the time she was being dragged. There was a nasty welt on her head where she had hit a rock when the horse jumped over the rock wall

Shelley arrived on the scene and we assessed her condition as to whether to move her or not. She truly seemed whole enough to at least pick her up and get her out of the dirt. There was a cold mountain river close by which we carried her down to and began cleaning her up and further assessing her condition. The Lord had been so kind for she had been drug by her right leg for approximately 500 feet and was alive, conscious, without broken bones or major lacerations and being a good sport about the whole thing."

Not to be redundant, but you can easily see why the single greatest request from our field-workers, is prayer! We praise Him always for watching over each one of them and their families.

Dr. Deborah Storie, Australian veterinarian, served as a veterinary missionary, in Afghanistan. CVM had given her a grant each year to help with expenses. She was leaving the field after five years of very difficult but distinguished service there. She served amid the conflict and civil strife that had devastated the lives of so many people.

She writes of her departure,

"Imagine yourself in this situation. You are about to relocate from a place where you have become established. You have invested much of yourself in the people and the place; your life, your time, your imagination and your labor. Your two worlds, the now and the future, are so different that it is difficult to credit the existence of one world while you are living in the other. Nobody in your current world can understand what your future life will involve; nobody in your new world can envisage, or empathize with, your experiences and learning over the years-although they do try.

When you leave, you are unlikely to ever return, not even to visit. There are no telephones, there is no postal service. You will probably never see or hear from your friends again. You will never know who marries whom, whose infant dies, who receives a job promotion. Imagine too, that life is very tenuous; the political situation is volatile, food scarce, anarchy rules and families live in fear. There are guns, bombs, weapons of mass destruction. You'll wonder who has survived each bout of fighting and what material losses they have sustained. You will wonder-you will never know."

October 27, 1998 is a historic day in the life of CVM. On this day, the first organizational charter was granted to Romania, as a CVM affiliate in Europe. Dr. Alex Popescu, an anatomy/physiology professor at Bucharest Veterinary School, serves as the director. Alex comes with good credentials: he is a committed Christian, professionally qualified, multilingual, with past knowledge and first hand experience of the evils of the communist system. He has a burning desire to see his country change for the better. What more could you ask?

The groundwork for this significant event was laid when a team of four veterinarians, Miron Costin, Charles Farho, Marion Hammarlund and I visited in May and June of '98. The idea surfaced when Miron attended, along with Marion, the CVM executive committee meeting in Reno, Nevada in 1997, in conjunction with the AVMA meeting. At the end of the day after he had listened to the discussions regarding the work of CVM, I turned to Miron and asked him if he thought it would have application for Romania. I have never received a more enthusiastic yes! From that moment forward, we began to explore dates and make plans for the visit.

It was a time of intense learning about Romania and the systems in place. To do this we met with leaders representing all phases of

L to R—Dr. Alex Popescu, Dr. Marion Hammarlund, Dr. Miron Costin, Dr. A. L. Dorminy, Dr. Chuck Farho.

political, religious, business, cultural and professional life in Romania. We traveled around the country, visiting three of the four state run veterinary schools and four of the five political districts. To learn about the veterinary profession we met with many veterinarians, those who were state employed, as district, regulatory, and laboratory veterinarians, plus a few in private practice. It was a fast paced crash course on Romania. It certainly met our first objective-to learn.

Secondly, as we met with veterinarians, both public and private, we learned where they stood professionally. It became obvious the communist system had taken its toll. They were behind the times professionally, and much of the livestock industry from which they derived their income had been decimated. We decided, that, as has happened in Mongolia, we could most definitely help them in upgrading their skills, with some specialists doing shuttles. That has proven to be very true.

The third objective was more or less left to them to make a decision, and that was whether they wanted to pursue a CVM Romania chapter or not. We carefully explained that we did not come laden with gifts, but rather, desirous to help if we could. They took the initiative and have come a long way toward developing a viable organization. Admittedly, the average veterinarian in Romania makes such a pittance for a salary that is difficult to survive, much less support an organization. We are helping them now, with hopes they can become self-sustaining, over a period of four or five years.

Romania is a beautiful country, with tremendous potential for the agricultural industry and the veterinary profession. It possesses a rich heritage in culture and religion. Some of the churches that date from the 15th and 16th centuries still retain the art painted on the walls during those periods, both on the inside and out. It is an incredible treasure to behold. Most of these are located in the northern part of the country and are associated with convents and monasteries.

Some might pose the question, why CVM in Romania? It certainly cannot be considered a third world country. It and its people have much to contribute. But due to 50 years of the most oppressive form of communism, Romania has fallen behind the Western world. Currently, the political environment, the scientific and technical resources, or the money are not present to move forward to where they should be. In all these areas, some progress is being made, but the transition is agonizingly slow.

A particularly rewarding and exciting aspect of this visit was the opportunity to meet with veterinary students. One particular event happened in Lasi (pronounced yash). This school has on its faculty, a world-renowned veterinary anatomist, Dr. Cotzofan. His anatomical drawings were incredible. He gave each of us one to take home. Maybe if I had had him for my anatomy professor, I would have learned more.

We were able to meet with about 15 faculty members and 35 students, on a strictly voluntary basis. I told them,

"It is wonderful that you are able to study veterinary medicine, to gain knowledge that will help the people of Romania and help you make a living for yourselves but—unless you gain wisdom with that knowledge you will have an unsuccessful life. And wisdom only comes from knowing God! If you doubt that, look at your country's plight. Look at the degradation displayed in movies and the media from the U.S. In both countries it shows what happens when people lose their moral compass."

A faculty member, Dr. Ovidu Popescu, volunteered in the meeting to serve as advisor to the students interested in forming a fellowship group and Dr. Constatin Alexandrescu, who had studied at a seminary in the U.S., volunteered to do Bible study with them. I pray that the Lord will bless that effort.

When we asked different people, *"What per cent of Romanian veterinarians are Christian?"* We got answers from 5% all the way up to 90%. We determined the difference to be this: if I attend worship service regularly, involve my self in a way to actively live out my faith, then the lower end of the scale. If my family was ever a member of the Orthodox Church, that makes me a Christian, hence the higher figure. Do we ever play games like that in the U.S.?

One of the ways we thought that we could help the faculty and students to gain more professional and CVM information was through the internet. We have provided them with funds for each school to do that. I hope that through the CVM Web Site www.vetmission.org, that we will be able to promote a worldwide fellowship of veterinarians and students.

Stefani Ewert joined the CVM central office staff. She is a graduate of Washington State University. She and Diane Marshall shift the majority to the Cougars! That could be dangerous. Stefani has served on short-term mission trips with Campus Crusade. She brings youth, energy and enthusiasm to the staff and all are welcome.

The 18th annual meeting was held in Baltimore. On Saturday morning, Dr. George Mixon started the executive board meeting off with an excellent devotion on relationships. The business portion of the meeting was chaired by Dr. Jim Rosenberger. Time was spent on long-term planning and defining CVM's values.

Sunday's meeting was very well attended. It was dedicated to Dr. Bob and Karen Hott and their family, who recently returned from Nepal and to Dr. John Fletemeyer who had served the past 2-1/2 years as Director of Short Term Missions and was retiring from that position. Dr. George and Martha Mixon showed their self-produced video "On the Road Again" It was fantastic! I think it inspired some of those present to consider doing long-term work. Dr. Janice Fuquay added a South American flavor with her slides of Peru. Dr. LeRoy Roemer provided information on the new home ministry program "Pet Pals".

CHAPTER 25

Finishing the First 25 Years

The CVM Board met in Seattle, January 27-30,1999. All members were present except Dr. Wendell Cantrell, Texas, who was still settling into a practice situation after returning from overseas. Dr. Gary Baker, California, served as chairman of the Board. Gary first represented CVM as region representative for the southwestern United States. He is a classmate of Peter Quesenberry and has been quite supportive of his work.

Gary and his wife, Lynette, take quite seriously their Christian commitment. One of the things Gary initiated this year is the Experiencing God study by Blackaby, for the board members. He posts questions on the Internet regarding the lesson each day, asking for response by board members through E-mail. Gary has visited with the Christian Medical and Dental Society, studying their approach to ministry, to see if any of it has application to CVM.

The Board finished the values exercise orchestrated by Susan Stewart. The results agreed upon were nine. CVM is to be:

Christ Centered;
Veterinary Focused;
Participatory;
Demonstrate Integrity and Accountability;
Model Servant Leadership;
Do Training that Sustains;
Seek Appropriate Partnerships;
And do Holistic Sustainable Development.
The idea behind these values that were adopted is to keep the
    direction of CVM on track.

259

The five year planning goals that are to be guided by these values are:

Christ Centered Ministry;
Effective organizational structure;
Transformed communities and changed lives through Holistic
    ministry;
Effective training and educational materials;
Increased numbers of long-term project sites;
Encouraging and developing global affiliates and fellowships;
Financial strength;
And a ministry to and through the veterinary community.
(Later Susan, Kit and I worked on indicators of evidence of CVM
    values at work in the organizational projects.)

In addition, there was some adjustment of committees for more efficient work. A summary of them shows the following structure. The Executive Committee is responsible for overall leadership and accountability. The evaluation, support systems, training and accountability of field-workers and staff come under the jurisdiction of the Personnel Committee. And, of course, it falls to the Finance Committee to work with budgets and financial reporting. The Outreach Ministries committee is responsible for relationship building, the cement that binds the organization together. Long-term and short-term ministries overseas come under the aegis of the Program Committee. The good news is that there are men and women available for these roles who take them seriously.

Dr. Karen Studemann, Illinois, asked to step down from the board. She and her husband, John, have been faithful supporters of CVM. They have two small children, thus making it difficult to attend the meetings. Dr. Dennis Sundbeck, Texas, completed his second term and was desirous to come off the board so he could work more with the student program. The board voted to hold the meeting in Athens, Georgia, in the year 2000.

❦

Dr. Kent and Marie Freer, Washington, have been long time friends of CVM and personal friends as well, as have Dr. Dave and

Karen Anderson. Tina and I have on occasion, enjoyed salmon with them that Dave had caught. He is an expert fisherman and has shared his fishing skills with Haitians. He has shared very generously with CVM.

Kent was originally a 'cowboy type' from Wyoming, where he occasionally took on wild horses and possibly a few men who challenged him. During his pre-Christian years Kent may be described as a 'Diamond in the Rough'. Kent has participated in many challenging, non-professional pursuits. He once accidentally landed in Puget Sound with a small light plane. He was able to "walk" away but I think it got his attention. Horses he can handle, but not light aircraft.

Kent has gone on several shuttles to Haiti. He and Marie went to Honduras together and more recently to the Navajo Reservation. They have two daughters who, when at home, filled their rooms with trophies from horse show competition during their high school years. Kent and Marie, once took several CVM folks on a most successful crabbing expedition in the Sound. Marie cooked them and it is still being debated on who ate the most. I think it came down to either Kit Flowers or Wendell Cantrell.

• ❧ •

Dr. Riddick Ricks, North Carolina, went to Haiti in February to work with Dr. Keith Flanagan and had an outstanding shuttle experience. Riddick arrived in Port au Prince with over three hundred pounds of pharmaceuticals and supplies. Luckily Keith had dispatched someone to see him safely through customs and the waiting crowd outside. As you would expect with Keith escorting, John hit the ground running. First thing he did was to treat a 100-pound Rottweiller for scrotal dermatitis and, as Riddick describes it, the dog was not a happy camper!

Riddick had met Keith and Jan the previous year in Baltimore at the AVMA meeting. They are kindred spirits and easily identify with one another. Riddick became involved in all the activities of the work. He started out by helping to stock and organize the pharmacy, which was added to with the supply he brought. He then totally immersed himself in whatever opportunities that surfaced. It is with this kind of attitude that shuttles have an enormously rewarding experience.

Riddick comments on his experiences,

"Because of the life of love displayed by Keith and Jan and my experiences with the lovely Haitians, who I can now call my friends, I am closer to the Lord and will ever be more sensitive to the needs of others. I have come to realize, that being a missionary is not crossing the sea, but seeing the cross. When we understand the meaning of the cross, God will use us in mighty ways!"

❦

When the first full time CVM worker, Tammy Dodd, walked in my office with Kit, and broke the news to me that she was leaving, I could not believe my ears. I had made the statement many times to Tammy, "I don't know what CVM would do without you and I hope we never find out". She was more than a worker. She was the embodiment of the wonderful family of CVM! So many people knew her personally and depended on her for so many things. Her skills were numerous and professional, all that was needed to make CVM marketing function efficiently and effectively.

How in the world she kept track of all the things assigned to her, I will never know. She handled the desktop publishing of the newsletters, updates, prayer letters. She kept track of the Loveline Program, updated displays, designed, bought and shipped hats and T-Shirts. She kept track of birthdays for staff and fieldworkers and remembered them with affection.

She was and will remain the "First Lady" of CVM. I will forever be in debt to her for helping launch CVM's work as a separate entity within the context of the World Concern/CRISTA family. We wish her, husband Ed, daughters, Melissa, Bethney and son Chris the best the Lord has to offer. I find it interesting that CVM has hired two additional workers, Janice Whitaker and Julie Logan, to try and take up the slack

❦

Dr. Scott Karper, Pennsylvania, made application in May, 1987 to do a shuttle and he went to Haiti in '88. In that same year, Scott and Diane applied for long-term service with CVM. We could never make it happen at that time. They eventually went to St. Thomas on their own for a couple of years, with their two sons, Jes and Trev. They hosted some shuttles for us while serving there.

In 1998 they had another false start with CVM. They explained,

"Since last February we have been gearing up to leave for the mission field once again. At that time our plans were to go to Tonga, a South Pacific island that was overrun by dogs. This project, to get the dog population under control, was privately funded. Just before Christmas, that funding fell through-after we had sold the practice, quit our job, sold our vehicles, and farmed out our furniture in preparation for departure. But we are thankful to be working for God, who is faithful. He has opened another door for us to serve where the need is greater.

We will be heading to Honduras in the spring. This is a new project, with so many possibilities for service. We will be working in the third neediest country in this hemisphere."

Afterwards they report from Guatemala where they were in language school,

"Our Spanish is improving-not by leaps and bounds but bit by bit. We are anxious to go into the Mosquitia area of Honduras to check out sites, needs and possibilities."

There is so much need in this area of Honduras that it was difficult to know where to settle. One particular place that interested them was, Wampusirpi. Isn't it interesting to see how, when one keeps their heart, mind and soul on the Lord and His work, He will guide us through. Am I that faithful? Are you that faithful?

There you have it! I hope that I have conveyed correctly the Lord's call and the response by the vast number of people involved in this work, here and overseas. Obviously, I could not include in the narrative everyone who was involved, but I have tried to give from my perspective those crucial times and events that were pivotal to the success of the ministry. I have used quotes from many people, as I think they can tell their story better than anyone else. It's the next best thing to being there.

For those who have not been mentioned, please accept my apologies. I just know that I have left out some very important stuff. But I have included in the book lists of very important groups, to try and overcome that deficit. One group that I have not included, and I feel badly about it, are those faithful and generous donors who have supported the ministry for many years and for some, sacrificially. I know they do not give to get their name in a book or on a list, but they are vital partners. Without them there would have been no CVM work. The Lord knows them and will reward them.

Finally, it is the story of ordinary men and women who are accomplishing extraordinary things for God, through His grace and power. It is truly amazing what these dedicated servants of the profession are doing. I am continually reminded of two things; the appropriateness of veterinarians for mission work and the desire by so many to serve in this manner. The profession was really hungry for involvement.

Veterinarians are, by nature of their training, experience and background, suitable candidates for mission work. To prosper in the profession, and even to survive, they must be creative and innovative. Of necessity, they must be problem solvers. Conditions in the developing world demand this. One thing in common between veterinary practice and working in the Third World is the fact that nothing is ever ideal.

I think the fact that the profession still operates in the world of reality, tends to keep our minds on a more practical focus. There is a limit to charges for service, whether for pets or food animal medicine. And I like to think that this fact also encourages us to recognize that we still need God in our lives. Some may dispute this but I believe it to be so. I think it is easy in this age of sophistication and high technology to think of ourselves as self-sufficient, but until someone discovers a way to get out of this world alive, it is just whistling in the dark.

Because we do work in those countries where the Quality of Life (QOL) index shows to be the worst, the work is more difficult. Living conditions are much more harsh and often times dangerous. Many times the reason for the low QOL index is civil strife. A case in point is Haiti. They have had so many tyrannical rulers. Sometimes the cause may be a natural disaster as in a severe drought. An example could be the drought in Kenya, or a flood, as in Honduras. Sometimes tradition, as with the Maasai, or superstition, as in Haiti with their Voodoo worship, help to prevent more sensible solutions.

The reasons may be varied and multiple. Whatever the reason, natural, man caused, ignorance or self inflicted, the need is there. I observed that nowhere in the Bible did I ever find that Jesus failed to help people in need. As Proverbs puts it, "He who works his land will have abundant food, but he who chases fantasies lacks judgment." Jesus knew their hearts but he still had compassion.

In my humble opinion, CVM has succeeded for the following reasons:

1. God gave the vision and ordained it to be so. Otherwise no amount of hard work would have made it succeed.
2. It was wonderful in its simplicity! Nothing complicated, nothing to join, come bring your gifts, affirm the basic statement of faith and let's go to work for the Lord!
   [Simply put, it was a new and unique form of Christian Missions. It would fill a great need that was not being filled at that time. It also proved that professional laymen could fill that need on a short or long term basis without costly and lengthy, time consuming preparation when they could be working in the field.]
3. It was highly focused, both as to work (veterinary skills) and to those areas overseas that had a tremendous need. We never tried to do those things that others were doing and could do better.

We need to remember these things!

After all these years of involvement in the veterinary profession, I still think it is one of, if not the most, difficult profession in the world. I was in a mixed practice and can remember the challenges I faced. I have told this story many times but it still illustrates the point. I had just finished pinning a femur on a two-pound Chihuahua and then was called outside to semen test a 2,000 pound Brahma bull! It did take making a big adjustment.

I have been asked many times and I have reflected on it often myself, how is it that such skilled professional people will go and give of themselves to help others under such difficult circumstances? There is only one answer, they are dedicated and committed Christians. They are responding to God's call on their lives. They have been touched by the Master. It leaves them restless. There is no peace in their souls until they respond to His call. It does not matter whether that call places them in such ungodly places as Rwanda, Haiti or Bangladesh; they know that is where God wants them to be.

I don't think any of them would consider doing it for financial gain. They certainly don't for CVM. We wish for them to break even in the process. Many don't even do that. There is always a cost to discipleship. Jesus promised that. But you know I don't think many or any of our overseas workers consider themselves deprived but rather fortunate that the Lord has called them to be workers in His vineyard. Now that is what blows the unbeliever's mind. They just don't get it.

I don't know if you are a veterinarian, student, or veterinary technician. Or whether you are someone with a different profession or vocation. But, I hope that whomever you are, that you seriously consider giving your gifts in service to the Lord. I Peter 4:10, says, "Each one should use whatever gift he has received to serve others, faithfully administering God's grace in its various forms." Isn't that amazing? We are dispensing God's grace. That is quite a responsibility.

Sometimes it is quite difficult to get into those areas of need to work, and not always is it appreciated. Again Peter 3:14,17 reminds us, "But even if you suffer for what is right, you are blessed. It is better, if it is God's will, to suffer for doing good than for doing evil." So the reason for service is not accolades or rewards. But, rather the satisfaction that we are sharing our skills with those who need them and we are honoring Him! Our neighbor, 95 year old, Mr. Frank Crouch, spent much time, making different gifts to give children and friends. He used to say, "Ain't nothing no good until you give it away." What do you have to give away in the name of the Lord?

During the summer Olympics in Atlanta in 1996, we watched the Marathon come down Peachtree Street on TV. When the runners got within a mile of us we ran outside to see them come by. They came in front of the complex where my son Blair and his wife Betsy lived, with their son and our grandson, Sterling. This was at about the 20-mile point in the race and the leaders were still doing close to a five-minute mile. Incredible!

The stress of the race was, unmistakably, revealed in their faces. One runner began to falter and had to drop out and was immediately picked up by an ambulance. The others struggled on. The crowd cheered each one regardless of their position in the race or what country they were from. The last person in the race was more than an hour behind the leader but was encouraged to continue on by the crowd. My mind immediately thought of Paul's admonition to the Corinthians (1-9:24) Run for the prize as the runner in the game does. Our prize is not gold but an everlasting one. We are to train for the race we are to run-witness and work for His Kingdom's sake!

This past December marked 50 years that Tina and I have been married. If you saw the January 1999 issue of Update, you can see the beginning of our journey. For half of those years, we have been involved, in some fashion, with Christian Veterinary Missions. It was 25 years ago that we felt God calling us to ministry, which, obviously, was CVM. He has watched over us and blessed us and has allowed us to see His guiding hand throughout it all. We are most thankful for that. We hope that it has been, is, and will be, a blessing to you.

ald

Dr. and Mrs. Leroy Dorminy.

267

Long Term Workers

Dr. Bill Baker and Mary Jo, Ar
Dr. Ivan Barineau and Mary, FL
Dr. Maureen Birmingham, IL
Dr. Catherine Botcherby, Scotland
Dr. Mark Bounds, TN
Dr. Bob Brabrook and Ann, WA
Dr. Wade Bradshaw and Chryse, TX
Dr. Dave Bremner and Nikki,
  South Africa
Dr. Wendell Cantrell and Jann, TX
Dr. Glenn Craft and Lisa, CA
Dr. Ed Cushing, NV
Dr. Ray Dayton and Vicki, MN
Drs. Charles Dodd and Lisa, MO
Dr. Keith Flanagan and Jan, OK
Dr. John Fletemeyer and Elaine, CO
Dr. Kit Flowers and Jan, FL
Dr. Rod Frank and Nancy, IL
Dr. Brad Frye and Angela, CO
Dr. Janice Fuquay, OR
Dr. Fred Gardner, KS
Vet Tech. Faye Goodling, PA
Dr. Jean Grade, WI
Dr. Kevin Hasch, NE
Dr. Steve Hiett, OR
Dr. Mark Hinton and Audrey, MN
Dr. Frank Hooper, SC
Dr. Bob Hott and Karen, MI
Dr. Toby Hover and Cindy, AL

Dr. Scott Karper and Diane, PA
Dr. Brian Kersten and Karen, WI
Dr. Paul Kline and Amanda, TX
Dr. Scott Lubbers, OR
Drs. Monty Mathis and Shelly, WA
Dr. Gerald Mitchum and Frances, NC
Dr. George Mixon and Martha, GA
Dr. Jim Nash and Randy, FL
Dr. Peter Quesenberry and Mary, CA
Dr. Ronnie Sarratt and Sue, OK
Dr. Valerie Shean, OR
Dr. Kent Smith and Jo Ann, MN
Dr. Patrick Smith and Wendy, CA
Dr. Kim Stender, OR
Dr. Susan Stewart, CO
Dr. Mike Storer and Debra, WI
Dr. Deborah Storie, Australia
Dr. Ron Stoufer and Karen, CA
Dr. Bill Testerman and Anne, WA
Dr. Max Thornesberry and Brenda, MO
Dr. Bob Van Dyke and Doris, AR
Drs. Fred Van Gorkum and Vicki, WA
Dr. Floyd Votaw, CA
Dr. Tom Wanous and Betty, MN
Dr. Ken Weinland and Ket, IN
Dr. Bob Wilmarth and Janet, FL
Dr. Don Wilson and Marilyn, MO

These are those who have served on the field long term with CVM. The cut off date for the records is June 30, 1999.

IN MEMORY

CVM has been blessed to have many dedicated and faithful workers over the last 20 years. We want to always remember those who have passed away while serving in long term ministry or having retired from service with CVM.

Dr. Ray Dayton—Ray served with CVM from 1980 to 1984 working with the Maasai in Kenya, East Africa. He is still remembered for his impact on the Maasai through his love for the people and the ministry through veterinary medicine. Dr. Dayton is survived by his wife Vicki and three children who reside in Hastings, MN.

Dr. Kent Smith—Kent served for almost one year in Haiti at Hospital Albert Schweitzer. Even in this short time of service he served as a faithful witness of the love of Christ to the Haitian people in the Artibonite valley, He is survived by his wife Jo Ann and three children who reside in Minnesota.

Dr. Bill Baker— Bill served with CVM in Haiti from 1980 to 1984. He played a key role in the early development of the CVM programs in Haiti and the swine repopulation program. He is fondly remembered for his relational skills with people of all persuasions. He is survived by his wife Mary Jo and son. They live in Arkansas.

Dr. Mark Bounds— Mark served faithfully in Bolivia with his wife Dr. Susan Stewart from 1988 until his death in September 1995. Mark and Susan served as a team in the leadership role of the WC/CVM programs in Latin America. Their work in developing training programs and techniques is recognized by many as the standard. Susan continues in the work.

Dr. Mike Storer—Mike served with CVM from 1985 until his death in September of 1995. His initial service was with the Navajo in Arizona. The Storer family then served five years in Haiti prior to their return to ministry with Native Americans in New Mexico. Mike's quiet gentle spirit is remembered by all who knew him. His wife Debra and three children continue to live in NM.

SHUTTLES

Abbott	Terrance	Dr.	PA
Ackerman	Chad	S	MI
Adams	John	Dr.	MO
Alford	Booker	Dr.	NJ
Alfred	Andrea	S	Can
Alspach	Adair	Dr. & Marah	FL
Amen	Jack	Dr.	MD
Amex	Edward	Dr. & Mrs.	IL
Anderson	David	Dr.	WA
Anderson	Gwen	S	IL
Armstrong	James	Dr.	RI
Arnaboldi	Joseph	Dr.	NY
Arnquist	Kristi	S	WI
Aspelund	Per	Dr.	Nor
Bair	Richard	Dr.	NB
Baker	Larry	Dr. & Mrs.	IL
Baker	Amy	S	CO
Barcelow	Laurie	Dr.	VT
Barea	Nilda	Dr.	TN
Barineau	Ivan	Dr. & Mrs.	FL
Basinger	Mark	Dr.	OH
Bastian	Robert	Dr. & Mrs.	PA
Bateman	Beverly	S	Can,
Bechert	Ursula	Dr.	OR
Beck	Natalie	Dr. & Mr.	KS
Beede	Bob	Dr.	ID
Belden	Matt	Dr.	TX
Bellhorn	Ted	Dr.	FL
Bender	Jeff	Dr.	MN
Bendick	Fred	Dr. & Mrs.	MO
Bennett	Heather	S	TN
Bensenhaver	John	Dr.	VA
Bentley	Jim	Dr. & son	OK
Berglund-Fosdick	Lee Ann	S	MI
Berry	Shana	S	TX

Berthlesen	John	Dr.	IA
Billings	Angela	S	VA
Birmingham	Maureen	Dr.	NY
Blackwell	David	Dr.	CT
Bley	Jack	Dr.	VA
Boldingh	Terry	Dr.	MN
Book	Brad	S	TX
Borgerson	Lara	Dr.	IL
Bossart	Greg	Dr.	FL
Botcherby	Catherine	S	UK
Bounds	Mark	Dr.	OR
Boyce	Charles	Dr.	IL
Brabrook	Bob	Dr.	WA
Bracht	Jeff	S	DE
Bradley	Sarah	S	OK
Braswell-Sisson	Cheryl	Dr.	GA
Bregitzer	Lee	Dr.	CO
Brooks	Lee	Dr.	GA
Brown	Steve	Dr.	OR
Brown	Phillip	Dr.	NZ
Buckland	Lori	S	GA
Bullard	Ted	Dr	AL
Burch	Jerry	Dr.	TN
Burns	Clyde	Dr.	NC
Burnsteel	Cinny	Dr.	MD
Burrichter	David	Dr. & Mrs.	PA
Bush	Eric	S	MI
Bushhouse	Sally	Dr.	MN
Busman	Paul	Dr. & Mrs.	WI
Buzby	Julie	S	KS
Byerly	David	S	KS
Camacho	Mark	S	NC
Cantrell	Wendell	Dr.	TX
Carlson	Jim	Dr. & Mrs.	CO
Carson	John	Dr.	WI
Carver	Deirdre	Dr.	TN
Cashin	Margaret	T	WA

Castellan	David	Dr.	CA
Caudle	Corina	T	NC
Chappell	Duane	Dr.	IN
Chatham	Willis	Dr.	KS
Chesson	Mike	Dr.	VA
Chong	Roger	Dr.	Aus
Clader	John	Dr.	TX
Clark	Catherine	T	NY
Clark	Teri	Dr.	OR
Clark	John	Dr.	MO
Claybrook	Huey	Dr.	TN
Clemons-Chevis	Connie	Dr.	MS
Cline	Beryl	Dr.	TX
Cobb	Charles	Dr.	LA
Coble	Jodi	S	NC
Colley	Jerry	Dr. & Mrs.	AL
Collier	Jim	AG	GA
Collinge	Irwin	Dr.	KS
Collins	Mary Jo	Dr.	IL
Cook	Dave	S	MN
Cornelius	Jim	Dr.	AR
Costin	Miron	Dr.	CA
Cragg	Alan	Dr. & Mrs.	OH
Cunningham	Paul	Dr. & Mrs.	MO
Davidson	Ann		LA
Davis	Alan	Dr.	IL
Davis	Joanna	Dr.	GA
Deisher	Bill	Dr. & Mrs.	IL
DeLaune	Scarlett		TX
Delinks	Don	Dr.	MA
Demumbrum	Lisa	Dr.	WI
Detweiler	Maureen	Dr.	CO
Dippel	Peter	Dr.	PA
Dixon	Jim	Dr. & Mrs.	CO
Dodd	Charles & Lisa	Drs.	MO
Dorminy	Leroy	Dr. & Mrs.	GA

Downes	Steven	Dr.	UK
Dugdale	Suzanne	T	OH
Dunbar	Michael	Dr.	TX
Dunlap	Alex	Dr.	TN
Durfee	John	Dr.	TX
Eckert	Jack	Dr.	MO
Emch	Scott	S	IN
Enderle	Wayne	Dr.	OH
Englund	Jessica	S	MA
Epp	Edward	Dr.	KS
Erickson	Fred	Dr.	CA
Eubank	James	Dr. & Mrs.& son	KS
Evans	Ralph	Dr.	OH
Faber	Scott	S	IN
Farho	Charles	Dr.	MI
Fife	Rebecca	S	Can
Flanagan	Keith	Dr.	OK
Fletemeyer	John	Dr. & Mrs.	CO
Flowers	Kit	Dr. & Mrs.	FL
Ford	Alton	Dr. & Mrs.	FL
Foreman	Max	Dr.	AL
Forester	Cricket	Dr.	GA
Frank	Rodney	Dr. & Mrs.	IL
Freeman	Tom	Dr.	KY
Freer	Kent	Dr. & Mrs.	WA
Frusher	Stephen	Dr. & Mrs	SD
Fuller	Anthony	Dr. & Mrs.	AL
Funk	Daryl	Dr. & Mrs.	IA
Funk	Nathan		IA
Funk	Renee		IA
Fuquay	Janice	Dr.	OR
Gaines	Glenn	Dr.	TX
Ganz	Dan	T	WI
Gardner	Fred	Dr.	KS
Garlichs	Stephanie	S	WA
Garza	Dave	Dr.	TX

Gasaway	Charles	Dr.	OK
Geiger	Garrell	Dr. & Jason	WI
Gentry	Daniel	S	AL
Gerstner	Melvin	Dr.	CA
Geshwiler	Erin	S	MA
Gessert	Mary	Dr.	WI
Gibson	James	Dr.	UK
Gillaspie	Tom	Dr. & Mrs.	FL
Gilmore	Steven	Dr.	MN
Goodling	Fay	T	PA
Goodman	Earle	Dr.	SC
Goodnough	Dawn	Dr.	CA
Goring	Jonas	Dr.	Can
Gracey	Rodger	Dr. & Mrs.	KS
Grade	Jean	Dr.	WI
Green	Ashby & Eleanor	Drs.	MS
Gregory	Howard	Dr.	VA
Grey	Cathy	Dr.	NY
Griffin	Scott	S	GA
Grimes	George	Dr.	TN
Grimley	William	Dr.	TX
Grimm	Dan	Dr. & Mrs.	IN
Gross	Todd	S	TN
Gunther	John	Dr.	WI
Gutberlet	Lena	S	VA
Haase	Loraine	S	WI
Haffner	Johnny	Dr.	TN
Hager	Billy	Dr.	NC
Hale	Jennifer	S	MN
Hall	Brenda	T	TX
Hall	Aime	S	NC
Halls	Edward	Dr.	MN
Halls	Ed	Dr.	MN
Hamilton	Tanya	Dr.	TN
Hammarlund	Marion	Dr.	CA
Hansen	Mark	Dr.	WA

Hargreaves	Robert	Dr.	CA
Hargreaves	Robert	Dr.	CA
Harty	Terry	Dr.	FL
Hayward	Brett	Dr.	Can
Hebert	Loree	Dr.	TX
Heiden	Daniel	Dr.	MN
Heimsoth	Don	Dr.	MO
Henriksen	Peter	Dr.	CA
Heuser	Walt	Dr.	Can
Hill	Robert	S	GA
Hinkle	Don	Dr. & Mrs.	NC
Hoffman	Elizabeth	Dr. & son	AK
Hofmeister	Judy	Dr.	KY
Holland	Mary Ann	T	TN
Hooper	Frank	S	SC
Hoover	Toby	Dr.	AL
Howlett	Jeff	Dr.	WA
Huddleston	Mac	Dr.	MS
Hunt	Devin	Dr.	Can
Hunter	Bruce	Dr.	Can
Hurd	Amy	Dr.	MA
Hurt	Yvonne	S	VA
Huston	Dick	Dr. & son	MN
Hyler-Booth	Connie	Dr. & Mr.	MI
Innis	James	S	MI
Jarmon	Lloyd	Dr.	TX
Jeans	Roland	Dr.	WI
Jeppesen	Julie	S	WA
Jepsen	Bill	Dr.	OR
Jewell	Nick	Dr.	AR
Johnston	Russell	S	TX
Johnston	Kathy	Dr.	NC
Jones	Howard	Dr.	FL
Jones	Floyd	Dr.	TX
Jones	Sara	S & Mr.	TN
Jones	Kerry	Dr. & Tom	OK
Jordan	Frank	Dr.	KS

Jorgesen	Keith	Dr.	Can
Karklins	Julie	S	OH
Karper	Scott	Dr. & Diane	
Kays	Jennifer	S	Can,
Keefer	Susan	S	VA
Kelly	Jim	Dr. & Mrs.	FL
Kennedy	Robert	Dr.	MS
Kimberling	Cleon	Dr.	CO
Kirkpatrick	James	Dr.	MN
Kline	Paul	Dr.	TX
Knight	Wally	Dr. & Son	VT
Koelsch	Bill	Dr. & Mrs.	MI
Koenig	Charles	Dr. & Mrs.	PA
Kononoff	Wally	Dr.	Can
Kononoff	Paul	MS	Can
Koskinen	Paul	Dr.	MN
Kraayenbrink	Darrel	Dr.	SD
Krahwinkel	D.J.	Dr.	TN
Kruckeberg	John	Dr.	TN
Krukeberg	John	Dr. & Friend	TN
Krusekopf	Kurt	S	AR
Kruser	Kurt	Dr.	PA
Kuchera	Craig	Dr.	OK
Kwantes	Louis	S	Can
Lane	Tom	Dr.	FL
Lane	Merle	Dr.	IA
Lanz	Ralph	Dr.	OH
LaRocca	Gina	Dr.	WI
Larsson	Deron	Dr. & Kathy	CA
Lauerman	Lloyd	Dr.	AL
Laurence	Greg	Dr.	MN
Lazalrony	Doris	Dr.	CO
Legge	Suzanne	Dr.	Can
LeMoine	Terese	T	WA
Lempka	Stacy	S	KS
Lewis	Doug	Dr. & Mrs.	PA
Ley	Bill	Dr.	VA

Lindsey	Rocky	S	LA
Litchfield	Stephen	S	IL
Lloyd	Herbert	Dr. & Mrs.	FL
Loafman	Tom	Dr.	MO
Logas	Laurel	S	IL
Long	Walter	Dr.	NE
Lucas	Hope	Dr.	NC
Maag	Trisha	S	KS
Mack	Anne	S	Can
Maddux	Regina	S	MS
Mahoney	Allison	S	KS
Marcus	M'Risa	S	TX
Maroney	Maureen	T	CA
Marshall	Diane	Dr.	WA
Marshall	Gary	Dr.	WA
Mathis	Monty	Dr.	WA
Mathis	Shelly	Dr.	WA
McDonald	George	Dr.	TX
McNally	Mike	Dr.	TX
Mersch	Robert	Dr.	MN
Meyer	Steven	Dr.	MN
Meyers	Kathleen	Dr.	OH
Mikolon	Andrea	Dr.	CA
Millar	David	Dr. & Mrs.	Can
Miller	John	Dr.	NM
Miller	Sophia	Dr.	MN
Minier	Dave	S & Mrs.	MI
Minnema	Murray	Dr.	CA
Mitchell	DeAnna	Dr.	VA
Mitchum	Gerald	Dr. & Mrs.	VA
Mitchum	Kevin	S	NC
Mixon	George	Dr.	GA
Moe	Tom	Dr.	ID
Molloy	Lisa	Dr.	CO
Moore	George	Dr.	TX
Moore	Heidi	S	PA
Morse	Brent	Dr.	MD

Moser	Ned	Dr.	MD
Muchna	Mark	Dr.	IA
Mueller	Bruce	S	OR
Mueller	Art	Dr. & Mrs.	WI
Mullins	Steve	Dr.	TN
Munn	Ken	T	AL
Murphy	Duane	Dr.	IN
Murray	John	Dr.	SC
Myers	Billy	Dr.	GA
Neilson	Shannon	S	OR
Nelson	Melissa	S	MN
Newhart	Katherine	S	VA
Nichols	Warren	Dr.	IL
Norman	Dina	Dr.	Nor
Nutsch	Robert	Dr.	IA
Oliphant	Rodney	Dr.	KS
Olson	Jerry	Dr.	CO
Olson	Patricia	Dr.	CO
Orel	Robert	Dr.	VA
Orfely	Christine	S	AL
Orta	Wanda	Dr.	TN
Otto	Bob	Dr. & Mrs	WA
Otto	Bob	Dr.	WA
Owens	Clint	Dr.	TX
Parris	Lorraine	Dr.	DE
Pasche	Katy	Dr,	CA
Paulo	Dan	Dr. & Family	PA
Pawlisch	Ray	Dr.	WI
Payton	Charles	Dr.	AL
Peak	Patricia	S	WA
Peng	Winnie	Stdt.	CO
Penner	Virgil	Dr.	ID
Pierson	Andrew	S	IL
Pierson	Bill	Dr. & Mrs.	VA
Plummer	William	Dr.	NC
Poirrier	Renee	Dr	LA
Pol	Jan	Dr.	MI

Polson	Dale	Dr.	IA
Poock	Scott	Dr. & Mrs.	WI
Price	Susan	Dr.	WI
Pugh	David	Dr.	GA
Pulvermacher	Carol	S	WI
Pust	Melody	S	MN
Quillin	Steve	Dr.	OK
Ratajczak	Christina	Dr.	PA
Read	Richard	Dr.	AUS
Reid	Malcom	AG	GA
Rhodes	James	Dr.	TX
Rice	Terri	T	WA
Richardson	Jim	Dr.	TX
Ricks	Riddick	Dr.	MC
Riddle	Mandy	Dr.	TX
Ridolfo-Masheimer	Michelle	T	IL
Righetti	Timothy	Dr. & Mrs.	CA
Rishel	William	Dr.	NE
Ritersbacher	Dave	AG	ID
Roach	Brad	S	OK
Roach	Kara	S	TN
Robertson	Edwin	Dr.	TN
Robinson	Robbie	Dr.	VA
Robinson	Beth	Dr.	LA
Robinson	Lauri	S	IN
Rodewald	Shelly		PA
Roehr	Keith	Dr. & Mrs.	CO
Rogers	Glenn	Dr.	TX
Rogers	Arnos	Dr.	GA
Rose	Ruben	Dr.	Aus
Rosenbaum	Lee	Dr. & Barbara	
Rosenberger	James	Dr. & Mrs.	OH
Rosenbluth	Peggy	Tech. Family	OH
Rudenberg	Paul	Dr.	MA
Rudenberg	Paul	Dr.	MA
Sardinia	Michael	S	WA
Sarratt	Ronnie	Dr.	OK

Scheinbein	Allan	Dr.	Can
Schilling	Hannah	S	Can
Schlierf	Heidi	Dr.	MA
Schmidt	Susan	Dr.	OH
Schmuck	Larry	Dr. & Mrs	PA
Schneller	John	Dr.	WI
Schoenborn	Phillip	Dr	MN
Schoenfeld	Angela	Dr.	LA
Schultz	Angelique	S	OK
Schulze	James	Dr.	TX
Schwenk	Barry	S	KS
Scott	Karen	T	KY
Shey	Daniel	Dr.	IA
Sims	Michael	Dr.	TN
Skinner	Steve	S	VA
Slater	Barry	Dr.	Can
Sletten	Wayne	Dr. & Mrs.	SD
Smalley	Bob	Dr.	GA
Smalley	Robert	Dr.	AL
Smialek	Dennis	Dr.	CO
Smith	Kent	Dr.	MN
Smith	Patrick	Dr.	NH
Smith	Laurie	Dr. & Mr.	TX
Smith	Greg	Dr.	CA
Smith	Chad	S	IA
Snowden	Karen	Dr.	UK
Solis	Wendi	T	FL
Staller	Heather	S	CO
Stanger	Bethany	S	MI
Stanley	David	Dr.	VA
Starcher	Joe	Dr.	WV
Staudinger	Mike	Dr.	WI
Steepe	Michael	S	MI
Stewart	Susan	Dr.	OR
Stewart	Keith	Dr.	AUS
Stocker	Jack	Dr.	IL
Stolt	Daniel	T	WI

Storey	Eric	S Mrs.	AL
Stoufer	Karen	Dr. & Mr.	CA
Strock	Barbara	Dr.	PA
Stuedemann	Karen	Dr.	IL
Stuttgen	Dennis	Dr.	WI
Sundbeck	Dennis	Dr.	TX
Sylvester	Robert	Dr.	FL
Sylvester	Don	AG	NM
Tavenner	Valerie	T	WA
Terra	Ron	Dr.	CA
Thayer	Don	Dr.	WI
Thayer	Debbie	S	WI
Thomas	Elden	S	IN
Thompson	Earl	Dr.	MN
Thompson	Margaret	Dr.	TX
Thomson	John	Dr.	IA
Trimble	Scott	T	NY
Trinh	Kent	Dr. & son	TX
Truex	Scott	S	FL
Tucker	Neil	T	AR
Tutt	Sonny	Dr. & Mrs	TX
Ulrich	Tim	Dr.	NC
Ulrich	Paula	Dr.	NC
Underwood	Wendy	S	NC
Underwood	Ann	Dr.	TX
Van Dijk	Conrad	Dr.	Can
Van Dyke	Bob	Dr. & Mrs.	AR
Van Meter	Tom	Dr. & Mrs.	WA
Vanderhoof	Bob	Dr.	CA
Varhus	Janet	Dr.	CO
Ver Steeg	Eugene	Dr. & M + D	IA
Verberg	Anje	Dr.	VT
VerSteeg	Eugene	Dr.	IA
Vesco	Beth	Dr.	OH
Vitanza	Lisa	S	TX
Wade	Emily	T	NC
Walker	Donna	S	OH

Walker	Vernie	Dr.	OK
Walker	Gerald	Dr. & Mrs.	CA
Walker	Lori	Dr.	OR
Waller	Susan	T	CA
Wanous	Tom	Dr. & Mrs.	MN
Ward	Denise		IA
Watts	Merle	Dr.	AZ
Weaver	Dick	Dr.	OH
Wendell	Sharon	T	NB
Wennerstrom	Brian	S	OH
Wilbur	Roger	Dr.	TX
Wilkerson	Kelley	S	AL
Willis	Lonnie	Dr. & Mrs.	KS
Wilmarth	Bob	Dr.	FL
Wilson	Don	Dr. & Mrs.	MO
Wilson	Warren	Dr.	WI
Wilson	Susan	Dr.	AZ
Winzer	David	Dr. & Mrs.	WA
Wood	Kevin	Dr.	TN
Woodworth	Kelley	S	VA
Wright	Laurel	Dr.	WA
Wright	Dave	Dr.	MN
Wyatt	David	Dr.	RI
Yee	Jennifer	S	OK
Yoder	Bill	AG	PA
Yoo	Henry	Dr.	OH
York	Dorothy	Dr.	CA
Yost	Tom	Dr.	CO
Zamora	Karen	T	KY
Zander	Rick	Dr.	CA
Zarle	Gretchen	S	TN
Zehnder	Mark	Dr. & Mrs	Can
Zicker	Steve	Dr. & Mrs.	CO

S = Student T = Technician.

Note: Information current through 6-30-99.

Veterinarians who have served as
Region Representatives and on the CVM Board

Terry Abbott
James Armstrong
Gary Baker
Mary Ballenger
Don Barnum
Robert Beede
Fred Bendick
David Blackwell
Tim Blair
Jerry Burch
Wendell Cantrell
Edmund Cushing
Don Delinks
Floyd Jones
Earl Goodman
Rod Frank
Toby Hoover

Devin Hunt
John Kruckeberg
Walt Long
George Moore
Bob Otto
Dan Paulo
Susan Price
James Rosenberger
Wayne Sletten
Karen Stuedeman
Dennis Sunbeck
Conrad Van Dyke
Gerry Walker
V.R. Walker
Laurie Wallace
Don Wilson

Veterinarians who have served as
CVM State Representatives

Alabama
Toby Hoover, Larry Swango, Steve Swaim, Jerry Colley, Scott Griffin, Charles Young
Alaska
Elizabeth Hoffman
Arizona
Susan Wilson and George Miller
Arkansas
Bill Terry, Derrell Wood, Richard Allen
California
Floyd Votaw, Robert Dickerson, Tim Righetti, Bob Vanderhoof, Lorraine Beaumont, Marion Hammarlund
Colorado
Bob Pierson, Dennis Smialek, James Carlson, John Fletemeyer, Glenn Cook
Connecticut
William Haines
Delaware
Donald Gooss, Lorraine Parris, Geneva Spence

Florida
Ken Weinland, Bruce Keene, Tom Gillaspie
Georgia
Q.L. Darbyshire and Felix Smith
Hawaii
Craig Hanney
Idaho
Robert Bryant, Gary McIntosh, Bob Beede
Illinois
Bruce Williams, Bill Diesher, Richard Dhuse
Indiana
John Clark, Max Brand, Mike Maroney, John Petscher, Roy Coolman
Iowa
E.D. Ver Steeg, Daniel Downing, David Smidt, Daniel Shey
Kansas
Rodney Oliphant
Kentucky
Duane Miksch, William Payne
Louisiana
Frederick Michaelson, Walter Ernst, Sheldon Bivin
Maine
Langdon Davis, Charles Gauger
Maryland
Ed Ruebush, Steven Sragner, Marvin Meinder, Mary Campbell
Massachusetts
Dennis Sweet, Don Delinks, Ray Claxton
Michigan
Jan Pol, Tom Yonkers
Minnesota
Milton Bauer, Tom Wanous
Mississippi
Eleanor and Ashby Green, Robert Kennedy, Robert Arline,
Lowell Rogers, Jim Watson
Missouri
Tom Loafman, Max Thornesberry, Fred Bendick, Don Wilson,
Wanda Pipkins
Montana
Elmer Davis, Robert Syvrud
Nebraska
Walt Long
Nevada
Ed Cushing

New Hampshire
  Patrick Smith, James Grayson, Dennis Sweet
New Jersey
  Michael Bush, Robert Meuller, Robert Goldsboro, Booker Alfred,
    Kim Taylor
New Mexico
  Donna Harper, Stan Agenbroad, Robert Blake, Roy Stewart
New York
  Joel Edwards, Robert Moore, John Sangiorgio
North Carolina
  Clyde Burns
North Dakota
  L.A. Dunn
Ohio
  Dick Weaver, James Rosenberger
Oklahoma
  Vernie Walker, Keith Flanagan, Ronnie Surratt, Charles Gasaway,
    Mary Ballenger
Oregon
  *Mr. Andy Parker, Donald Hansen, Bill Jepsen, Leo Van Dijk,
    Steve Brown
Pennsylvania
  Harold Landis
Rhode Island
  James Armstrong
South Carolina
  Earle Goodman
South Dakota
  Wayne Sletten
Tennessee
  George Grimes, Jerry Burch, Huey Claybrook, Kevin Wood
Texas
  John Terrall, Glenn Rogers, Dennis Sunbeck, Sonny Tutt
Utah
  Clark Vanderhoof
Vermont
  David Baldwin, Ronald Veenema, Anje Verburg Degraaf
Virginia
  Howard Gregory, Robbie Robinson, Anita Foote, James Gates,
    Charles Hickey

---

*Not a veterinarian.

Washington
  Bob Otto, Bill Testerman
West Virginia
  Ernest Benner, Joe Starcher
Wisconsin
  Sue Price, Steve Dirks, Donald Dykhouse, Phil Schoenborn
Wyoming
  R.E. Fuschsel, Margery Hanfelt
Canada
  Don Barnum
Alberta
  Richard Bibby, Ed Neufield
British Columbia
  Norman Lowes, A.F. Gill, Brett Hayward
Ontario
  Conrad Van Dyke, Elroy Mann, Murray Gordon, Ron Downey,
    Cate Dewey
Manitoba
  Wayne Lees
Newfoundland
  Conrad Van Dyke
Quebec
  Jean-Louis Forgues
Saskatchewan
  Wally Kononoff

Veterinarians who have served as
School Representatives

Auburn University
  Larry Swango, Marshall Putman, Steve Swaim, Bruce Gray,
    Lloyd Lauerman, Lynn Hagood
University of California
  Donald Jasper, Donald Strombeck, Dallas Hyde
Colorado State
  Patricia Olsen, Jerry Olsen, Robert Pierson, Steven Roberts, Brad Frye
    Phillip Steyn
Cornell University
  Fred Scott, James Richards
University of Florida
  Tom Lane
University of Georgia
  David Tyler, Lisa Williamson, *John McCall

University of Illinois
  Arnold Smith
Iowa State University
  Mel Swenson, Joseph Hayes
Kansas State University
  Marvin Samuelson, Bob Taussig, Keith Beeman, Michael Sanderson
Louisiana State University
  Joe Newton, Sheldon Bivin, Dan Paulson, David Baker
Michigan State University
  Charles Gibson, Patrick LaBlanc, John Milo Kruger, Curtis Probst
University of Minnesota
  Donald Johnson, Alan Leman, Vic Cox
Mississippi State University
  Eleanor and Shelby Green, Mac Huddleston, Lee Tyner,
    Ann Kraus-Hansen, Gerald Radde, Richard Hopper
University of Missouri, College of Veterinary Medicine
  Stuart Nelson, Don Schmidt, Laurie Wallace, Alex Bermundez
University of Montreal
  Laslo DeRoth
North Carolina State University
  Karen Snowden, Edward Henry, Mark Comacho, Kathy Ann Spaulding,
    Kip Berry
Ohio State University
  James Burt, Richard Slemons
Oklahoma State University, College of Veterinary Medicine
  Fayne Oberst, Lloyd Faulkner, J.W. Alexander, Kenneth Clinkenbeard,
    Gaymen Helman
Ontario Veterinary College, University of Guelph
  Don Barnum, John Deen, Gary Partlow
College of Veterinary Medicine at Oregon State University
  Donald Mattson
University of Pennsylvania
  Richard Bartholomew, Don Abt, *Peter Dodson Ph.D., Robert Whitlock
University of Prince Edward Island, Atlantic Veterinary College
  Patty Scharko, Earnest Hovingh
Purdue University, School of Veterinary Medicine
  Roger Lukens, William Van Alstine, H.L.Thacker
University of Saaskatoon, Western College of Veterinary Medicine
  Wally Kononoff
University of Tennessee
  D. J. Krahwinkel

*Ph.D. not a veterinarian.

Texas A & M, College of Veterinary Medicine
  Kenneth Pierce, Michael Willard
Tufts University, School of Veterinary Medicine
  Robert Cook
Tuskegee University, School of Veterinary Medicine
  George Heath, Otto Williams, Winston Felton, Fred Tippetts
Virginia Tech and University of Maryland,
Virginia-Maryland Regional College of Veterinary Medicine
  Phillip Sponenberg
Washington State University, College of Veterinary Medicine
  Myron Person, Lynette Corbeil, Duane Mickelson, James Evermann
University of Wisconsin-Madison, School of Veterinary Medicine
  Sue Price, Garrett Oetzel

Publishing Dates

Book	Date Published	Revisions	ISBN#	Copyright
Pig Book	1984	Oct '88 1/10/95	1-886532-00-1	10/5/92
Dr. Earl Goodman, SC				
Rabbit Spanish Edition '96 Dr. Sheldon Bivin, LA, Dr. William King, LA	7/15/88	7/28/94	1-886532-01-X	10/5/92
Fish Dr. Lydia Brown, UK and Miss State Aquatic Task Force; Dr. Lora Petrie-Hanson, MS, Dr. Larry Hanson, MS	8/18/88	Nov '96	1-886532-05-2	10/5/92
Beef Cattle Dr. James Carlson, CO	1/1/90	'96	1-886532-06-0	10/5/92
Poultry	2/9/90	5/7/94 Reprint 4-98	1-886532-02-8	10/5/92
Spanish edition 7-'95 Malcolm Reid, Ph.D., GA, Gene Pesti, Ph.D., GA, Dr. M.A. Hammarlund,CA, Dr. Pran Vohra,CA				
Goat Spanish May '98 Dr. Bob Vanderhoof, CA	9/20/90	June '97	1-886532-04-4	10/5/92
Dairy Cattle Dr. Bill Testerman, WA	Sept '95		1-886532-03-6	2/20/96

Book	Date Published	Revisions	ISBN#	Copyright
Sheep	Jan '98	1-886532-07-9		4/19/98
Dr. Cleon Kimberling, CO, Dr. Mary Gessert, CO, Deborah Marsh, CO				
Drugs and Their Usage	April '98	1-886532-08-7		12/23/98
Dr. Will Grimley, TX, Dr. Randy Lynn, NC, Dr. Beth Blevins, MT, Dr. Beth Robinson, TX				

In Progress:

Horse—Dr. Bob Beede, ID (ISBN assigned) 1-886532-09-5

Where Their is No Vet—
   Dr. Maureen Birmingham, IL and Dr. Peter Quesenberry, CA
   (ISBN assigned) 1-886532-10-9

Buffalo Husbandry—Dr. Ben Benjamin, India and Dr. Bob Hott, MI

Bee Keeping—Dr. Randy Lynn, NC

Slaughter and Preservation of Meat—Dr. Dave Dressen, GA and
   Dr. Sandol Johnson, CO

Note: Information current through 6-30-99.

In addition to our series of books on Raising Healthy Animals, our fieldworkers have developed country specific training manuals, that reflect the needs and culture sensitivity. All these books illustrate the talents, language skills, adaptability, interaction and involvement of our field-workers with the people with whom they work.

   Haiti-Creole—by Dr. Maureen Birmingham
   Raising Healthy Pigs, Goats, Chickens, Cattle, Horses.
   Haiti-Creole—Dr. Maureen Birmingham and Dr. Rod Frank
   Principles of Veterinary Medicine.

   Bolivia-Spanish—Dr. Maureen Birmingham
   Raising Healthy Pigs, Sheep and Goats, Chickens, Cattle, Guinea
      Pigs, Llamas, Rabbits and Veterinary Principles.
   Bolivia-English and Spanish, Dr. Susan Stewart

Raising Healthy Sheep, Cattle in the Tropics.
The Agricultural Worker's Participatory Sourcebook published
   by HPI.

Nepal—Dr. Peter Quesenberry
English—
Raising Healthy Pigs in the Hills of Nepal-published by UMN.
JTA Handbook of Animal Health-published by UMN
Nepali—
Raising Healthy Pigs in the Hills of Nepal-published by UMN
Livestock Anatomy and Physiology-published by UMN
Animal Health Book for Nepal-published by UMN
Nepal—

English and Nepali—Dr. Karen Stoufer, Henk-Peter Dijkema,
   Narayan Ojha, Dhanajaya Paudel, and Goma Shrestha.
The Village Animal Health Worker (Spiral Flash)
Liver Fluke (Spiral Flash)
Primary Textbook for Village Animal Workers
Medicines Used for Animals
(CVM copyright)

Nepal—Dr. Bob Hott-English
Training Village Animal Health Workers in Nepal (Part I and
   Part II)

U.S.-Patrick Smith-English and Spanish-Illustrations by Dr. Todd
   Cooney
Raising Healthy Calves.
All these books represent great talent, much hard work and a
   Christian commitment by the field workers to use their skills
   in service to others.

Those who served as directors and advisors when the organization first became a national entity in the years 1977 to 1983.

Dr. James Armstrong
Dr. Tim Blair
Dr. W.F. Bozeman
Dr. Mike Chesson
Dr. M.J. Christopher
Dr. Ed Cushing
Dr. Bob Dickerson
Dr. A.L. Dorminy
Dr. Earl Goodman
Dr. Howard Gregory
Dr. Gordon Hatcher
Dr. Harold Landis
Dr. Tom Loafman

Dr. Clarence Mannasmith
Dr. Bob Otto
Dr. Dick Perkins
Dr. Bob Pierson
Dr. James Rosenberger
Dr. Fred Scott
Dr. Felix Smith
Dr. Steve Swaim
Dr. Larry Swango
Dr. Dave Tyler
Dr. Bob Vanderhoof
Dr. Floyd Votaw
Dr. Tom Wanous

A list of those veterinarians and others attending the first breakfast at Jekyl Island, Georgia, June, 1976.

Mr. Campbell Ansley
Dr. Dilmus Blackman
Dr. Horace Blalock
Dr. David Bedell
Dr. J.R. Bloodworth
Dr. Bill Bozeman
Dr. Raiford Claxton
Dr. Charles Cooper
Dr. Larry Corry
Dr. Q.L. Darbyshire
Dr. Charles Dobbins
Dr. L.H. Ellington
Dr. P.D. Ellison
Dr. P.M. Epple
Dr. Dan Fincher
Dr. C.B. Gaskins
Dr. Charles Graham

Dr. James Jarrett
Dr. T.W. Jenkins
Dr. Paul Lindsey
Dr. Paul May
Dr. J.T. Mercer
Dr. W.C. Mitchell
Dr. Don Nunn
Dr. George Patton
Dr. Brett Phillips
Dr. Arnos Rogers
Dr. Kelly Robinson
Dr. Felix Smith
Dr. James Strickland
Dr. D.E. Tyler
Dr. Preston Wall
Dr. Billy Weeks